Big Data Analytics for Sustainable Computing

Anandakumar Haldorai
Sri Eshwar College of Engineering, India

Arulmurugan Ramu
Presidency University, India

A volume in the Advances in Data
Mining and Database Management
(ADMDM) Book Series

Published in the United States of America by
    IGI Global
    Engineering Science Reference (an imprint of IGI Global)
    701 E. Chocolate Avenue
    Hershey PA, USA 17033
    Tel: 717-533-8845
    Fax: 717-533-8661
    E-mail: cust@igi-global.com
    Web site: http://www.igi-global.com

Library of Congress Cataloging-in-Publication Data

Names: Haldorai, Anandakumar, 1983- editor. l Ramu, Arulmurugan, 1985- editor.
Title: Big data analytics for sustainable computing / Anandakumar Haldorai
  and Arulmurugan Ramu, editors.
Description: Hershey, PA : Engineering Science Reference, an imprint of IGI
  Global, [2020] l Includes bibliographical references and index.
Identifiers: LCCN 2019007880l ISBN 9781522597506 (hardcover) l ISBN
  9781522597513 (softcover) l ISBN 9781522597520 (ebook)
Subjects: LCSH: Big data.
Classification: LCC QA76.9.B45 B5475 2020 l DDC 005.7--dc23 LC record available at https://
lccn.loc.gov/2019007880

This book is published in the IGI Global book series Advances in Data Mining and Database Management (ADMDM) (ISSN: 2327-1981; eISSN: 2327-199X)

British Cataloguing in Publication Data
A Cataloguing in Publication record for this book is available from the British Library.

All work contributed to this book is new, previously-unpublished material.
The views expressed in this book are those of the authors, but not necessarily of the publisher.

For electronic access to this publication, please contact: eresources@igi-global.com.

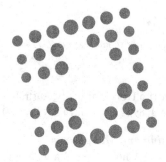

Advances in Data Mining and Database Management (ADMDM) Book Series

ISSN:2327-1981
EISSN:2327-199X

Editor-in-Chief: David Taniar, Monash University, Australia

MISSION

With the large amounts of information available to organizations in today's digital world, there is a need for continual research surrounding emerging methods and tools for collecting, analyzing, and storing data.

The **Advances in Data Mining & Database Management (ADMDM)** series aims to bring together research in information retrieval, data analysis, data warehousing, and related areas in order to become an ideal resource for those working and studying in these fields. IT professionals, software engineers, academicians and upper-level students will find titles within the ADMDM book series particularly useful for staying up-to-date on emerging research, theories, and applications in the fields of data mining and database management.

COVERAGE

- Educational Data Mining
- Data Analysis
- Data quality
- Enterprise Systems
- Data Mining
- Factor Analysis
- Data Warehousing
- Neural Networks
- Database Testing
- Predictive Analysis

IGI Global is currently accepting manuscripts for publication within this series. To submit a proposal for a volume in this series, please contact our Acquisition Editors at Acquisitions@igi-global.com or visit: http://www.igi-global.com/publish/.

Titles in this Series

701 East Chocolate Avenue, Hershey, PA 17033, USA
Tel: 717-533-8845 x100 • Fax: 717-533-8661
E-Mail: cust@igi-global.com • www.igi-global.com

Table of Contents

Detailed Table of Contents

Chapter 1
> *Naciye Güliz Uğur, Sakarya University, Turkey*
> *Aykut Hamit Turan, Sakarya University, Turkey*

In today's world, it is necessary to use data or information available in a wise manner to make effective business decisions and define better objectives. If the information available is not utilized to its full extent, organizations might lose their reputation and position in this competitive world. However, data needs to be processed appropriately to gain constructive insights from it, and the heterogeneous nature of this data makes this increasingly more complex and time-consuming. The ever-increasing growth of data generated is far more than human processing capabilities and thus computing methods need to be automated to scale effectively. This chapter defines Big Data basically and provides an overview of Big Data in terms of current status, organizational effects (technology, health care, education, etc.), implementation challenges and Big Data projects. This research adopted literature review as methodology and refined valuable information through current journals, books, magazines and blogs.

Chapter 2
> *Saranya N., Sri Eshwar College of Engineering, Coimbatore, India*
> *Saravana Selvam, PSR Engineering College, India*

After an era of managing data collection difficulties, these days the issue has turned into the problem of how to process these vast amounts of information. Scientists, as well as researchers, think that today, probably the most essential topic in computing science is Big Data. Big Data is used to clarify the huge volume of data that could exist in any structure. This makes it difficult for standard controlling approaches for mining the best possible data through such large data sets. Classification in Big Data is a procedure of summing up data sets dependent on various examples. There are distinctive classification frameworks which help us to classify data collections. A few methods that discussed in the chapter are Multi-Layer Perception Linear Regression, C4.5, CART, J48, SVM, ID3, Random Forest, and KNN. The target of this chapter is to provide a comprehensive evaluation of classification methods that are in effect commonly utilized.

    Sheik Abdullah A., Thiagarajar College of Engineering, India
    Priyadharshini P., Thiagarajar College of Engineering, India

The term Big Data corresponds to a large dataset which is available in different forms of occurrence. In recent years, most of the organizations generate vast amounts of data in different forms which makes the context of volume, variety, velocity, and veracity. Big Data on the volume aspect is based on data set maintenance. The data volume goes to processing usual a database but cannot be handled by a traditional database. Big Data is stored among structured, unstructured, and semi-structured data. Big Data is used for programming, data warehousing, computational frameworks, quantitative aptitude and statistics, and business knowledge. Upon considering the analytics in the Big Data sector, predictive analytics and social media analytics are widely used for determining the pattern or trend which is about to happen. This chapter mainly deals with the tools and techniques that corresponds to big data analytics of various applications.

    Vinay Kellengere Shankarnarayan, Dayananda Sagar College of
        Engineering, India

In recent years, big data have gained massive popularity among researchers, decision analysts, and data architects in any enterprise. Big data had been just another way of saying analytics. In today's world, the company's capital lies with big data. Think of worlds huge companies. The value they offer comes from their data, which they analyze for their proactive benefits. This chapter showcases the insight of big data and its tools and techniques the companies have adopted to deal with data problems. The authors also focus on framework and methodologies to handle the massive data in order to make more accurate and precise decisions. The chapter begins with the current organizational scenario and what is meant by big data. Next, it draws out various challenges faced by organizations. The authors also observe big data business models and different frameworks available and how it has been categorized and finally the conclusion discusses the challenges and what is the future perspective of this research area.

Chapter 5
Donald Douglas Atsa'am, Department of Mathematics, Statistics, and Computer Science, University of Agriculture, Makurdi, Nigeria

A filter feature selection algorithm is developed and its performance tested. In the initial step, the algorithm dichotomizes the dataset then separately computes the association between each predictor and the class variable using relative odds (odds ratios). The value of the odds ratios becomes the importance ranking of the corresponding explanatory variable in determining the output. Logistic regression classification is deployed to test the performance of the new algorithm in comparison with three existing feature selection algorithms: the Fisher index, Pearson's correlation, and the varImp function. A number of experimental datasets are employed, and in most cases, the subsets selected by the new algorithm produced models with higher classification accuracy than the subsets suggested by the existing feature selection algorithms. Therefore, the proposed algorithm is a reliable alternative in filter feature selection for binary classification problems.

Chapter 6
Sheik Abdullah A., Thiagarajar College of Engineering, India
Abiramie Shree T. G. R., Thiagarajar College of Engineering, India

Each day, 2.5 quintillion bytes of data are generated due to our daily activity. It is due to the vast amount of use of the smart mobiles, Cloud data storage, and the Internet of Things. In earlier days, these technologies were utilized by large IT companies and the private sector, but now each person has a high-end smartphone along with the cloud and IoT for the easy storage of data and backup. The analysis of the data generated by social media is a tedious process and involves a lot of techniques. Some tools for social network analysis are: Gephi, Networkx, IGraph, Pajek, Node

XL, and cytoscope. Apart from these tools there are various efficient social data analysis algorithms that are far more helpful in doing analytics. The need for and use of social network analysis is very helpful in our current problem of huge data generation. In this chapter, the need for the analysis of social data along with the tools that are needed for the analysis and the techniques that are to be implemented in the field of social data analysis are covered.

Chapter 7

Technological advances in computing, data storage, networks, and sensors have dramatically increased our ability to access, store, and process huge amounts of data. "Big data" as a term has been the biggest trends of the last few years, leading to an elevation in research, as well as industry and government applications. The problem with current big data analysis faces any one of the following challenges: heterogeneity and incompleteness, scale, timeliness, privacy, and human collaboration. It's an undeniable fact that "data" forms the basis for geospatial industry. With technological advances in the collection, distribution, management, and access of data, there is an exponential increase in the amount of geospatial information. Computational intelligence techniques such as machine learning optimization and advanced data analytics can help make faster decisions. This chapter analyses how geospatial data is driving software and services market as a "big data challenge" and how biologically inspired techniques are effective in analyzing remote sensing data.

Chapter 8

Monitoring application virtualization environments for auto-scaling purposes have become an important requirement in today's computing world. In this chapter, the authors introduce the design and implementation of resource monitoring and management software architecture for application virtualization environments. They also present a prototype application of the proposed architectures with details. They discuss the performance evaluation of prototype implementation. All the results were observed to be successful.

Chapter 9

Suriya Murugan, KPR Institute of Engineering and Technology, India

Sumithra M. G., KPR Institute of Engineering and Technology, India

Cognitive radio has emerged as a promising candidate solution to improve spectrum utilization in next generation wireless networks. Spectrum sensing is one of the main challenges encountered by cognitive radio and the application of big data is a powerful way to solve various problems. However, for the increasingly tense spectrum resources, the prediction of cognitive radio based on big data is an inevitable trend. The signal data from various sources is analyzed using the big data cognitive radio framework and efficient data analytics can be performed using different types of machine learning techniques. This chapter analyses the process of spectrum sensing in cognitive radio, the challenges to process spectrum data and need for dynamic machine learning algorithms in decision making process.

Chapter 10

*Arulkumar Varatharajan, Computer Science and Engineering, Sri
    Krishna College of Engineering and Technology, Coimbatore, India*

Selvan C., National Institute of Technology, Tiruchirappalli, India

*Vimalkumar Varatharajan, Cognizant Technology Solutions,
    Coimbatore, India*

Big Data has changed the way we manage, analyze and impact the data information in any industry. A champion among the most promising zones where it will, in general, be associated with takeoff progress is therapeutic medicinal administrations. Administration examinations can diminish costs of treatment, foresee flare-ups of pestilences, keep up a key separation from preventable diseases and improve individual fulfillment overall. The chapter depicts the beginning field of a huge information investigation in human services, talks about the advantages, diagrams a design structure and approach, portrays models revealed in the writing, quickly examines the difficulties, and offers ends. A continuous examination which targets the utilization of tremendous volumes of remedial data information while combining multimodal data information from various sources is discussed. Potential locales of research inside this field which can give noteworthy impact on medicinal administrations movement are in like manner dissected.

Chapter 11

Sumit Arun Hirve, VIT-AP University, India

Pradeep Reddy C. H., VIT-AP University, India

Being premature, the traditional data visualization techniques suffer from several challenges and lack the ability to handle a huge amount of data, particularly in gigabytes and terabytes. In this research, we propose an R-tool and data analytics framework for handling a huge amount of commercial market stored data and discover knowledge patterns from the dataset for conveying the derived conclusion. In this chapter, we elaborate on pre-processing a commercial market dataset using the R tool and its packages for information and visual analytics. We suggest a recommendation system based on the data which identifies if the food entry inserted into the database is hygienic or non-hygienic based on the quality preserved attributes. For a precise recommendation system with strong predictive accuracy, we will put emphasis on Algorithms such as J48 or Naive Bayes and utilize the one who outclasses the comparison based on accuracy. Such a system, when combined with R language, can be potentially used for enhanced decision making.

Chapter 12

Ankit Shah, Shankersinh Vaghela Bapu Institute of Technology, India

Mamta C. Padole, The Maharaja Sayajirao University of Baroda, India

Big Data processing and analysis requires tremendous processing capability. Distributed computing brings many commodity systems under the common platform to answer the need for Big Data processing and analysis. Apache Hadoop is the most suitable set of tools for Big Data storage, processing, and analysis. But Hadoop found to be inefficient when it comes to heterogeneous set computers which have different processing capabilities. In this research, we propose the Saksham model which optimizes the processing time by efficient use of node processing capability and file management. The proposed model shows the performance improvement for Big Data processing. To achieve better performance, Saksham model uses two vital aspects of heterogeneous distributed computing: Effective block rearrangement policy and use of node processing capability. The results demonstrate that the proposed model successfully achieves better job execution time and improves data locality.

Preface

INTRODUCTION

Big Data consists of data sets that are too large and complex for traditional data processing and data management applications. Therefore, to obtain the valuable information within the data, one must use a variety of innovative analytical methods, such as web analytics, machine learning, and network analytics. As the study of big data becomes more popular, there is an urgent demand for studies on high-level computational intelligence and computing services for analyzing this significant area of information science.

Big Data Analytics for Sustainable Computing is a collection of innovative research that focuses on new computing and system development issues in emerging sustainable applications. Featuring coverage on a wide range of topics such as data filtering, knowledge engineering, and cognitive analytics, this publication is ideally designed for data scientists, IT specialists, computer science practitioners, computer engineers, academicians, professionals, and students seeking current research on emerging analytical techniques and data processing software.

OBJECTIVE OF THE BOOK

This book deliberates the methods of implementing big data applications in data analytics in Cloud Computing, Cognitive Analytics, Cyber Security, Data Filtering, Knowledge Engineering, Machine Learning, Real-Time Data, Scalable Data Management, Smart Grid, Ubiquitous Data and Future Advancements in Big data analytics.

ORGANIZATION OF THE BOOK

The book consists of 12 chapters that are organized as shown below.

Chapter 1

In today's world, it is necessary to use the data or the information available in a wise manner to make effective business decisions and define better objectives. If the information available is not utilized to its full extent, organizations might lose their reputation and position in this competitive world. However, data needs to be processed appropriately to gain constructive insights from it, and the heterogeneous nature of this data makes this increasingly more complex and time-consuming. The ever-increasing growth of data generated is far more than human processing capabilities and thus computing methods need to be automated to scale effectively. This chapter defines Big Data basically and provides an overview of Big Data in terms of current status, organizational effects (technology, health care, education, etc.), implementation challenges and Big Data projects. This research adopted a literature review as a methodology and refined valuable information through current journals, books, magazines, and blogs.

Chapter 2

This chapter studies about different big data techniques that have been used in classification analysis. The chapter elaborates about different types of classification algorithms and implementation procedures. The author also compared similar big data classification methods and recommends the most suitable method for the dataset to be analyzed also composed of classification processes, issues in classification, different classification algorithms and examines the different classification algorithms.

Chapter 3

Big Data analytics is the mechanism of examining complex process with different types of data sets in order to determine the hidden pattern or information, correlations, and data preferences to make decision at proper level. Various forms of techniques are available to process large amount of data, but the success lies at the applicability of right platform for the data set chosen. This chapter focuses towards the tools, applications and techniques that correspond to the field of big data analytics. Also, this chapter covers the security aspects of data handling mechanism such as threats, attacks and its services towards data analytics in a big data platform. The process of clients, server and its affordable attacks in a big data platform has also been addressed.

Chapter 4

Today, Big Data is used in every business, hence the data analytics tools and techniques are in demand that is widely used to analyze big sets of structured or unstructured data. The literature selected for this paper clearly discusses the various scenarios where big data analytics have been successfully implemented or could see possible usage. Big data has the potential to revolutionize every domain, whether it is Education, Research or even health care sector. This paper is aimed to showcase the insight of big data and its tools and techniques the companies have adopted to deal with data problems. The article is divided into seven sections. In the first section "Introduction to Big World", this includes an introduction part and why it is very essential in the present-day scenario. Second Section "Research Scope" deals with the scope of the study and challenges evolved around this technique. "Big Data Business Model" and various open-source big data "Frameworks" have been discussed in the Third, Fourth and Fifth sections. Sixth section "The role of Government in Big Data", showcase how can a government can store and analyze established and unstructured statistics in an effort to maximize its cost. "Limitations" and "Suggestion for future research" has been discussed in the Seventh and an eighth section were drawn a series of conclusions, concerning the various reviews and the possible future investigations are also indicated.

Chapter 5

In this chapter, a filter feature selection algorithm was developed and its performance tested. In the initial step, the algorithm dichotomizes the dataset, transforming all input and output values to binary. Then, the algorithm separately computes the association between each binary predictor and the binary class variable using relative odds (odds ratios). The value of the odds ratios represents the importance ranking of the corresponding explanatory variable in determining the output. Variables with higher values of odds ratios indicate their importance in classification modeling. Logistic regression classification was deployed to test the performance of the new algorithm in comparison with three existing feature selection algorithms: Fisher index, Pearson's correlation, and varImp function. A number of experimental datasets were employed and in most cases, the subsets selected by the new algorithm produced models with higher classification accuracy than the subsets suggested by existing feature selection algorithms. Classification accuracy was evaluated using 10-fold cross validation. The classification accuracy results showed that the proposed algorithm is a reliable alternative in filter feature selection. It is therefore recommended for use in feature selection for binary classification problems.

Chapter 6

The amount of data generated everyday seems to be increasing day to day based on various activities and application in real time data processing. The process of understanding the data, modeling the requirements seem to be a difficult task in data handling and its applications. Some of the data has been managed and monitored in cloud-based storage for frequent access and retrieval. But most of the data resides at repository and on servers which can be localized to different platforms. Among all the analytics in action the phenomenon of social network analysis has becoming trending and needed with regard to applicability of real time issues and the decision-making process. This chapter completely covers the techniques and tools that preferably correspond to social network analysis and its applications.

Chapter 7

This chapter analyses the challenges of Big Data like heterogeneity and incompleteness, scale, timeliness, privacy and human collaboration. The chapter also discusses about the advances in computing, data storage, networks and sensors have dramatically increased our ability to access, store and process huge amounts of data. The impact of big data processing in the field of remote sensing is elaborated using computational intelligence techniques. Finally, this chapter analyses how geospatial data is driving software and services market as a "Big-Data challenge" and how biologically inspired techniques are effective in analyzing remote sensing data.

Chapter 8

In this chapter, the authors focus on software architectures, which include resource usage monitoring for application virtualization environments. In particular, they propose a software architecture, which dynamically monitors and manages the application virtualization environments according to instantly changing resource needs. The proposed real-time resource management methodology analyzes the streaming performance data for auto-scaling purposes. We apply complex event processing on performance data collected from application virtualization environment. This approach is able to detect potential failures in application virtualization environments by continuously monitoring performance data. They also introduce details of a prototype application of the proposed software architectures and discuss its performance evaluation from the perspective of scalability and performance. The results of the evaluation are promising.

Chapter 9

This chapter highlights about how Cognitive Radio (CR) has emerged as a promising candidate solution to improve spectrum utilization in next generation wireless networks. The significance of spectrum sensing and utilization is analysed for addressing big data applications. Also, various machine learning techniques are studied that be applied for big data cognitive radio framework. The process of spectrum sensing in cognitive radio, the challenges to process spectrum data and need for dynamic machine learning algorithms in making efficient decision-making process are explored in this chapter.

Chapter 10

This chapter highlights the idea of how Big Data is always showing signs of change. Contemporarily genomics and post genomics innovations produce enormous measures of crude information about complex biochemical and administrative procedures in life forms. In this chapter, three territories of big information investigation in prescription are examined. These three regions do not completely mirror the utilization of big information examinations in medicine, these are image processing diagnosis, therapy assessment, and planning; medical signal processing volume and speed hindrances; and Big Data analytics in healthcare for big data in insurance. Privacy and security in Big Data analytics for human services and medication are important protection of the patients. Information management and integrity difficulties span the whole range of the Big Data lifecycle. Big Data analytics in drug and human services is the promising procedure of incorporating, investigating, and breaking down of huge sum complex heterogeneous information with various natures.

Chapter 11

In this chapter, the authors propose an R-tool and data analytics framework for handling a huge amount of commercial market store data and discovers knowledge patterns out of the dataset for conveying the derived conclusion. They elaborate on pre-processing a commercial market dataset using the R tool and its packages for information and visual analytics. They suggest a recommendation system based on the data which identifies if the food entry inserted into the database is hygienic or non-hygienic based on the quality preservation attributes. For a precise recommendation system with strong predictive accuracy, we will put emphasis on Algorithms such as J48 or Naive Bayes and utilize the one who outclasses the comparison based on accuracy. Such a system, when combined with R language, can be potentially used for enhanced decision making.

Chapter 12

This research work aims to optimize Big Data processing time on a heterogeneous distributed environment. Hadoop MapReduce framework is the most popular framework for Big Data processing. To improve Hadoop performance, HDFS is an imperative component. HDFS not only allows to store the big data but also provides handy support to distribute and process the huge amount of data. Default HDFS block placement policy requires a major improvement in terms of placing of data replicas and processing. This work contributes to the block rearrangement algorithm along with the proposed "Saksham" model for performance optimization of Big Data processing. The proposed approach, Saksham: block rearrangement policy leverages the processing capacity of CPU, during block placement. This approach helps MapReduce to minimize the internode and inter-rack transfer. The research work demonstrates that data blocks of a specific file can be placed on the specified nodes. This approach will not affect the overall load balancing of a cluster as other remaining files will not be affected.

Anandakumar Haldorai
Sri Eshwar College of Engineering, Coimbatore, Tamilnadu, India

Arulmurugan Ramu
Presidency University, Bangalore, Karnataka, India

Acknowledgment

The editors would like to acknowledge the help of all the people involved in this project and, more specifically, to the authors and reviewers that took part in the review process.

The editors would like to thank each one of the authors for their contributions. Our sincere gratitude goes to the chapter's authors who contributed their time and expertise to this book. We believe that the team of authors provides the perfect blend of knowledge and skills that went into authorizing this book. We thank each of the authors for developing their time, patience, perseverance and effort towards this book.

A special thanks to the publisher team, who showed the editors, ropes to start and continue. The editors would like to express their gratitude to all the people support, share, talked things over, read, wrote, offered comments, allowed us to quote their remarks, and assisted in editing, proofreading, and design through the book journey.

Chapter 1
Understanding Big Data

Naciye Güliz Uğur
Sakarya University, Turkey

Aykut Hamit Turan
Sakarya University, Turkey

ABSTRACT

In today's world, it is necessary to use data or information available in a wise manner to make effective business decisions and define better objectives. If the information available is not utilized to its full extent, organizations might lose their reputation and position in this competitive world. However, data needs to be processed appropriately to gain constructive insights from it, and the heterogeneous nature of this data makes this increasingly more complex and time-consuming. The ever-increasing growth of data generated is far more than human processing capabilities and thus computing methods need to be automated to scale effectively. This chapter defines Big Data basically and provides an overview of Big Data in terms of current status, organizational effects (technology, health care, education, etc.), implementation challenges and Big Data projects. This research adopted literature review as methodology and refined valuable information through current journals, books, magazines and blogs.

DOI: 10.4018/978-1-5225-9750-6.ch001

Figure 1. Market predictions on big data (USD Billion)
Source: IDC (2015)

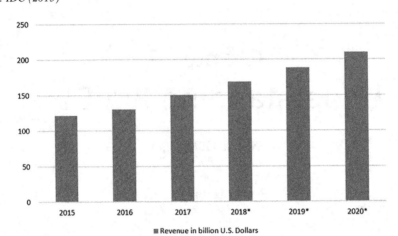

■ Revenue in billion U.S. Dollars

INTRODUCTION

Big data has been one of the major areas of focus in the field of data management. Big data provides the business solutions which help the organizations making their decisions. Current growing value for the data helps organizations innovate quickly the optimum usage of data and keep up the edge (Lukoinova and Rubin, 2014).

Implementation of methodologies should be in context with a technology base that is growing to be a moving target. The main technology behind fostering the rate of innovation in big data platforms and solutions is the open source technology development and delivery model. Organizations face challenges with evolving business needs and technologies, organizations hold the flexibility for the platforms, solutions, and evolving their capabilities so that they derive value and positive insights from their big data investments (Nimmagadda and Dreher, 2013).

According to the latest Worldwide Semiannual Big Data and Analytics Spending Guide from International Data Corporation (IDC), worldwide revenues for big data and business analytics (BDA) will grow from $130.1 billion in 2016 to more than $203 billion in 2020 (IDC, 2015).

Organizations which handle the big data and implement its methodologies are expected to make 40% more profits than regular software industry does in the current scenario. The increasing value for big data makes it easier to predict the gains for the organization in the future. Organizations currently lack the human resource and talent which can give them the best big data engineering experience and help them grow.

The era of big data has established a new path for exploring data in newer forms and finding different ways to handle the data on a large scale. Although processing and maintaining a large data is a challenge, big data challenges have given the scope to find a solution for these challenges and implement them for a better data environment (Chen et al., 2013). Big data has been into existence since the 1990s and data integration has been one of the major challenges since then. Data Integration in large: Challenges of Reuse, a research paper which was published in 1994 signifies the existence of big data from 1990s.

This chapter defines Big Data basically and provides an overview of Big Data in terms of current status, organizational effects (technology, health care, education etc.), implementation challenges and Big Data projects. This research adopted literature review as methodology and refined valuable information through current journals, books, magazines and blogs.

BACKGROUND

Evolution of large data sets from major industries is termed as big data in the field of data science. The first large-scale methods for metadata creation and analysis (an arrangement of clay tablets revealing data about livestock) has been linked to the Sumerian people, active in the early Bronze Age (Erikson, 1950). Similarly, card catalogs, and other information methods used in libraries (Lee, Clarke and Perti, 2015), are forerunners to the large-scale digitized metadata collections of today, as they too were technologies used for gathering and storing facts about data in comprehensive and systematized ways (Lee, Clarke and Perti, 2015). The rise in digital technology is leading to the overflow of data (Gog et al., 2015), which constantly requires more updated and faster data storage systems (Sookhak, Gani, Khan, and Buyya, 2017). The recognition of data excess started as early as the 1930s but was not actually named Big Data until the mid-1990s by John Mashey (Kitchin and McArdle, 2016). The sudden increase in the U.S. population, the dispensing of social security numbers, and the wide-ranging increase of knowledge (research) required more detailed and organized record-keeping (Gandomi and Haider, 2015).

Big data can be classified as the large volumes of data-sets with a higher complexity level. Gandomi and Haider (2015), IDC, IBM, Gartner, and many others have contributed with an excellent summary regarding Big Data characteristics. Clearly, size is the first characteristic that comes to mind considering the question "what is big data?" (Gandomi and Haider 2015). Following that, the Three V's

Figure 2. 5V's of big data

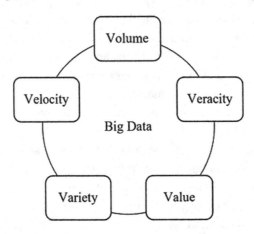

have emerged as a common framework to describe big data (Chen, Chiang, and Storey, 2012; Kwon, Lee, and Shin, 2014): Volume, Variety, and Velocity. There have been more additions: IBM, White (2012) introduced Veracity – the fourth V, SAS introduced Variability and Complexity, the fifth V and Oracle introduced Value as the sixth V. While these are commonly used today there are possibilities with further enhancements more may be added or defined further contextually. There is even the possibility of having "smarts" added to this volume of data as well. There are questions about the usefulness and life of the data as well.

The concept of big data has been described as "a phenomenon defined by the rapid acceleration in the expanding volume of high velocity, complex, and diverse types of data. Big Data is often defined along three dimensions -- volume, velocity, and variety" (TechAmerica Foundation, 2012, p. 7). Many authors will refer to those three characteristics as the 3V's. Others define big data as "datasets whose size is beyond the ability of typical database software tools to capture, store, manage, and analyze" (MGI, 2012, p. 3).

Despite big data 3V's characteristics - volume, velocity. and variety, some authors write about multiple fourth V's such as variability, vulnerability, veracity, and value. The fundamental definition is not affected by many V's, but all together they do provide a better understanding of different aspects of big data (Seddon and Curie, 2017). It is anticipated that volume of data will increase 44 times by 2020; velocity will increase as data is brought in from every imaginable device, and variety will increase due to a greater diversity in the data being collected. (Fernandes, O'Connor, and Weaver, 2012).

In order to define Big Data, we look at the definitions for each of the 5 Vs below as they seem to characterize Big Data broadly:

- *Volume* - Volume is the large data-sets that represent big data. Volume makes a huge difference for an organization as the huge data is what they require to make business decisions.
- *Variety* - This represents the different types of data available, such as text, numbers, images, videos, documents, spreadsheets, etc. This signifies the category or type of data something belongs to. The big data comes from different sources which makes it very unpredictable and consists of different forms which are ideally unstructured, structured and semi-structured. The unstructured data has the log files, HTML tags. Structured data consists of the relational database data which is represented in tables. Semi-structured data consists of XML files and data from other text files.
- *Velocity* - Velocity represents the speed of data at which it is transmitted and received from the source and destination. Velocity plays a crucial role in data management as the process flows in the business are highly impacted by the speed of data transfer.
- *Veracity* - Veracity represents the uncertainty of the data as it comes from an untrusted source and needs more optimization. Veracity ideally is characterized by raw data.
- *Value* - Value represents the revenue and market value gained by an organization using the big data. Value is measured in terms of revenue and business's success with their clients using the tools for generating the value for data.

The five v's of big data impact the scope, time, and budget for any project which deals with big data (Yin and Kaynak, 2015). The opportunity cost, ambiguity, and collection ability play a role in authenticity/reliability of the data, the inconsistencies behind gathering and gaining the data and the value derived and implementation costs from the data.

In summary, having gone through the definitions that exist in literature today and having looked at characteristics to date, we are still not close to agreeing on the definition of the term, Big Data.

Figure 3. Big data market by service (USD million)
Source: Grand View Research (2016)

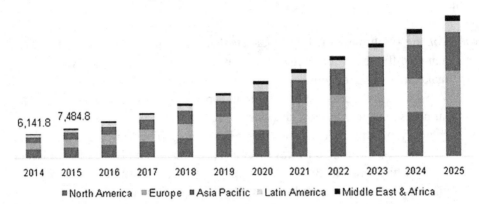

CURRENT STATUS

IT departments do not measure the growth of Big Data by the number of records that are in storage but by the amount of space required to store the records (Kitchin, and McArdle, 2016). To illustrate this point Abbasi, Sarker, and Chiang (2016) noted this space now consists of "Gigabytes, Terabytes, Exabytes, and Petabytes" (p. 5) versus previous traditionally records based number approaches to data management. As well as the expanding data size, the monetary value of Big Data also increases with a very high rate. The global big data market size was valued at USD 25.67 billion in 2015 and is expected to witness a significant growth over the forecast period (Grand View Research, 2016).

This widespread growth pattern stems from many different sources such as social networking sites, wired and wireless broadband access, and the widespread use of search engine sites (Hashem, et al., 2015). Additional non-interactive devices are also filling storage such as radio frequency identification (RFID) and sensors associated with the Internet of Things (IoT) (Reimsbach-Kounatze, 2015). Expanding market also affects software markets. Big Data market is shared by analytics, database, visualization and distribution tools, and software. Database related products are the main driver of the commercial transactions.

This growth is so rapid that both practitioners and academics are trying to keep up with newer and faster analytics and statistics (Gandomi and Haider, 2015). Since the majority of Big Data is unstructured (approximately 95%), the data is harder to process (Gandomi and Haider, 2015). While IoT and Big Data analytics appear to

Figure 4. Big data market share by software (USD million)
Source: Grand View Research (2016)

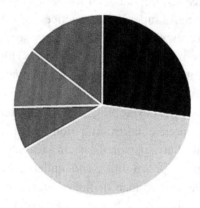

■ Analytics ▪ Database ■ Visualization ▪ Distribution Tools ■ Others

have incredible potential for converting various businesses, many academics and industry experts are struggling to comprehend these ideas and capture the business value in joining IOT and big data analytics (Riggins and Wamba, 2015). In addition, very few academic studies exist assessing the real potential of IoT and Big Data analytics (Riggins and Wamba, 2015). However, as noted previously, there are many different projects underway to resolve the difficulty of converting raw data into information and then into knowledge.

In recent years, the explosive growth of data has been observed in numerous industries like e-commerce, health, social networks, etc. Access to preferred data in such massive datasets necessitates sophisticated and effective gathering methods. In the past, special algorithms have served as common descriptors for numerous tasks including image cataloging and recovery (Ahmad et al., 2018). The algorithms perform extremely well when equated to hand-crafted queries and filters. However, these algorithms are typically high dimensional, necessitating a lot of memory and CPU for indexing and gathering. For extremely large datasets, use of these high dimensional algorithms in raw usage becomes infeasible (Ahmad et al., 2018).

Boone, Skipper, and Hazen (2017) conducted a study to Increase request for receptive, cost effectual, and maintainable procedures that necessitated service parts deliberation and acceptance of new industry models and resolutions that cover the complete life-cycle of merchandises. Many organizations are looking to big data information. Though service parts supervisors have long trusted examination and optimization, big data information is thought to be more incorporating and thus particularly capable. Hereafter, big data and its associated uses are suggested as a means of refining service parts supervision practices. More precisely, information gathered from consultations with service parts supervisors is used to build a basis describing the encounters of service parts supervision. This background then aids as the foundation for big data connected suggestions for overcoming the emphasized encounters. Thus, the examination answers the demand for service parts supervision connected backgrounds while developing a starting point for suggestions for supervisorial thought and intellectual examination (Boone et al., 2017).

The advance of Big Data that of personal data, in particular, dispersed in numerous data sources presents huge opportunities and understandings for companies to discover and influence the importance of linked and assimilated data. However, privacy fears impede distribution or trading data for connection across diverse organizations (Vatsalan et al., 2017). Privacy-preserving record linkage (PPRL) purposes to address this situation by recognizing and joining records that match to the identical real-world individual across numerous data sources stored by diverse parties without revealing any sensitive data about these individuals (Boyd et al., 2017). PPRL is progressively being required in numerous practical application areas. Instances include public health, observation of crime, deception exposure, and national security. Big Data and PPRL creates numerous challenges, with the three main ones being (a) scalability to several large data warehouses, due to their considerable volume and the movement of data within Big Data solutions, (b) attaining high quality and effects of the link in the occurrence of variety and veracity of Big Data, and (c) maintaining discretion and confidentiality of the individuals represented in Big Data pools (Vatsalan et al., (2017).

IT departments have encountered several new skills due to Big Data, including how to gather, allocate, accumulate, clean, examine, filter, examine, portion, protect, and envision data (Purdam, 2016). Considering the problem of accumulating and saving big data, an array of new systems emerged in recent years to handle these kinds of big data encounters (Gudivada, Baeza Yates, and Raghavan, 2015). Big Data computational analysis is considered an important aspect to be further enhanced to intensify the operational margin of both public and private initiatives and signifies the next frontier for their modernization, competition, and throughput (Esposito et al., 2015). Big Data is typically formed in different sectors of private and public organizations, often physically distributed throughout the world, and are categorized by a large size and variety (Rajan, 2015). Therefore, there is a solid need for strategies handling larger and faster amounts of data in settings characterized by multifaceted event processing programs and multiple mixed sources, dealing with the numerous issues related to resourcefully gathering, examining, and distributing them in a fully controlled manner (Esposito et al., 2015). This necessity leads to newer, faster, and better software (Kim et al., 2016).

Developing and running software creates large quantities of raw data about the development process and the end user usage. This information can be turned into creative perception with the assistance of skilled data scientists (Kim et al., 2016). Unfortunately, data scientists with the skills to analyze these very large data-sets are difficult to come by (Hilbert, 2016). Data scientist comes in many different forms such as Insight Providers, Modeling Specialists, Platform Builders, Polymaths, and Team Leaders (Kim et al., 2016).

Many "big data" and "fast data" analysis methods such as Hadoop, Spark, and Storm have come from the Apache foundation (Dimopoulos, Krintz, and Wolski, 2016). These programs are used by analysts to implement a variety of applications for query support, data mining, machine learning, real-time stream analysis, statistical analysis, and image processing (Dimopoulos, Krintz, and Wolski, 2016). Another software platform named R is a free, prevailing, open source software platform with widespread statistical computing and graphics abilities (Xu, et al., 2016). Due to its advanced expressiveness and many domain explicit packages, R has become the 'lingua franca' for many parts of data analysis, acquiring power from community-developed packages (Xu et al., 2016).

With the extremely rapid growth of information and intricacy of systems; artificial intelligence, rapid machine learning, and computational intelligence methods are highly required. Many predictable computational intelligence methods face constraints in learning such as intensive human involvement in addition to connection time. However, effective learning algorithms offer different yet significant benefits including rapid learning, ease of execution, and minimal human involvement. The need for competent and fast execution of machine learning methods in big data and dynamic changing methods poses many research encounters (Sun et al., 2017). Big Data, from an industry point of view, is leading the way to newer and better methods of doing business (Shin and Choi, 2015). The common view, in most industries, is that growth of Big Data, though difficult now, will achieve a status that is manageable and thus controllable in the future (Kitchin and Lauriault, 2015). German officials and scientist believe this so strongly that they are referring to Big Data as the Fourth Industrial Revolution and calling it "Industrie 4.0" (Yin and Kaynak, 2015). Akter and Wamba (2016) used the phrase "the next frontier for innovation, competition, and productivity." Industries such as retail, are utilizing Radiofrequency Identification (RFID) marked merchandises to develop marketing campaigns based on the movement of merchandise (Cao, Chychyla, and Stewart, 2015).

ORGANIZATIONAL EFFECTS

Akter and Wamba (2016) stated the definition of Big Data is more than merely larger storage or the gathering of data from social media sites with millions of members. Bigness is an indication of scalability issues in one or more extents — the four Vs of variety, velocity, veracity, and volume (Abbasi, Sarker, and Chiang, 2016). Big data is an inaccuracy, suggesting that bigness is a fundamental characteristic of a dataset. Rather, Big Data defines the association between a dataset and its usage framework (Akter and Wamba, 2016). A dataset is too large for a specific use when it is computationally not feasible to convert the data using traditional or outdated software tools (George et al., 2016). With the immense amounts of data currently available, businesses in nearly every industry are focusing on manipulating data for the competitive benefit (He et al., 2015). A key challenge for IT researchers and IT experts alike is that data growth rate is exceeding the ability to maintain the required hardware and necessary software to manage the high volume of data (Saltz, 2015). Simply stating, analyzing "data in motion" creates new encounters because the anticipated patterns and perceptions are moving targets, and this is not the situation for static data (Abbasi, Sarker, and Chiang, 2016). Junque de Fortuny et al. (2013) noted the growth rate is approximately 50% annually or doubling every two years.

Gobble (2013) and Manyika et al., (2011) identify big data as the next big thing in innovation and the next frontier for innovation, competition, and productivity, respectively. Strawn (2012) called it the fourth paradigm of science. Furthermore, McAfee and Brynjolfsson (2012) appropriately categorized their article on Big Data as a management revolution similar to what Ann Keller et al., (2012) termed Big Data as bringing a revolution in science and technology.

The emergence of new technologies, new processes, threats, regulations and thought leadership all affect the organization more than ever. Organizations which handle the big data and implement its methodologies are expected to make 40% more profits than regular software industry in the current scenario. The increasing value for big data makes it easier to predict the gains for the organization in the future. Organizations currently lack the human resource and talent which can give them the best big data engineering experience and help them grow.

Technology is now being established that is able to process enormous amounts of organized and unorganized data from various causes and sources. This information is often denoted to as big data, and opens new areas of study and uses that will have a growing impact in all parts of society (Marvin et al., 2017). Big Data and its velocity are being applied in the food safety area and acknowledged several encouraging trends particularly the speed by which the information is being transmitted. In numerous parts of the world, governments encourage the publication on the Internet of all information produced in publicly financed research projects. This program opens new chances for interested parties dealing with food safety to report issues which were not conceivable before. The use of mobile phones as exposure devices for food safety and the communication of social media as early caution of food safety situations are a few instances of the new improvements that are conceivable due to Big Data (Marvin et al., 2017).

Big data will also offer new potentials for research by allowing access to linked data, medical information, and social media. The total extent of information, however, does not remove and may even intensify systematic inaccuracy. Therefore, procedures addressing systematic error, scientific knowledge, and underlying theories are more significant than ever to confirm that the indicator is apparent behind the noise (Ehrenstein et al., 2017).

The era of big data has established a new path for exploring data in newer forms and finding different ways to handle the data on a large scale. Although processing and maintaining a large data is a challenge, big data challenges have given the scope to find a solution for these challenges and implement them for a better data environment (Du, 2013). Big data has been into existence since the 1990s and ways to success have been one of the major mysteries since then. Data Integration in large: Challenges of Reuse, a research paper which was published in 1994 signifies the existence of big data challenges from the 1990s.

Technology

Netflix analyzes millions of real-time data points that its viewers create, thus helping the firm determine if a pilot will become a successful show (Xu et al., 2015). Facebook hosts over 500 terabytes of data every day – including uploaded photos, likes and users' posts (Provost and Fawcett, 2013). Google alone contributed roughly $54 billion to the US economy in 2009 (Labrinidis and Jagadish, 2012). Akamai Technologies Inc, a leading global Content Delivery Network provider collects and analyzes petabytes of data every day to help its customer base with cloud performance and security initiatives. Amazon, another e-commerce/technology company, utilizes its various data points to ensure personalized experiences for its client base.

Machine learning (ML) is constantly releasing its influence in a wide collection of applications. It has been pressed to the front in current years somewhat owing to the arrival of Big Data and its velocity. ML procedures have never been better guaranteed while tested by Big Data. Big Data empowers ML procedures to expose more fine-grained configurations and make more opportune and precise forecasts than ever before; yet it creates major tests to ML such as model scalability and distributed computing (Zhou et al., 2017). The framework of Big Data is balanced on ML which follows the stages of preprocessing, knowledge, and assessment. In addition, the framework is also comprised of four other components, namely big data, consumer, realm, and method (Zhou et al., 2017).

Healthcare

Burg (2014) argued that Big Data can enable a better and transparent healthcare system. Allouche (2014) identified cost saving and unnecessary procedure reducing capabilities from Big Data. Tormay (2015), identifies pharmaceutical RandD as the engine that fuels the pharmaceutical industry. He claims this engine has been declining in productivity over the last 20 years with increasing costs, demands for better standard care, and concomitant productivity challenges. He believes that data, specifically the fast and voluminous nature along with technological advances will help revitalize this engine. Furthermore, Groves et al. (2013) document the innovations identified because of Big Data projects. Another organization, Intel, announced its Collaborative Cancel Cloud in August of 2015 to enable diagnosing of cancer patients based on their specific genome sequencing and tailor a precision treatment plan for them all based on the concept of Big Data.

Education

Erwin (2015) insists students to be more literate in their abilities to use data. He argues that there is a growing call for students to develop data literacy. His theory is more of a project-based learning where students solve real-world problems with data that is provided to them will enable them to build skills and be able to meet the current demands of business. Similarly, Rijmenam (2014) reasoned changes in the education systems by using Big Data to change the way that students and teachers interact. A more practical example, Gwinnett, in suburban Atlanta, Georgia, is the 14th largest school system in the United States, has 23,000 employees and transports more people every school day than the locally based carrier, Delta Air Lines. All that activity generates information, more and more of it captured digitally and in 2002, as the school system's leaders continued seeking fresh educational solutions, they began to explore how analytics could help how all that information could be investigated for patterns, relationships, dependencies, and predictors.

Public Sector (Government)

Gamage (2016), in his article, examines the opportunities presented by effectively harnessing big data in the public-sector context. He talks about the impact of Big Data and how it will play an important role in the future. Furthermore, he also outlines key challenges to be addressed to adapt and realize the benefits of Big Data in the public sector. Similarly, another article, stemming from SAP's partnership within the Middle East governments, documents high level of Big Data production, consumption and the need to train public sector to be successful at these opportunities.

Miscellaneous

The Big Data Strategy framework in Servitization as proposed by Opresnik and Taisch (2014) is focusing on new revenue streams and decreasing product-service costs in manufacturing. An optimization model for green supply chain management based on Big Data proposed by Zhao et al. (2017) is a scheme that minimizes the inherent risk of hazardous materials, associated carbon emissions and economic cost. The Cebr (Center of Economics and Business Research) (2012) has anticipated that the benefits of big data innovation opportunities would contribute £24 billion to the UK economy between 2012 and 2017. These opportunities are described to be identifying hidden patterns, better decision making, improving business processes and developing new business models (Halaweh and Massry 2015). There are many more examples of such initiatives and values across industries that organizations are realizing and going back to the accumulation of data is reaching out to every industry and organization across geographies.

IMPLEMENTATION CHALLENGES

The growth in big data comes along with unstructured data which dominates the data mainly. Therefore, organizations tend to find new methods for handling the unstructured data in large volumes. Organizations implement technologies like Hadoop to handle this data, currently as Hadoop is the only big data tool currently in the market. Hadoop is an open source currently being provided by two organizations Hortonworks and Cloudera. However, some of the tools in Hadoop are not available in the services provided by Cloudera. Big data tools are used individually for different tasks based on the requirement. Some of the big data tools are MapReduce, Yarn, Pig, Hive (Seay et al., 2014).

Another important aspect of big data is the integration services and the storage. Big data integration services include the tools which are used to integrate the data from different sources to gain meaningful insights. Big data integration plays a major role as it provides the organization with necessary data which stands as a base to make the business decisions. KARMA and Talend stand as the best data integration tools currently in the market and Talend has been used by Groupon, one of the largest e-commerce organizations. The different data jobs from different sources were implemented using Talend which gave them good profits on a whole.

The storage of big data has been another important aspect, where the data is generated every second. A load of huge data chunks has to be managed efficiently in order to make use of this data. The storage servers and third-party storage providers bridge the gap between big data and storage. But securing this data is much important for organizations. Accordingly, they tend to use different security measures to prevent the data breach (Ives et al., 1999).

Menon and Hegde (2015) wrote that the indication of the growth of knowledge as an approaching storage and retrieval problem came in 1944 when Fremont Rider, a Wesleyan University librarian, estimated that university libraries in America were doubling in size every sixteen years. Given this growth rate, Rider estimated that in 2040 the Yale Library would contain approximately 200,000,000 volumes, stretching over 6,000 miles of shelves and requiring a cataloging staff of over six thousand people to maintain. While the development of knowledge was generally considered good for humanity, it was leading to a major storage and retrieval situation for libraries (Menon and Hegde, 2015). As the amount of data continued to multiply in the ensuing decades, organizations began to design, comprehend, and execute centralized computing methods that would allow them to automate their inventory systems (Erikson, 1950). As these methods began to mature across organizations and develop within enterprises, organizations began to apply the analysis of the data to avail themselves with solutions and insight that would allow them to make improved business judgments i.e., business intelligence (Wang, 2016).

Wixom et al. (2014) believed that with business intelligence continuing to grow rapidly, the challenge of management and storage quickly became a real issue within IT departments. To offer more functionality, digital storage had to become more cost-effective (Chang, and Wills, 2016). This challenge led to the advent of Business Intelligence (BI) platforms (Wang, 2016). As these BI platforms continue to develop, the data gathered enabled and will enable companies, scientific and medical researchers, our national defense and intelligence organizations, and other organizations to create innovative breakthroughs (Wixom et al., 2014).

At the same time as it problematized data overflow, the Big Data industry was also involved in spreading the myths such as, methodological issues no longer mattered, Big Data provided a comprehensive and unbiased source of data on which to base decisions about data, and in hyping the promises of Big Data sets (Kimble and Milolidakis, 2015). Like Wes Nichols (2013), co-founder and CEO of MarketShare, a predictive-analytics company based in Los Angeles, many market researchers placed a great amount of confidence in the usability of large datasets that concurrently produced and analyzed data. In the past, associating sales data with a few dozen isolated advertising variables used to be acceptable (Oh and Min, 2015). However, many of the world's biggest companies are now deploying analytics 2.0 (Jobs, Aukers, and Gilfoil, 2015), a set of practices that compute through terabytes of data and hundreds of variables in real time to define how well advertising touch points interact (Fesenmaier et al., 2016). This resulted in 10 to 30 percent improvements in marketing performance.

Instead of data storage and integration issues, big data visualization has also been one of the major challenges for organizations. Therefore, they tend to build data samples to build on the tools for data visualization. Visualizations help to understand the data better than its original form. Visual analytics can be integrated with big data to understand and implement the data for a better business.

Some of the data visualization challenges identified is given by:

Meeting the need for speed: Many organizations use data for their business growth. And this data comes from numerous sources. Organizations tend to use different methods to keep this data organized to derive the insights. Few of these methods are discussed below:

- Visualization of data which helps them to perform the analysis more efficiently.
- As the challenge grows with more granularity constraints, some of the organizations are using parallel processing hardware units to grab the large crunch of data at once. This helps them to perform data optimization quickly.
- Grid computing has been another approach to grab a large amount of data in smaller units of time.

Understanding the data: Getting a meaningful insight from the data is a huge task as the data comes from different sources. For an instance, data coming from a social networking site, where it is important to know the user from whom the data is gathered from. Implementation of visual analytics without the proper context can prove useless for organizations. Expertise at domain level is very much needed in this case as the analytics team needs to be aware of the data sources and the understanding of consumers' data usage and interpretation.

Addressing data quality: Although the data is collected and processed quickly to serve the purpose, it is very likely that a data which has no context is of no value to the consumer. To address this challenge, organizations need to have an information management team to analyze the data and assure that the data is clean. Visualizing this analyzed data can be of a huge value and source of information for organizations and the consumers.

Displaying meaningful results: Graphical representation of huge data is a common challenge faced by organizations. For an instance, consider the data from a huge retail business. When the stock-keeping unit (SKU) data which has more than a billion plots, it's difficult to have a look at each plot and speculate. Therefore, data needs to be split into clusters and the small data is to be separated from the big ones to derive the insights.

Dealing with outliers: Big data can be represented in the form of tables and sets as well, but this would be a challenge to viewers. The efficient way of displaying the big data would be by implementing the visual analytics and represent the data in the form of graphs and charts. This would make it easier for the viewers to understand and spot the growth.

On a whole, data visualization plays a key role in big data as this is the main source of information for organizations. The simpler the form of representation is, the simpler would be the analysis and derivations from this data.

Organizations face many challenges with big data in terms of storage, visualization or integration, therefore they look for new solutions and tools which can handle the big data efficiently. This clearly states that big data is the new challenge which needs more research for its development.

SOLUTIONS AND RECOMMENDATIONS

In today's world, it is necessary to use the data or information available in a wise manner to make effective business decisions and define better objectives (Laudon and Laudon, 2016). If the information available is not utilized to its full extent, organizations might lose their reputation and position in this competitive world. However, data needs to be processed appropriately to gain constructive insights from it, and the heterogeneous nature of this data makes this increasingly more complex and time-consuming (Ang and Teo, 2000). The ever-increasing growth of data generated is far more than human processing capabilities and thus computing methods need to be automated to scale effectively (Das et al., 2015).

Variety, velocity, and volume were identified as three key attributes of Big Data by Laney in 2001. Many authors and business specialists modify these attributes. In 2012, IBM added a fourth dimension to this called veracity. Ebner et al. (2014) define Big Data as "a phenomenon characterized by an ongoing increase in volume, variety, velocity, and veracity of data that requires advanced techniques and technologies to capture, store, distribute, manage, and analyze these data." Big Data helps to unlock potentials of different fields like predictive modeling, data integration, network analysis, natural language processing, etc. Thus, Big Data technologies have huge economic potential that should be harnessed by executives in a proper manner. Questions related to the IT infrastructure, capturing crucial information, analytical requirements, etc. should be asked by the executives to determine the way in which way Big Data solution needs to be handled.

In recent times, the research on Big Data has been always concentrated toward creating better algorithms and designing robust data models (Saltz and Shamshurin, 2016). However, not much work has been done regarding finding out the best methodology for executing such projects (Ahangama and Poo, 2015) (Saltz, 2015). The exploratory nature of Big Data projects demands a more specific methodology that can handle the uncertain business requirements of such projects (Saltz, 2015). According to a survey carried out by Kelly and Kaskade (2013), "300 companies reported that 55% of Big Data projects don't get completed and others fall short of their objectives." The reasons for such project failure can be identified at the beginning of the project or can be reduced at a later stage by some coordination methodology (Saltz, 2015).

A well-defined Big Data analysis project methodology would help to address different issues like roles and responsibilities of team members, project stakeholders, expected project outcome, relevant data architecture or infrastructure, approaches for validation of results, etc. (Saltz, 2015). It might be a notion that there is no need for such a methodology to be defined since; Big Data projects are often open-ended in nature. Agile methodology can be used for such projects instead. The sheer goal of finding the "value in data" is not enough. There needs to be communication between the team regarding the next steps (Saltz, 2015).

Different process methodologies have been defined in other domains. The Software Development Life Cycle (SDLC) is used in the software development domain. Optimizing business processes is used in the operations research domain, while statistical analysis is used in quantitative research. Big Data projects do not always fall specifically in these categories, although they might be similar to them. Software projects have less focus on the data aspect. A large number of extract-transform-load (ETL) processes need to be performed. Determining the relevant data sources is a crucial task in Big Data projects. This step is not a part of the SDLC. Kaisler et al. (2013) found out that "trend analysis may not require the precision that traditional database (DB) systems provide." This shows that acceptable levels of data quality depend in most cases on data usage (Kaisler et al., 2013). Even if any software methodology was to be applied to Big Data projects, it would be difficult to determine which software methodology to use since different alternatives like waterfall or agile are in practice. Business Intelligence is another domain that deals with making effective business decisions by scrutinizing the data available. A business intelligence system that can react to unanticipated requirements also needs to be developed (Krawatzeck, Dinter, and Thi, 2015). Thus, any combined BI methodology cannot suffice a Big Data project thoroughly.

Goodwin (2011) noted that poor communication is a factor due to which 75% of corporate business intelligence projects face failure. Thus, Team Effectiveness is an essential aspect of any Big Data project. Hackman (1987) proposed a model that focuses on different factors from input to output. It is one of the most widely used models. While continuous improvement is one of the criteria in Hackman's model, a vital factor is measuring the team's performance. The model created by DeLone and McLean (1992) is based on system creation, usage, and consequences of use.

FUTURE RESEARCH DIRECTIONS

Further along the path of this chapter, there are several potential extensions and challenging directions to be explored regarding Big Data. New systems and solutions have been proposed in Big Data systems. Big Data's relation and integration with Industry 4.0, Artificial Intelligence and emerging Business Intelligence projects are brand new research areas, including different industry diversities. Researchers can examine how Big Data rules emerging technology trends.

CONCLUSION

Data is growing at a rate we never imagined. Large volumes of digital data are generated at a rapid rate by sources like social media sites, mobile phones, sensors, web servers, multimedia, medical devices and satellites, leading to a data explosion. The importance of capturing this data and creating value out of it has become more important than ever in every sector of the world economy. While the potential of creating meaningful insights out of big data in various domains like Business, Health Care, Public Sector Administration, Retail and Manufacturing are being studied, data science related technologies are expanding to capture, store and analyze big data efficiently.

This chapter clearly observed the various opportunities being explored, examined and extracted for the betterment and effectiveness of organizations across the different industries that have successful Big Data projects. Also Big Data is basically defined and an overview of Big Data is provided in terms of current status, organizational effects (technology, health care, education etc.), implementation challenges and Big Data projects. The main purpose of this research was to build on the current diverse literature around Big Data by contributing discussion and data that allow common agreement on definition, characteristics, and factors that influence successful Big Data projects. The research questions being investigated are based on the argument establishing Big Data be used as a tool for the organization by which to develop and create enterprise-wide efficiencies.

REFERENCES

Abbasi, A., Sarker, S., & Chiang, R. H. (2016). Big data research in information systems: Toward an inclusive research agenda. *Journal of the Association for Information Systems*, *17*(2), I–XXXII. doi:10.17705/1jais.00423

Ahangama, S., & Poo, C. C. D. (2015). Improving health analytic process through project, communication and knowledge management.

Ahmad, J., Muhammad, K., Lloret, J., & Baik, S. W. (2018). Efficient Conversion of Deep Features to Compact Binary Codes using Fourier Decomposition for Multimedia Big Data. *IEEE Transactions on Industrial Informatics*, *14*(7), 3205–3215. doi:10.1109/TII.2018.2800163

Akter, S., & Wamba, S. F. (2016). Big data analytics in E-commerce: A systematic review and agenda for future research. *Electronic Markets*, *26*(2), 173–194. doi:10.100712525-016-0219-0

Allouche, G. (2014). *How Big Data can Save Health Care*. Innovation Excellence. Retrieved from [REMOVED HYPERLINK FIELD]http://www.innovationexcellence.com/blog/2014/11/14/how-big-data-can-save-health-care/

Ang, J., & Teo, T. S. (2000). Management issues in data warehousing: Insights from the Housing and Development Board. *Decision Support Systems*, *29*(1), 11–20. doi:10.1016/S0167-9236(99)00085-8

Boone, C. A., Skipper, J. B., & Hazen, B. T. (2017). A framework for investigating the role of big data in service parts management. *Journal of Cleaner Production*, *153*, 687–691. doi:10.1016/j.jclepro.2016.09.201

Boyd, J., Ferrante, A., Brown, A., Randall, S., & Semmens, J. (2017). Implementing privacy-preserving record linkage: Welcome to the real world. *International Journal of Population Data Science*, *1*(1). doi:10.23889/ijpds.v1i1.153

Burg, N. (2014). How Big Data Will Help Save Healthcare. *Forbes Magazine, 10*.

Cao, M., Chychyla, R., & Stewart, T. (2015). Big Data analytics in financial statement Audits. *Accounting Horizons*, *29*(2), 423–429. doi:10.2308/acch-51068

Cebr. (2012). *The Value of Big Data and the Internet of Things to the UK Economy*. Retrieved from https://www.sas.com/content/dam/SAS/en_gb/doc/analystreport/cebr-value-of-big-data.pdf

Chen, H., Chiang, R. H., & Storey, V. C. (2012). Business intelligence and analytics: From big data to big impact. *Management Information Systems Quarterly, 36*(4), 1165–1188. doi:10.2307/41703503

Chen, J., Chen, Y., Du, X., Li, C., Lu, J., Zhao, S., & Zhou, X. (2013). Big data challenge: A data management perspective. *Frontiers of Computer Science, 7*(2), 157–164. doi:10.100711704-013-3903-7

Das, M., Cui, R., Campbell, D. R., Agrawal, G., & Ramnath, R. (2015). Towards methods for systematic research on big data. *Proceedings of the 2015 IEEE International Conference on Big Data* (pp. 2072-2081). IEEE. 10.1109/BigData.2015.7363989

Dimopoulos, S., Krintz, C., & Wolski, R. (2016). Big data framework interference in restricted private cloud settings. *Proceedings of the 2016 IEEE International Conference on Big Data* (pp. 335-340). IEEE. 10.1109/BigData.2016.7840620

Du, Z. (2013). Inconsistencies in big data: Cognitive Informatics & Cognitive Computing (ICCI* CC), 2013. *Proceedings of the 12th IEEE International Conference. IEEE.*

Ebner, K., Buhnen, T., & Urbach, N. (2014, January). Think big with Big Data: Identifying suitable Big Data strategies in corporate environments. *Proceedings of the 2014 47th Hawaii International Conference on System Sciences (HICSS)* (pp. 3748-3757). IEEE.

Ehrenstein, V., Nielsen, H., Pedersen, A. B., Johnsen, S. P., & Pedersen, L. (2017). Clinical epidemiology in the era of big data: New opportunities, familiar challenges. *Clinical Epidemiology, 9*, 245–250. doi:10.2147/CLEP.S129779 PMID:28490904

Erikson, E. H. E. (1950). *Childhood and society*. New York: Norton.

Erwin, R. (2015). Data literacy: Real-world learning through problem-solving with data sets. *American Secondary Education, 43*(2), 18–26.

Esposito, C., Ficco, M., Palmieri, F., & Castiglione, A. (2015). A knowledge-based platform for Big Data analytics based on publish/subscribe services and stream processing. *Knowledge-Based Systems, 79*, 3–17. doi:10.1016/j.knosys.2014.05.003

Fernandes, L. M., O'Connor, M., & Weaver, V. (2012). Big data, bigger outcomes. *Journal of American Health Information Management Association, 83*(10), 38–43. PMID:23061351

Fesenmaier, D. R., Kuflik, T., & Neidhardt, J. (2016). Rectour 2016: workshop on recommenders in tourism. *Proceedings of the 10th ACM Conference on Recommender systems* (pp. 417-418). ACM.

Gamage, P. (2016). New development: Leveraging 'big data' analytics in the public sector. *Public Money & Management*, *36*(5), 385–390. doi:10.1080/09540962.20 16.1194087

Gandomi, A., & Haider, M. (2015). Beyond the hype: Big data concepts, methods, and analytics. *International Journal of Information Management*, *35*(2), 137–144. doi:10.1016/j.ijinfomgt.2014.10.007

George, G., Osinga, E. C., Lavie, D., & Scott, B. A. (2016). Big data and data science methods for management research.

Gobble, M. M. (2013). Creating change. *Research Technology Management*, *56*(5), 62–66. doi:10.5437/08956308X5605005

Goodwin, K. (2011). *Designing for the digital age: How to create human-centered products and services*. John Wiley & Sons.

Grand View Research. (2016). *Big Data Market Size, Share Forecast, Industry Research Report, 2025*. Retrieved from https://www.grandviewresearch.com/industry-analysis/big-data-industry?utm_source=Pressrelease&utm_medium=referral&utm_campaign=abnewswire_05oct&utm_content=content

Groves, P., Kayyali, B., Knott, D., & Van Kuiken, S. (2013). The 'big data' revolution in healthcare. *The McKinsey Quarterly*, *2*(3).

Gudivada, V. N., Baeza-Yates, R. A., & Raghavan, V. V. (2015). Big Data: Promises and Problems. *IEEE Computer*, *48*(3), 20–23. doi:10.1109/MC.2015.62

Hackman, J. R. (1987). The design of work teams. In J.W. Lorsch (Ed.), Handbook of organizational behavior (pp. 315-342). Englewood Cliffs, NJ: Prentice-Hall.

Halaweh, M., & Massry, A. E. (2015). Conceptual model for successful implementation of big data in organizations. *Journal of International Technology and Information Management*, *24*(2), 2.

Hashem, I. A. T., Yaqoob, I., Anuar, N. B., Mokhtar, S., Gani, A., & Khan, S. U. (2015). The rise of "big data" on cloud computing: Review and open research issues. *Information Systems*, *47*, 98–115. doi:10.1016/j.is.2014.07.006

He, W., Shen, J., Tian, X., Li, Y., Akula, V., Yan, G., & Tao, R. (2015). Gaining competitive intelligence from social media data: Evidence from two largest retail chains in the world. *Industrial Management & Data Systems, 115*(9), 1622–1636. doi:10.1108/IMDS-03-2015-0098

Hilbert, M. (2016). Big data for development: A review of promises and challenges. *Development Policy Review, 34*(1), 135–174. doi:10.1111/dpr.12142

IDC. (2015). *Double-Digit Growth Forecast for the Worldwide Big Data and Business Analytics Market Through 2020 Led by Banking and Manufacturing Investments, According to IDC.* Retrieved from https://www.idc.com/url.do?url=/includes/pdf_download.jsp?containerId=prUS41826116&position=51

Ives, Z. G., Florescu, D., Friedman, M., Levy, A., & Weld, D. S. (1999, June). An adaptive query execution system for data integration. *SIGMOD Record, 28*(2), 299–310. doi:10.1145/304181.304209

Jobs, C. G., Aukers, S. M., & Gilfoil, D. M. (2015). The impact of big data on your firms marketing communications: A framework for understanding the emerging marketing analytics industry. *Academy of Marketing Studies Journal, 19*(2).

Junqué de Fortuny, E., Martens, D., & Provost, F. (2013). Predictive modeling with big data: Is bigger really better? *Big Data, 1*(4), 215–226. doi:10.1089/big.2013.0037 PMID:27447254

Kaisler, S., Armour, F., Espinosa, J. A., & Money, W. (2013). Big data: Issues and challenges moving forward. *Proceedings of the 2013 46th Hawaii international conference on System sciences (HICSS)* (pp. 995-1004). IEEE.

Keller, S. A., Koonin, S. E., & Shipp, S. (2012). Big data and city living–what can it do for us? *Significance, 9*(4), 4–7. doi:10.1111/j.1740-9713.2012.00583.x

Kelly, J., & Kaskade, J. (2013). CIOS & Big Data what your IT team wants you to know. Retrieved from http://blog.infochimps.com/2013/01/24/cios-big-data

Kim, M., Zimmermann, T., DeLine, R., & Begel, A. (2016). The emerging role of data scientists on software development teams. *Proceedings of the 38th International Conference on Software Engineering* (pp. 96-107). ACM. 10.1145/2884781.2884783

Kimble, C., & Milolidakis, G. (2015). Big data and business intelligence: Debunking the myths. *Global Business and Organizational Excellence, 35*(1), 23–34. doi:10.1002/joe.21642

Kitchin, R., Lauriault, T. P., & McArdle, G. (2015). Knowing and governing cities through urban indicators, city benchmarking and real-time dashboards. *Regional Studies. Regional Science*, 2(1), 6–28.

Kitchin, R., & McArdle, G. (2016). What makes Big Data, Big Data? Exploring the ontological characteristics of 26 datasets. *Big Data & Society*, 3(1).

Krawatzeck, R., Dinter, B., & Thi, D. A. P. (2015, January). How to make business intelligence agile: The Agile BI actions catalog. *Proceedings of the 2015 48th Hawaii International Conference on System Sciences (HICSS)* (pp. 4762-4771). IEEE.

Kwon, O., Lee, N., & Shin, B. (2014). Data quality management, data usage experience and acquisition intention of big data analytics. *International Journal of Information Management*, 34(3), 387–394. doi:10.1016/j.ijinfomgt.2014.02.002

Labrinidis, A., & Jagadish, H. V. (2012). Challenges and opportunities with big data. *Proceedings of the VLDB Endowment International Conference on Very Large Data Bases*, 5(12), 2032–2033. doi:10.14778/2367502.2367572

Laudon, K. C., & Laudon, J. P. (2016). *Management information system*. Pearson Education India.

Lee, J. H., Clarke, R. I., & Perti, A. (2015). Empirical evaluation of metadata for video games and interactive media. *Journal of the Association for Information Science and Technology*, 66(12), 2609–2625. doi:10.1002/asi.23357

Manyika, J., Chui, M., Brown, B., Bughin, J., Dobbs, R., Roxburgh, C., & Byers, A. H. (2011). *Big data: The next frontier for innovation, competition, and productivity*. McKinsey Global Institute.

Marvin, H. J., Janssen, E. M., Bouzembrak, Y., Hendriksen, P. J., & Staats, M. (2017). Big data in food safety: An overview. *Critical Reviews in Food Science and Nutrition*, 57(11), 2286–2295. doi:10.1080/10408398.2016.1257481 PMID:27819478

McAfee, A., & Brynjolfsson, E. (2012). Big Data: The Management Revolution. *Harvard Business Review*, 90(10), 60-66. PMID:23074865

Menon, S. P., & Hegde, N. P. (2015, January). A survey of tools and applications in big data. *Proceedings of the 2015 IEEE 9th International Conference on Intelligent Systems and Control (ISCO)* (pp. 1-7). IEEE. 10.1109/ISCO.2015.7282364

MGI. (2012). *Big Data: The next frontier for innovation, competition, and productivity*. Retrieved from https://www.mckinsey.com/~/media/McKinsey/Business%20 Functions/McKinsey%20Digital/Our%20Insights/Big%20data%20The%20next%20 frontier%20for%20innovation/MGI_big_data_exec_summary.ashx

Nichols, W. (2013). Advertising Analytics 2.0. *Harvard Business Review*, *91*(3), 60–68. PMID:23593768

Nimmagadda, S. L., & Dreher, H. V. (2013). Big-data integration methodologies for effective management and data mining of petroleum digital ecosystems. *Proceedings of the 2013 7th IEEE International Conference on Digital Ecosystems and Technologies (DEST)* (pp. 148-153). IEEE. 10.1109/DEST.2013.6611345

Oh, Y. K., & Min, J. (2015). The mediating role of popularity rank on the relationship between advertising and in-app purchase sales in mobile application market. *Journal of Applied Business Research*, *31*(4), 1311. doi:10.19030/jabr.v31i4.9318

Opresnik, D., & Taisch, M. (2015). The value of big data in servitization. *International Journal of Production Economics*, *165*, 174–184. doi:10.1016/j.ijpe.2014.12.036

Provost, F., & Fawcett, T. (2013). Data science and its relationship to big data and data-driven decision making. *Big Data*, *1*(1), 51–59. doi:10.1089/big.2013.1508 PMID:27447038

Purdam, K. (2016). Task-based learning approaches for supporting the development of social science researchers' critical data skills. *International Journal of Social Research Methodology*, *19*(2), 257–267. doi:10.1080/13645579.2015.1102453

Rajan, K. (2015). Materials informatics: The materials "gene" and big data. *Annual Review of Materials Research*, *45*(1), 153–169. doi:10.1146/annurev-matsci-070214-021132

Reimsbach-Kounatze, C. (2015). *"The Proliferation of "Big Data" and Implications for Official Statistics and Statistical Agencies: A Preliminary Analysis", OECD Digital Economy Papers, No. 245*. Paris: OECD Publishing. doi:10.1787/5js7t9wqzvg8-

Riggins, F. J., & Wamba, S. F. (2015). Research directions on the adoption, usage, and impact of the internet of things through the use of big data analytics. *Proceedings of the 2015 48th Hawaii International Conference on System Sciences (HICSS)* (pp. 1531-1540). IEEE. 10.1109/HICSS.2015.186

Rijmenam, M. (2014). *Think bigger: Developing a successful big data strategy for your business*. Amacom.

Rubin, V., & Lukoianova, T. (2013). Veracity roadmap: Is big data objective, truthful and credible? *Advances in Classification Research Online, 24*(1), 4. doi:10.7152/acro.v24i1.14671

Saltz, J. S. (2015). The need for new processes, methodologies and tools to support big data teams and improve big data project effectiveness. *Proceedings of the 2015 IEEE International Conference on Big Data (Big Data)* (pp. 2066-2071). IEEE. 10.1109/BigData.2015.7363988

Saltz, J. S., & Shamshurin, I. (2016). Big data team process methodologies: A literature review and the identification of key factors for a project's success. *Proceedings of the 2016 IEEE International Conference on Big Data (Big Data)* (pp. 2872-2879). IEEE. 10.1109/BigData.2016.7840936

Seay, C., Agrawal, R., Kadadi, A., & Barel, Y. (2015, April). Using hadoop on the mainframe: A big solution for the challenges of big data. *Proceedings of the 2015 12th International Conference on Information Technology-New Generations (ITNG)* (pp. 765-769). IEEE. 10.1109/ITNG.2015.135

Seddon, J. J., & Currie, W. L. (2017). A model for unpacking big data analytics in high-frequency trading. *Journal of Business Research, 70*, 300–307. doi:10.1016/j.jbusres.2016.08.003

Shin, D. H., & Choi, M. J. (2015). Ecological views of big data: Perspectives and issues. *Telematics and Informatics, 32*(2), 311–320. doi:10.1016/j.tele.2014.09.006

Sookhak, M., Gani, A., Khan, M. K., & Buyya, R. (2017). Dynamic remote data auditing for securing big data storage in cloud computing. *Information Sciences, 380*, 101–116. doi:10.1016/j.ins.2015.09.004

Sun, F., Huang, G. B., Wu, Q. J., Song, S., & Wunsch, D. C. II. (2017). Efficient and rapid machine learning algorithms for big data and dynamic varying systems. *IEEE Transactions on Systems, Man, and Cybernetics. Systems, 47*(10), 2625–2626. doi:10.1109/TSMC.2017.2741558

TechAmerica Foundation. (2012). *Demystifying Big Data: A practical guide to transforming the business of government*. Retrieved from http://www.techamerica.org/Docs/fileManager.cfm?f=techamerica-bigdatareport-final.pdf

Tormay, P. (2015). Big data in pharmaceutical R&D: Creating a sustainable R&D engine. *Pharmaceutical Medicine, 29*(2), 87–92. doi:10.100740290-015-0090-x PMID:25878506

Vatsalan, D., Sehili, Z., Christen, P., & Rahm, E. (2017). Privacy-preserving record linkage for big data: Current approaches and research challenges. In *Handbook of Big Data Technologies* (pp. 851–895). Cham: Springer. doi:10.1007/978-3-319-49340-4_25

Wang, C. H. (2016). A novel approach to conduct the importance-satisfaction analysis for acquiring typical user groups in business-intelligence systems. *Computers in Human Behavior, 54*, 673–681. doi:10.1016/j.chb.2015.08.014

White, T. (2012). *Hadoop: The definitive guide.* O'Reilly Media, Inc.

Wixom, B., Ariyachandra, T., Douglas, D. E., Goul, M., Gupta, B., Iyer, L. S., . . . Turetken, O. (2014). The current state of business intelligence in academia: The arrival of big data. CAIS, 34, 1.

Xu, W., Huang, R., Zhang, H., El-Khamra, Y., & Walling, D. (2016). Empowering R with high performance computing resources for big data analytics. In *Conquering Big Data with High Performance Computing* (pp. 191–217). Cham: Springer. doi:10.1007/978-3-319-33742-5_9

Xu, Z., Liu, Y., Mei, L., Hu, C., & Chen, L. (2015). Semantic based representing and organizing surveillance big data using video structural description technology. *Journal of Systems and Software, 102*, 217–225. doi:10.1016/j.jss.2014.07.024

Yin, S., & Kaynak, O. (2015). Big data for modern industry: Challenges and trends [point of view]. *Proceedings of the IEEE, 103*(2), 143–146. doi:10.1109/JPROC.2015.2388958

Zhao, R., Liu, Y., Zhang, N., & Huang, T. (2017). An optimization model for green supply chain management by using a big data analytic approach. *Journal of Cleaner Production, 142*, 1085–1097. doi:10.1016/j.jclepro.2016.03.006

Zhou, L., Pan, S., Wang, J., & Vasilakos, A. V. (2017). Machine learning on big data: Opportunities and challenges. *Neurocomputing, 237*, 350–361. doi:10.1016/j.neucom.2017.01.026

ADDITIONAL READING

Abbasi, A., Sarker, S., & Chiang, R. H. (2016). Big data research in information systems: Toward an inclusive research agenda. *Journal of the Association for Information Systems*, *17*(2), I–XXXII. doi:10.17705/1jais.00423

Akter, S., & Wamba, S. F. (2016). Big data analytics in E-commerce: A systematic review and agenda for future research. *Electronic Markets*, *26*(2), 173–194. doi:10.100712525-016-0219-0

Chen, H., Chiang, R. H., & Storey, V. C. (2012). Business intelligence and analytics: From big data to big impact. *Management Information Systems Quarterly*, *36*(4), 1165–1188. doi:10.2307/41703503

Fernandes, L. M., O'Connor, M., & Weaver, V. (2012). Big data, bigger outcomes. *Journal of American Health Information Management Association*, *83*(10), 38–43. PMID:23061351

Jobs, C. G., Aukers, S. M., & Gilfoil, D. M. (2015). The impact of big data on your firms marketing communications: A framework for understanding the emerging marketing analytics industry. *Academy of Marketing Studies Journal*, *19*(2).

Kimble, C., & Milolidakis, G. (2015). Big data and business intelligence: Debunking the myths. *Global Business and Organizational Excellence*, *35*(1), 23–34. doi:10.1002/joe.21642

Saltz, J. S., & Shamshurin, I. (2016). Big data team process methodologies: A literature review and the identification of key factors for a project's success. *Proceedings of the 2016 IEEE International Conference on Big Data (Big Data)* (pp. 2872-2879). IEEE. 10.1109/BigData.2016.7840936

Yin, S., & Kaynak, O. (2015). Big data for modern industry: Challenges and trends [point of view]. *Proceedings of the IEEE*, *103*(2), 143–146. doi:10.1109/JPROC.2015.2388958

KEY TERMS AND DEFINITIONS

Big Data: The large volumes of data-sets with a higher complexity level.

Value: Value represents the revenue and market value gained by an organization using the big data.

Variety: This represents the different types of data available, such as text, numbers, images, videos, documents, spreadsheets, etc.

Velocity: Velocity represents the speed of data at which it is transmitted and received from the source and destination.

Veracity: Veracity represents the uncertainty of the data as it comes from an untrusted source and needs more optimization.

Volume: Volume is the large data-sets that represent big data.

Chapter 2
A Detailed Study on Classification Algorithms in Big Data

Saranya N.
Sri Eshwar College of Engineering, Coimbatore, India

Saravana Selvam
PSR Engineering College, India

ABSTRACT

After an era of managing data collection difficulties, these days the issue has turned into the problem of how to process these vast amounts of information. Scientists, as well as researchers, think that today, probably the most essential topic in computing science is Big Data. Big Data is used to clarify the huge volume of data that could exist in any structure. This makes it difficult for standard controlling approaches for mining the best possible data through such large data sets. Classification in Big Data is a procedure of summing up data sets dependent on various examples. There are distinctive classification frameworks which help us to classify data collections. A few methods that discussed in the chapter are Multi-Layer Perception Linear Regression, C4.5, CART, J48, SVM, ID3, Random Forest, and KNN. The target of this chapter is to provide a comprehensive evaluation of classification methods that are in effect commonly utilized.

DOI: 10.4018/978-1-5225-9750-6.ch002

INTRODUCTION

Big data is which grows each year in a system. Invention in research, as well as scientific factors, has impacted the size of data that grows every day with the goal to enhance profitable activities. On the other hand, information accessibility and exploration of thoughts have resulted in the delivery of a completely progressive modification of the internet, which has been utilized in the most beneficial ways. As a result, billions of bytes of information are created every day hence throwing much information at regular intervals. Since newly provided data night is unstructured, structured or possibly confused; we need classification techniques in case of unstructured or complex data. A classification is an approach that allots data in a class to focus on Categories or groups (Owais & Hussein, 2016). The objective of grouping would be to precisely estimate the prospective class of every single file in the data.

Diverse Classification strategies make use of distinctive methods intended for finding the relationships among the list of data units. These types of relationships are generally compacted in a model, which may then have the ability to connect to an alternate dataset when class assignments are covered up. Classification models are broken down through differentiating the expected valuations as well as known values in a wide scope of test data (Revathy & Lawrance, 2017). The target data to get a classification model is normally isolated into several sets of data: one for understanding the genuine model; another for testing the actual model.

The overall classification technique is shown in Figure 1 below. The purpose of the learning stage is to assemble the classification model and testing stage. In the learning stage, a classification strategy is produced to portray a redid set of data classes. In both learning and training phase, the classification approach develops the classifier using a method of comprehension from the training dataset and the related class names.

Figure 1. Classification process

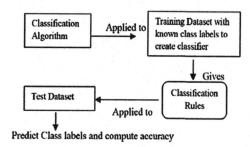

Organization of this Paper

This paper is composed of classification processes, issues in classification and different classification algorithms used to examine the different classification algorithms. Finally, the last section concludes the paper.

MACHINE LEARNING AND CLASSIFICATION PROCESS

Machine learning is a quickly developing area, which shows how computers able users to learn or enhance the performance to utilize data. Computer programs naturally figure out how we can distinguish patterns and settle on accurate decisions with respect to data (Wu, Zhu, Wu & Ding, 2013). We represent great issues in machine learning, which are profoundly identified with data mining and big data. There are three primary sorts of machine learning ideas as shown in Figure 2. These ideas are described as following:

Figure 2. Types of machine learning

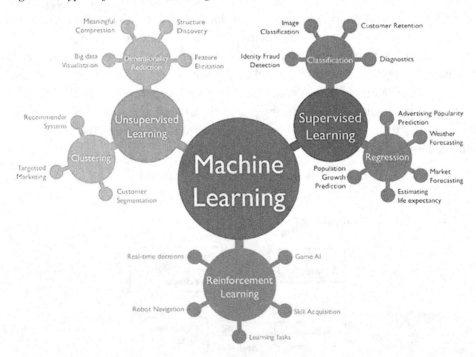

Supervised Learning

Supervised learning comprises of all the information for algorithms to figure out how output can be predicted from training dataset. This idea is utilized in the classification of problems (Revathy & Lawrance, 2017) e.g. Naive Bayes, Random Forest, Support Vector Machine (SVM).

Unsupervised Learning

Clustering-based techniques use unsupervised learning whereby information remains unlabeled. The output structure is figured out from the training datasets by the algorithms (Oliverio & Poli-Neto, 2017). We can utilize clustering to find the classes inside a dataset. Other unsupervised learning algorithms include K-implies and Neural Networks.

Reinforcement Learning

1. Reinforcement learning is concerned with making a reasonable move to augment rewards in a specific circumstance (https://en.wikipedia.org/wiki/Weka_(machine_learning))

In most case, the classification will likely be experimented using a laptop or a computer, together with the help of statistical classification and approaches (Çığşar & Ünal, 2019). Classification will probably be made by following the procedures given below:

- Defining Classification Classes: According to the target as well as the features of the information, the actual classification classes need to be clearly identified.
- Purpose of Characteristics: Characteristics, in order to segregate amongst the classes, must be recognized by making use of multi-spectral or multi-temporal attributes, surface types and so forth.

- A selection of Training Information; Training information should be tested in an attempt to find out suitable decision rules (Oliverio& Poli-Neto, 2017). Classification methods, as an example, based on training data sets learning method (either supervised or unsupervised) will be decided certainly at that time.

- Approximation of General Data: Numerous classification techniques would probably be contrasted along with the training information, with the purpose that an acceptable decision rule will be picked out based on the resultant classification.
- Classification relying upon the Decision rule: Almost all of the pixels tend to be grouped in an individual class. There can be two approaches for pixel by pixel depiction and per-field, with regard to segmented regions.
- Confirmation of Outcomes: The actual categorized solutions must be examined and checked for their exactness as well as durability. Some difficulties in classification and well-known classification algorithms will be cleared up in coming sessions.

ISSUES IN CLASSIFICATION METHODS

The supplementary issues are critical to be regarded throughout the classification for information pre-processing and algorithm contrast.

Pre-Processing of Data

The supplementary preprocessing stages have applied to the information to accomplish better, efficiency, accuracy, and versatility of the classification procedure: -

1. *Data cleaning:* It alludes to the pre-processing of information with the perspective of the treatment of missing values and evacuating or lessening noise.
2. *Relevance analysis:* The dataset might contain excess characteristics. The strategies like connection investigation can be utilized to see whether any two properties are factually related. Another importance analysis is a subset of attribute choice that finds a decreased set of characteristics, to such an extent that the accomplished likelihood distribution of classes (Gao & Li, 2012). This is the means by which we identify attributes that don't add to characterization. In principle, the time expended on analysis of relevant information, when included to the time consumed in learning from the inferred decreased set of attributes, ought to be not exactly the time consumed from learning the actual set of attributes. Subsequently, this progression can enhance classification effectiveness and adaptability.
3. *Data Transformation and Reduction*: At times, the dataset might be needed to be changed by standardization, particularly when calculation like "neural network system" is utilized which needs numerical qualities to be given to the

input layer, or calculation like "K-NN" which needs measuring of distance. Standardization is finished by scaling all estimation of a trait under consideration, so they exist in a predetermined range, for example, - 0.0 to 1.0.

Criteria for Comparing Classification

1. *Accuracy*: The precision of a classifier alludes to the capacity of an offered classifier to accurately foresee the class label of hidden information.
2. *Speed*: It alludes to the computational expense in the involved building model and utilizing it.
3. *Robustness*: The capacity of the classifier to produce the correct prediction, even if the information is noisy, and have some missing values.
4. *Scalability*: It is the capacity to build the model of classification productively, given a substantial measure of data.
5. *Interpretability*: This alludes to the straightforwardness or degree of understanding given by the classifier.

VARIOUS TYPES OF CLASSIFICATION ALGORITHMS

The types below are the effective systems of some classification algorithms applied to big data and the machine learning industry. The classification algorithms are generally split up into different types as demonstrated in figure 3.

Figure 3. Different classification algorithms

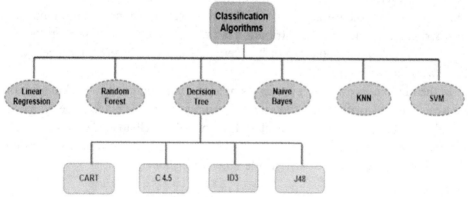

Linear Regression

Linear regression is actually a logistic model that anticipates a direct relationship between the input as well as the outcome variable. To train or understand the linear regression design, evaluate the coefficients esteems applied to the depiction for available information. At the level when there is a solitary input variable, at that time, the method is recognized as a simple linear regression. At the level when there are distinct input elements, then the strategy is referred to as multiple linear regressions (Gandhi & Deshpande, 2016). Distinctive approaches can be employed in order to plan or prepare the linear regression equation from the given data. A few of them tend to be gradient descent, regular minimum square, and regularization. Among this Regular Minimum Square is usually a standout amongst the most widely identified methods. It looks to restrict the total of squared residuals. It indicates offered a regression line from the information, determine the separation of each and every data point from the regression line, square them, and aggregate the vast majority of squared errors with one another (Thakor, 2017). This is the total that regular minimum squares turn to limit. Regularization approaches are the expansions of linear design training. These strategies make an effort to limit both the entire squared error on the training information and in addition to lower the design complexity.

Random Forest

The Random Forest method is really an accumulating supervised learning process which can be applied as an indicator of information with regard to classification and regression. In the classification procedure, algorithm fabricates several decision trees during the training period and develop the class this provides the technique of the class outcome with the use of each and every single tree (Çığşar & Ünal, 2019). Random Forest technique is a collection of tree indicators exactly where every single tree influenced by the estimations of an arbitrary vector examined autonomously together with the comparable distribution for all those trees within the forest. The main standard is that a gathering of "vulnerable valuations" can easily meet up to frame a "robust valuations".

In the random forest strategy, every single tree is formulated by making use of the associated Algorithm. Let the range of training cases a chance to be N, along with the number of elements in the classifier possibly be (Piao et al., 2014) We are informed the number m of input elements to be employed to determine the decision at a node of the tree; m must be considerably lower than M.

Box 1.

- Select a training set just for this tree by choosing n instances along with substitution from all N obtainable training instances. Utilize whichever is remaining of the instances to measure the error of the tree, through predicting their own classes.
- For each and every node of the tree, arbitrarily pick m elements on which to base the decision at that node. As specific want to know the best part relying on these m elements from the training set. Every single tree is totally developed and never pruned as done in constructing a regular tree classifier.

Random Forests are an accurate method to make predictions taking into consideration they do not over fit. Introducing the actual sort of irregularity makes them exact classifiers. Solitary decision trees frequently have excessive variance or big inclination. Random Forests endeavouring to direct the maximum difference difficulties and big inclination through averaging to obtain a feature balance between the two boundaries.

Decision Tree

The Tree framework has been employed to correlate with classification models. Decision tree algorithms are an inductive understanding process to make use of specific facts to create progressively summed up conclusions. Nearly all decision tree algorithms rely on a greedy top-down recursive strategy for tree progression. One noteworthy demerit of the Greedy search is that it typically prompts imperfect solutions.

Decision tree classifier can easily split an unpredictable decision-making method into a gathering of less complicated and simple decision. The difficult decision is usually subdivided into much easier decision. It isolates complete training set into little subsets. Obtained data, gain percentage, gain report is 3 vital portion criteria to decide an attribute as a splitting point. Decision trees could be built from genuine information they are regularly employed for rational evaluation just like a form of supervised learning. The algorithm is organized in a manner that it works with all the data which is obtainable and as possibly best (https://archive.ics.uci.edu/ml/datasets/Labor+Relations). There are several specific Decision tree algorithms. Some are discussed down below.

1. CART (Classification and Regression Tree)

CART process is determined by information query and prediction calculation. It creates regression or classification trees, no matter whether the actual variable is all out or even numerical. It could furthermore deal with lacking factors effectively.

Box 2.

- Check for base cases.
- For each attribute *A*, Find the standardized information gain from splitting on A.
- Let *A_best* be the attribute with the most elevated standardized information gain.
- Create a decision node that parts on *A_best*.
- Recurse on the sub records acquired by splitting on *A_best*, and include those nodes as children of the node.

CART is exclusive with regards to other Search structured computation. The binary tree developed via CART alludes as Hierarchical Optimal Discriminate Analysis (HODA) (Akinola & Oyabugbe, 2015). It employs binary decision tree computation that wills recursively segment data directly into 2 homogeneous subsets. An important element of CART is its capacity to produce regression trees

2. C4.5

C4.5 is an algorithm developed by Ross Quinlan. It produces Decision Tree that is often employed with regard to classification issues (Brijain et al., 2014). It enhances the ID3 algorithm through handling both equally ceaseless and discrete features, lacking factors and pruning trees soon after development. Since it is a supervised learning technique, it will require plenty of training designs and every model may very well be a pair: input object, as well as a perfect outcome valuation. The technique breaks down the training set along with fabricated classifier that has to possess the ability to successfully group each training and test samples (Al-Radaideh et al., 2006). C 4.5 produces a decision tree in which every node part of the classes is dependent on the data gain. The actual characteristic of all the big standardized information gain will be utilized for the reason that splitting criteria. Typically, the pseudo code with the standard Algorithm is as per the following:

3. ID3 (Iterative Dichotomiser 3)

ID3 is a straightforward decision tree learning calculation created by Ross Quinlan (1983). The fundamental concept of ID3 method is to build up the decision tree through the use of a greedy search with a top-down approach through actually offered models to evaluate every single feature at each tree node (Pitre & Kolekar, 2014). In order to choose the feature which is most a good choice for ordering a given set, information gain will be applied. To locate a perfect strategy to categorize a learning set, that which we should do is usually to restrict the actual queries requested. Hence, we demand a few functionalities which could gauge which queries provide the most fine-tuned splitting. (https://www.analyticsvidhya.com/blog/2015)

Box 3.

- Take every unused attribute and check their entropy concerning test examples.
- Choose attribute for which entropy is least (or, equally, information gain is high).
- Make node belonging that attribute.

The ID3 calculation could be abridged as shown in Box 3.

4.   J48

J48 is definitely an open source method. It is the Java usage of the actual C4.5 method (Dai &2014). J48 Decision Tree Classifier utilizes two stages.

5.   Naïve Bayes

The Bayesian Classification speaks to a supervised learning strategy just as a measurable technique for classification. Typically, the naive Bayesian classifier is a kind of probabilistic classifier. This strategy utilizes Bayes' hypothesis and furthermore expect that every single feature in a class is very independent, that is the presence of an element in a particular classification isn't associated with the addition of a few other components (Brindha, Prabha & Sukumaran, 2016). The naive Bayesian classification performance is determined by the earlier likelihood and probability of the tuple to some class. Assumes a hidden probabilistic design also it makes it possible to capture vulnerability regarding the type principally through determining possibilities of the outcomes. It will take care of symptomatic as well as prescient concerns.

Box 4.

---

a. Tree development
- Begins with the entire data index at the root
- Check the attribute of the data collection and partition them dependent on the accompanying cases
    ➢ Case 1: If the attribute value is clear and has a target value, at that point it ends the branch and allocates the value as Target value.
    ➢ Case 2: If the attribute, gives the most elevated data, at that point proceed till we get a get decision or run out of attributes.
    ➢ Case 3: If we run out of attributes or we are given questionable outcome, at that point assign the present branch as target value.
    ➢ Case 4: Disregard missing values.
b. . Tree Pruning
- Recognize and evacuate branches that reflects noise and anomalies to decrease classification errors.

Bayesian grouping gives functional understanding methods and earlier information as well as discovered information could be consolidated. Bayesian Classification gives a helpful standpoint to understand and also determining several learning algorithms (Gao & Li, 2012). It determines explicit possibilities with regard to the concept which is powerful in order to find noise in the information. Naive Bayes classification is generally used in text classification, online applications, Spam sifting, and Hybrid Recommender framework.

KNN (K-Nearest Neighbor)

KNN classifier is certainly an instance-based understanding Algorithm that usually depends on the distance functionality for sets associated with perceptions, for example, the Euclidean separation or Cosine (Gandhi & Deshpande, 2016). Additionally, it is known as a lazy algorithm. It means any generalization will not make use of the training data points. KNN is the least complex method for machine learning. In which object orders determined by the nearest training precedent from feature space. Their role verifiably figures the decision limitation; in fact, it is likewise feasible in order to process the decision expressly. The actual neighbours tend to be picked from the set of items for which the proper classification is considered (https://en.wikipedia.org/wiki/Weka_(machine_learning)). No unequivocal training stage is needed this could be regarded as the training set to the tactic. The KNN method is sensitive towards the nearby structure with the data collection. This is actually the exceptional scenario in case k = 1 is recognized as the NN (nearest neighbour) algorithm. The actual K nearest neighbour technique is easy to apply while connected to a smaller group of information, yet while connected to substantial amounts of information as well as higher dimensional information that produce slower performance. The calculation is actually insecure of the estimation of k also it influences typically the performance of the classifier.

SVM (Support Vector Machine)

SVM is a type of supervised learning-based strategy which is utilized for regression analysis, classification, and pattern recognition. It is especially utilized in noisy and complex spaces (Gorade, Deo & Purohit, 2017). This method is utilized for classification based on the training dataset. In the Support Vector Machine methodology, the information item is plotted in n-dimensional space. The value of each component is the value of a particular coordinate. The hyper plane ought to make in order to split the actual classes. 'n' is utilized for a no of features in training dataset along with the significance of every element getting the significance of a specific coordinate in space. When this occurs, we attain classification through finding and developing the hyper plane on a dataset which isolates the dataset into a pair of classes as appeared in figure 4.

Support Vectors are fundamentally the coordinates of individual reflection. SVM is used to isolate the two classes in a better way. This method characterized by linear information and non-linear information. On-linear classification a few sorts of transformation have done to the given training dataset. Linear classification is actualized utilizing hyper plane. After transformation, different strategies are endeavoring to utilize linear classification for the division (Yu, Yang & Han, 2003). There are 2 key executions of the SVM method that is scientific programming and piece work. Hyper plane isolates in a high dimensional space that information point of various classes.

DISCUSSION

There are so many researches are done to find a suitable classification algorithm based on the dataset and customer requirements (Cigsar & Ünal, 2019), has done research on TUIK dataset using WEKA software 3.9. A WEKA application was used to obtain 20,275 units of data containing 12 variables (work, gender, marital status, region, health, education, bills, home loan, class, house, individual revenue), one of

Figure 4. Hyper plane of SVM

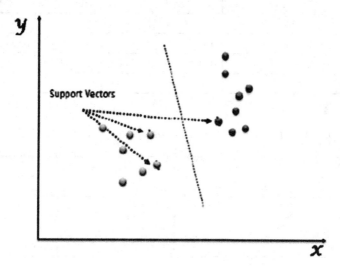

which is a class variable. This research used to find the best suitable classification algorithm to get best credit risks and estimate the difficulties. The performances of the algorithms were compared according to accuracy, Recall, F-measure, and precision criteria, and the linear regression classification algorithm was found to be the best algorithm. The results are shown in table 1.

Another research has been done by Vinicius (Oliverio & Poli-Neto, 2017). based on the data set of Clinics Hospital of Ribeirao Preto of the University of Sao Paulo (HCFMRP/USP). This data set contains 346 patients as instances. 106 attributes (constipation, painful bladder, pelvic congestion, etc.) are taken from the form filled by the doctors. Here the classification algorithms naïve Bayes, C4.5, KNN, and SVM are analyzed based on the accuracy, specificities, and sensibilities. As shown in table 2, the algorithm performed better based on accuracy is SVM, based on the specificities C4.5 is best and based on the sensibilities Naïve Bayes is best.

From this paper, we have seen that every algorithm has its advantages and disadvantages. Naive Bayes' performs well if it has restrictive freedom between attributes. It isn't generally the situation and takes less time. Decision tree gives understandability in describing to classification model which takes less time. Support vector machine takes extensively less expectation time though the number of attributes is huge. It likewise gives better exactness and works for directly indistinguishable information also; the unpredictability of learned SVM classifier relies upon a number of support vectors.

Table 1. Comparison of classification algorithm based on the TUIL dataset with WEKA software

Algorithm	Accuracy	Precision	Recall	F-Measure
Naïve Bayes	82.532	0.824	0.825	0.824
Linear Regression	83.108	0.822	0.831	0.824
J48	82.47	0.818	0.825	0.821
Random Forest	82.11	0.809	0.821	0.814

Table 2. Comparison of classification algorithm based on the HCFMRP/USP dataset

Algorithm	Accuracy	Specificities	Sensibilities
Naïve Bayes	87.78%	0.898	0.602
C4.5	88.77%	0.948	0.403
SVM	89.19%	0.945	0.437
KNN	86.83%	0.912	0.468

K-nearest neighbor is a lazy algorithm and gives poor precision in the event that it is provided with noisy or futile attributes. Its exactness can be enhanced by feature extraction. Figure 5 depicts the benefits and negative marks of various classification methods in detail with their complexity. Where n is the number of training test, p is the number of features, n_{trees} is the number of trees and n_{sv} is the number of support vectors.

Table 3. Comparison of classification algorithms based on their overall merits and demerits

Algorithm	Merits	Demerits	Complexity	
			Training	Prediction
Linear Regression	Linear regression implements a statistical model that, when relationships between the independent variables and the dependent variable are almost liner, shows optimal results	1. Linear regression is often inappropriately used to model non-linear relationships. 2. Linear regression is limited to predicting numeric output. 3. A lack of explanation about what has been learned can be a problem	$O(p^2n+p^3)$	$O(p)$
Random Forest	1.Can handle large set of data with high dimensionality 2. Useful in the case of missing data	1. Fit for some datasets with noisy classification /regression tasks. 2. Classifications made by random forests are difficult to interpret.	$O(n^2pn_{trees})$	$O(pn_{trees})$
CART	1.In-built features that deal with missing attributes. 2. Variable selection can be done automatically	1. Data is sorted at every node to determine the best splitting point. 2. The linear combination splitting criteria is used during the regression analysis.	$O(n^2p)$	$O(p)$
C4.5	1. Produces accurate result 2. Takes less memory 3.Less model-built time 4. Short searching time	1. Can lead to empty branches 2. It may generate insignificant branches 3. It gives problem of over fitting	$O(n^2p)$	$O(p)$
ID3	1. produces the more accuracy result than the C4.5 algorithm 2. Uses nominal attributes for classification with no missing values 3.Produces false alarm rate and omission rate decreased, increased the detection rate	1. Has long searching time. 2. Takes the more memory than the C4.5 to large program execution	$O(n^2p)$	$O(p)$
J48	1. All data are examined and categorized 2. Larger programs are split into more than one class	1. Ignores missing values 2. computation is slower	$O(n^2p)$	$O(p)$
Naïve Bayes	1. To improves the classification performance by removing the unrelated options. 2. Good Performance 3. It is short computational time	1. Requires very large number of records to obtain good result. 2. It is instance based or lazy in that they store all of the training samples	$O(np)$	$O(p)$
KNN	1. It is an easy to understand 2. Training is very fast. 3. Robust to noisy training data.	1. Sensitive to the local structure of the data. 2. It has Memory limitation. 3. Being a supervised learning lazy algorithm i.e., runs slowly.	–	$O(np)$
SVM	1. High accuracy 2. Avoid over fitting 3. Flexible selection of kernels for nonlinearity and accuracy 4. Performance are independent of number of features 5. Good generalization ability 6.Rrobust to noise. 7. Memory-intensive.	1.SVM is a binary classifier. To do a multi-class classification, pair wise classifications can be used 2. Computationally expensive based on the dataset.	$O(n^2p+n^3)$	$O(n_{sv}p)$

CONCLUSION

The past few years have produced a dramatic pace, which makes it difficult to classify these types of data, especially for the common man. The leading purpose of the classification algorithm is always to develop a framework which often classifies the information while relying on a training Data list. There are many related types of researches based on different classification tactics. However, it has not been discovered if a single approach is much better than others. Challenges like accuracy, flexibility, training time and several others play a vital role in choosing the right method to classify the data for mining. The lookup for the most practical way of classification, even presently, remains to be the research place. In this paper, we have made an extensive investigation on various classification methods including Decision tree, linear regression, Random forest, Naive Bayes, SVM, and KNN classifier. Distinct classification strategies provide a unique outcome on the base of exactness, training time, accuracy and recall. Every approach seems to have its very own pros and cons as given in this paper. One of the classification methods can be preferred based on specified application conditions. In future work, various big data analytics methods can be employed along with classification algorithms to further improve overall performance, as well as high accuracy.

REFERENCES

Akinola, S. O., & Oyabugbe, O. J. (2015). Accuracies and training times of data mining classification algorithms: An empirical comparative study. *Journal of software Engineering and Applications*, 8(9), 470.

Al-Radaideh, Q. A., Al-Shawakfa, E. M., & Al-Najjar, M. I. (2006, December). Mining student data using decision trees. *Proceedings of the International Arab Conference on Information Technology (ACIT'2006)*, Yarmouk University, Jordan. Academic Press.

Brijain, M., Patel, R., Kushik, M., & Rana, K. (2014). A survey on decision tree algorithm for classification.

Brindha, S., Prabha, K., & Sukumaran, S. (2016, January). A survey on classification techniques for text mining. *Proceedings of the 2016 3rd International Conference on Advanced Computing and Communication Systems (ICACCS)* (Vol. 1, pp. 1-5). IEEE. https://www.analyticsvidhya.com/blog/2015

Çığşar, B., & Ünal, D. (2019). Comparison of Data Mining Classification Algorithms Determining the Default Risk. *Scientific Programming*.

Dai, W., & Ji, W. (2014). A mapreduce implementation of C4. 5 decision tree algorithm. International journal of database theory and application, 7(1), 49-60.

Gandhi, B. S., & Deshpande, L. A. (2016, August). The survey on approaches to efficient clustering and classification analysis of big data. *Proceedings of the 2016 International Conference on Computing Communication Control and automation (ICCUBEA)* (pp. 1-4). IEEE. 10.1109/ICCUBEA.2016.7859993

Gao, S., & Li, H. (2012, August). Breast cancer diagnosis based on support vector machine. *Proceedings of the 2012 2nd International Conference on Uncertainty Reasoning and Knowledge Engineering* (pp. 240-243). IEEE.

Gorade, S. M., Deo, A., & Purohit, P. (2017). A study of some data mining classification techniques. *International Research J. of Engineering and Technology (IRJET), 4*.

Labor Relations dataset. (n.d.). UCI. Retrieved from https://archive.ics.uci.edu/ml/datasets/Labor+Relations

Oliverio, V., & Poli-Neto, O. B. (2017, April). Case Study: Classification Algorithms Comparison for the Multi-Label Problem of Chronic Pelvic Pain Diagnosing. *Proceedings of the 2017 IEEE 33rd International Conference on Data Engineering (ICDE)* (pp. 1507-1509). IEEE.

Owais, S. S., & Hussein, N. S. (2016). Extract five categories CPIVW from the 9V's characteristics of the big data. *International Journal of Advanced Computer Science and Applications*, 7(3), 254–258.

Piao, Y., Park, H. W., Jin, C. H., & Ryu, K. H. (2014, January). Ensemble method for classification of high-dimensional data. *Proceedings of the 2014 International Conference on Big Data and Smart Computing (BIGCOMP)* (pp. 245-249). IEEE. 10.1109/BIGCOMP.2014.6741445

Pitre, R., & Kolekar, V. (2014). A Survey Paper on Data Mining With Big Data. *International Journal of Innovative Research in Advanced Engineering*, 1(1), 178–180.

Revathy, R., & Lawrance, R. (2017). Comparative Analysis of C4. 5 and C5. 0 Algorithms on Crop Pest Data. *Int. J. Innov. Res. Comput. Commun. Eng*, 5(1), 50–58.

Thakor, H. R. (2017). A Survey Paper on Classification Algorithms in Big Data. International Journal Of Research Culture Society, 1(3).

Wikipedia. (n.d.). Weka (machine learning). Retrieved from https://en.wikipedia.org/wiki/Weka_(machine_learning)

Wu, X., Zhu, X., Wu, G. Q., & Ding, W. (2013). Data mining with big data. *IEEE Transactions on Knowledge and Data Engineering*, 26(1), 97–107.

Yu, H., Yang, J., & Han, J. (2003, August). Classifying large data sets using SVMs with hierarchical clusters. *Proceedings of the ninth ACM SIGKDD international conference on Knowledge discovery and data mining* (pp. 306-315). ACM. 10.1145/956750.956786

Chapter 3
Big Data and Analytics

Sheik Abdullah A.
Thiagarajar College of Engineering, India

Priyadharshini P.
Thiagarajar College of Engineering, India

ABSTRACT

The term Big Data corresponds to a large dataset which is available in different forms of occurrence. In recent years, most of the organizations generate vast amounts of data in different forms which makes the context of volume, variety, velocity, and veracity. Big Data on the volume aspect is based on data set maintenance. The data volume goes to processing usual a database but cannot be handled by a traditional database. Big Data is stored among structured, unstructured, and semi-structured data. Big Data is used for programming, data warehousing, computational frameworks, quantitative aptitude and statistics, and business knowledge. Upon considering the analytics in the Big Data sector, predictive analytics and social media analytics are widely used for determining the pattern or trend which is about to happen. This chapter mainly deals with the tools and techniques that corresponds to big data analytics of various applications.

DOI: 10.4018/978-1-5225-9750-6.ch003

INTRODUCTION

Big Data is a huge number of data sets. In the recent year, most of the organizations and industries generated a large amount of data known as big data. Big data is designed and focused on the volume aspect of extreme data-set maintenance (Abdullah, Gayathri & Selvakumar, 2017). The data volume then goes to process usual database but cannot be handled as a traditional database. Big Data is stored among structure, unstructured, and semi structured data. Big data is often retrieved from multiple sources and comes in multiple formats for Big Data analytics to be processed in varied datasets.

An organization generates and manages a large amount of volume data, which makes big data analytics tools to be the most important tool in enterprises. The Big data analytics tool should be expanded when analysing data cleaning, data mining, data duplicates, and data visualization. Big data does not change only in predictive analysis but also changes our power of thinking and knowledge. These techniques are used in quickly analysing the real time organization's and industries' data set. These technologies change the world's business and also help in good decision-making. This is an emerging technology for companies and it has been applied to analyse big data analytics in cloud, Hadoop, deep learning, and no SQL and in-memory analytics. Banking and securities, communications & media, healthcare, education, insurance, consumer trade, transportation are the top sectors used by Big Data analytics.

For example, the global spread of the Ebola virus strains have been identified in different countries, using a data analytics tool. The collected datasets and subsequently surveys were used in the research (Abdullah, Gayathri & Selvakumar, 2017). For the datasets to be analysed accurately, it required experts to apply some skills like programming, data warehousing, computational frameworks, quantitative aptitude and statistics, and business knowledge. The predictive analytics is a perfect analytics process in the current state and defines the correlation and source to obtaining the quality of data. In the process, IT and digital agencies are involved in applying different types of tools. These tools are recognised when solving various dataset issues such as determining whether the right data will be enough for a system. Identifying Big data solutions for data processing recommend using the popular open source. Tools include Apache Hadoop, Apache Spark, Apache Strom, Apache Cassandra, Mango Db, R programming Environment, Neo4j, and Apache SAMOA. However, there are many big data analytics tools available in recent years.

The next level of mobile app will use the current demographics. The main challenges of big data analytics are security and privacy. Collecting datasets potentially comes with data risks, which means that data security and privacy is mostly needed for data analytics. Some available security techniques are also available in evaluating the Big Data context. However, security technologies are only applicable on static data and cannot be applied on dynamic data. Unfortunately, big data analytics risks running out of cloud-based storage and data mining collection techniques. Data needs to be stored in storage medium since the stored data include sensitive information. This media also enables users to determine the origin and access control of data being stored. So, big data base threats and vulnerability security should be ensured in an organization. These are all hot topics explained in detail in this book chapter.

BIG DATA

Big data analytics is a one of the complex datasets in which process to complex or huge amount of sensitive data are analysed. These sets help organizations to make proper decisions. Data analytics mainly concentrate on big data since it includes gathering large amount of unstructured data. So, data analytics sort to classify datasets by specific data items (Abdullah et al., 2018).

BIG DATA APPLICATION

The Internet of things (IOTs) is a network-connected object. The IOTs model contains communication devices, which are embedded sensor devices in real world. These are interconnected with Sensor devices and objects, which are used to communication technologies. In these technologies are: RFID, Bluetooth, Wi-Fi and GSM. An IOT object is also able to collect and transfer sensitive data. With this technology, data transfer over the internet does not need human to human or human to computer interaction. The main critical component in the IoTs process is data. Data transmission from communication devices to remotely control devices (Abirami et al., 2018) is focused on the volume aspect based on a lot of data set maintenance.

The IOT application, along with the ability to gather data from physical and virtual sensor nodes, continuously defines the importance of big data in handling velocity dimensions. The data volume goes to processing usual database but cannot be handled as a traditional database. Big Data is stored among structure, unstructured, and semi structured data. The usage of Big Data in IOTs is to process of large amount of data in real time whereby the major applications used will be data storage and data security. The two major system privacy issues that arise in big data are the IOTs.

One of the Big Data analytics tool is used to restore private information while the other one is used in unidentified user generating data. Data Security perspective dedicated software is needed for data processing in websites. Software performance will be exposed to threats and attacks in the future hence making the connected devices to be at risk. This is because it will be necessary to store a lot of unstructured data in big data systems hence making it vulnerable. IOT and big data have a data analytics tool used to provide knowledge about sensor network infrastructure and related information based on the process of decision making.

Analysing data refers to creating graphs, charts and tables, which enables well-organized decision making. The IoTs and big data analytics focus on infrastructure size and performance. Big data analytics performance on a large amount of stream data may depend on event correlation and statistic operation but data should not always be stream data. However, IoT applications include different levels of analytics methods used in real time, off line, memory and business intelligent level analytics. The main challenges of big data in IOT are related to data management, data integrity, data quality, and data discovery. Currently, most industries and research societies are embracing the IoT big data technologies (Abdullah, Gayathri & Selvakumar, 2017). The real-time applications include smart transportation, smart health care, smart grid, smart inventory, smart cities, smart manufacturing, smart retail, and smart agriculture. The big data in IoTs includes one of the applications in smart homes. Moreover, there are IoTs devices enabled in smart home environments such as security cameras, automatic sensor lighting, computer, sensor water tabs and home applications.

BIG DATA ANALYTICS

Big data analytics are processed in varied data set. An organization generates and manages a large amount of volume data, which makes big data analytics tools to be the most important tool in enterprises. The Big data analytics tool should be expanded when analysing data cleaning, data mining, data duplicates, and data visualization. Big data does not change only in predictive analysis but also changes our power of thinking and knowledge (Abdullah et al, 2018). These techniques are used in quickly analysing the real time organization's and industries' data set. These technologies change the world's business and also help in good decision-making. This is an emerging technology for companies and it has been applied to analyse Big Data analytics in the cloud, Hadoop, deep learning, and no SQL and in-memory analytics. Banking and securities, communications & media, healthcare, education, insurance, consumer trade, transportation are the top sectors used by big data analytics.

BIG DATA ANALYTICS TOOLS

Real time data analytics includes a process of the classification, modelling, and transferring data to discover important information. Important stages for data analytics are data requirement, data collection, data pre-processing and data cleaning (Abdullah, Gayathri & Selvakumar, 2017).

Big data solution for the data processing recommends using the popular open source. These tools such as Apache Hadoop, Apache Spark, Apache Strom, Apache Cassandra, Mango Db, R programming Environment, Neo4j, and Apache SAMOA are used. There are many big data analytics tools available in recent years, but the next generation of mobile app will use the current demographics. These Data analytics tools are R programming, Weka, and rapid miner (Abdullah et al., 2017).

ANALYTICS TOOL DEMO

See Figures 1-3.

Figure 1. Data set for heart disease

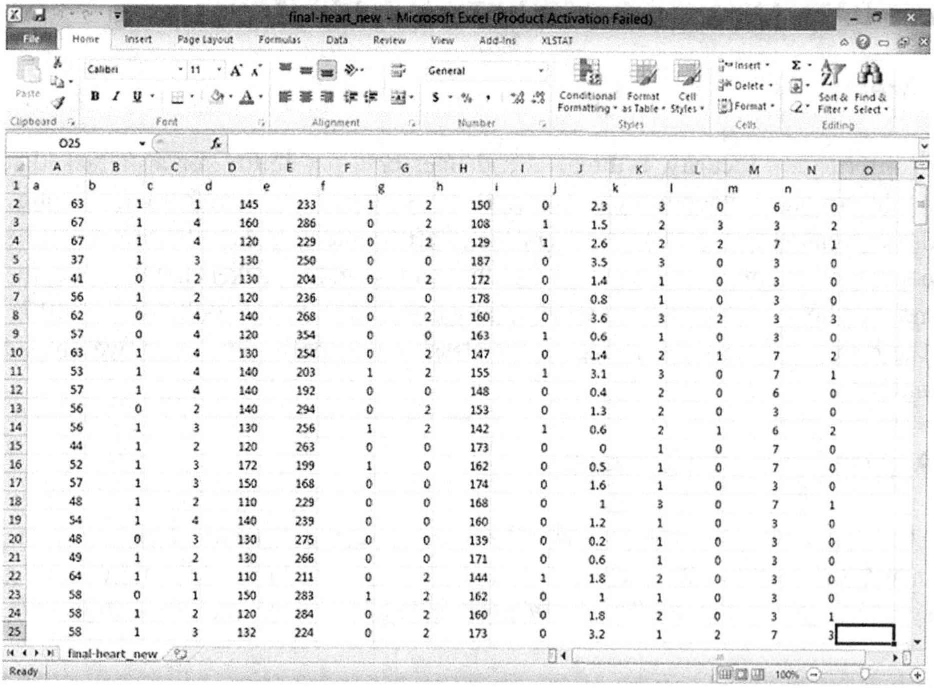

a	b	c	d	e	f	g	h	i	j	k	l	m	n
63	1	1	145	233	1	2	150	0	2.3	3	0	6	0
67	1	4	160	286	0	2	108	1	1.5	2	3	3	2
67	1	4	120	229	0	2	129	1	2.6	2	2	7	1
37	1	3	130	250	0	0	187	0	3.5	3	0	3	0
41	0	2	130	204	0	2	172	0	1.4	1	0	3	0
56	1	2	120	236	0	0	178	0	0.8	1	0	3	0
62	0	4	140	268	0	2	160	0	3.6	3	2	3	3
57	0	4	120	354	0	0	163	1	0.6	1	0	3	0
63	1	4	130	254	0	2	147	0	1.4	2	1	7	2
53	1	4	140	203	1	2	155	1	3.1	3	0	7	1
57	1	4	140	192	0	0	148	0	0.4	2	0	6	0
56	0	2	140	294	0	2	153	0	1.3	2	0	3	0
56	1	3	130	256	1	2	142	1	0.6	2	1	6	2
44	1	2	120	263	0	0	173	0	0	1	0	7	0
52	1	3	172	199	1	0	162	0	0.5	1	0	7	0
57	1	3	150	168	0	0	174	0	1.6	1	0	3	0
48	1	2	110	229	0	0	168	0	1	3	0	7	1
54	1	4	140	239	0	0	160	0	1.2	1	0	3	0
48	0	3	130	275	0	0	139	0	0.2	1	0	3	0
49	1	2	130	266	0	0	171	0	0.6	1	0	3	0
64	1	1	110	211	0	2	144	1	1.8	2	0	3	0
58	0	1	150	283	1	2	162	0	1	1	0	3	0
58	1	2	120	284	0	2	160	0	1.8	2	0	3	1
58	1	3	132	224	0	2	173	0	3.2	1	2	7	3

Figure 2. Design for rapid miner tool

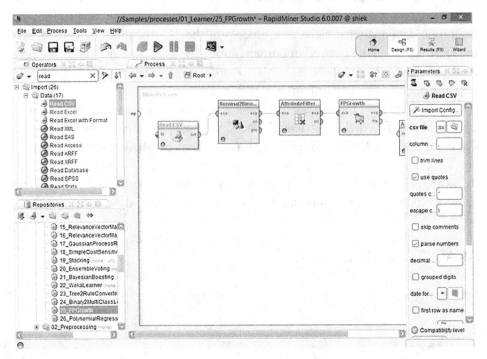

BIG DATA ANALYTICS SECURITY AND PRIVACY

Threats

In information security, a threat is a danger or a possibility for an attack that might exploit a vulnerability to breach security system and therefore cause a huge damage onto a system. These threats can either be intentional or accidental. As the population of smartphone users is rapidly increasing, the hackers are targeting the mobile phones, which have a wide variety of applications (Abdullah et al, 2017). There are many types of threats and are classified as application-based, web-based and server-side threats.

Application-Based Threats

The number of malware and spyware has been increased in mobile devices by more than 600% since 2012, whereby over 250.000 malware in the Android operating system are evident alone. The malware is malicious software and refers to viruses,

Figure 3. Result analysis for data set

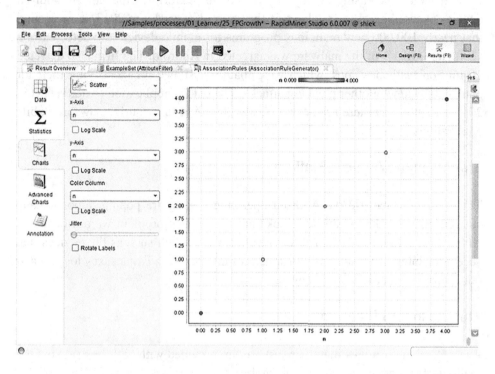

worms, Trojan horses, ransomware, which cause a deviation from the normal behaviour of a system. The malware has many types of malicious behaviors which include leaking sensitive data or stealing credentials, restricting device usage, mobile distributed denial of service etc.

The recent malware is the root exploits (jailbreak exploits), which enables an attacker to gain access to certain privileges. In mobile devices, the official application stores such as Google play and apple app store will scan the application they offer for traces of malware, spyware and remove the application if any threats are detected. The main threat lies during application installation and application handling in the mobile devices. The security of the mobile users would not end once an application has been installed or when the user is asked to make a decision regarding the security and privacy while handling the application. However, it is essential to ask the user for permission to access the information in the mobile device. The application installed tends to update automatically and can even change the permission settings, which becomes a major threat to users. If the infected smartphones were to be used in the workplace or a company, hackers could obtain corporate secrets. Nowadays even the government sectors are subjected to the many attacks (Harsheni et al, 2019).

Threats are increasing day by day in mobile platforms, especially in android devices. According to the analysis of threats by Kaspersky in 2013, it was found that nearly 100,000 new malicious programs for mobile devices are detected in a year. Here, 98.1% of the malware was targeted in Android. The firm also detected 10 million malicious apps, which were mainly designed for identifying theft for bank details among other phishing attacks. The cenzic application trends report in 2014 also says that there has been a steady growth in the security flaws in mobile applications.

Threats in the Android Platform

The devices which use the Android operating system are popular among many customers. With this, malware attacks are the biggest problem we are facing in android platform. The risk of threat has become so high such as the devices that access the internet are subjected to attacks or infections by Trojans, key loggers and other forms of malware and spyware.

Threats in IOS Platform

Every Apple user thinks that their systems are provided with high security, but the reality is that iPhone and other Apple mobile devices are also a target for the attacks. In September 2015, one the most serious threats occurred, which affected the app store. When this was discovered, a large number of trojanized IOS apps were being hosted on the service. Here, the apps were developed using a malicious version of Xcode, in addition to this, the organized apps are capable of receiving commands from coca servers in order to carry out phishing attacks. One of the major threats in IOS is jail breaking, by which the attackers can escalate the privileges by removing the software restrictions imposed by Apple on IOS. It can be done using kernel patches (Abdullah et al., 2019).

Threats in Windows Platform

The mobile devices with the Windows OS are less used when compared with other Android and iOS, due to its compatibility. It is also subjected to many types of attacks, which are mainly the command injection attacks thereby stealing the credentials. Currently, Microsoft is seeking to unify their applications, which means that many developers are remaking their applications as universal windows apps as the ROI on maintaining a stand-alone windows phone app is too little. The windows app store will have only a smaller number of applications than in android.

The report found that privacy violation and excessive privileges appear in most of the mobile applications. In order to prevent cyber war through the smartphones, Korea internet and security agency of South Korea has organized a cooperative mobile security defence group. It acts as a defence against malicious software (Abdullah, Gayathri & Selvakumar, 2017).

Web-Based Threats

In today's world, the mobile device offers a high level of convenience. At any location (office, home, hotel, playground, road, or anyplace in the world) the mobile user can fulfil their daily needs, including buying, communication searching, selling, entertainment, making payments etc. by means of web applications in mobiles. Threats related to such activity is a major concern and it became a serious problem for the mobile users. This extreme level of comfort brought an extreme level of security issues and threats. Some of the web-based threats are described below.

Mobile Browsing

The best feature of the mobile device is browsing, which provides the best use of internet applications. Normally in mobiles the user cannot see the entire web address or the domain address, hence it is difficult to check whether the URL is secure or not. It becomes a threat for a phishing-related attack.

Multiple User Logging

Due to the progressive growth of social networking sites and single sign-on in the mobile application ecosystem, it has been found that 60% of the application is insecure due to the use same login credentials for multiple website or applications moreover in mobile devices the user login to the application once, and they never log out mainly in Gmail account, it become serious threat to mobile devices (Suganya et al., 2018), by which the attackers can acquire the credentials and can gain access to a user's profile page.

Client-Side Injection

As the mobile devices are accessing the internet for every action there may be a chance of executing the malicious program without the knowledge of the user, it occurs by mobile applications or web browsing client-side injection. There are many types of client-side injection some of them are HTML injection, SQL injection etc. In this way, any data can be injected.

Improper Session Handling

Session handling is identified as an important security concern for web applications in mobile devices. Improper session handling is a major threat when the mobile devices are accessing the internet over any platform. The application with long expiry sessions is often subjected to the attack especially in a mobile device (Karaolis et al., 2010). This poor management session provides a way for an attacker to unauthorized access by session hijacking

Weak Authentication and Brute Force Attack

Today, almost every application relies on password-based authentication. Who are using this application will not enforce strong passwords and does not provide security for the application. Thus, the user itself exposes themselves to a host of threats for an attacker. With the brute force attack, the hacker gains the credentials of the user due to the weak authentication mechanism.

Web-Based Threats in Different Mobile Platforms

The possibility of attacks is larger in the mobile devices of android platforms When compare with other Operating systems. In apple IOS only a few numbers of applications are free of cost and other application can be used only by paying money, hence the user will be considered that there can be some security feature in it. Then the windows and blackberry OS are rare in usage by the user, but in every platform, the possibility of an attack is increasing day by day (Chang-Sik et al., 2012).

Network-Based Threats

The mobile devices provide the best support to cellular networks and wireless LAN IEEE 802.11. In both the networks we have different types of threats for the mobile users. Some of the network-based threats are described as follows,

Network Exploits

This threat occurs in the mobile devices due to the faults in the operating system and other applications in the mobile. When the mobile device is connected to the network there is a possibility of installing some malicious software on the user's device without the knowledge of the users

Mobile Network Services

The network provides a lot of services like SMS, MMS, voice calls, multimedia transmission, etc., by means of these services the hacker can launch the attack. For example, a phishing attack can be launched by the attacker in which he impersonates a legitimate user and communicates with the target.

Wi-Fi Sniffing

It is one of the major threats in wireless technology. Here every device communicating in the wireless medium is a target for the attack. By intercepting the communication (i.e. man in the middle attack) or by simply monitoring the attacker gain the access. Then by placing a rogue access point with the strong signal, the hacker can steal the sensitive information, therefore communication in the wireless medium is a big risk, unencrypted data can easily be stolen by the attackers.

ATTACKS

The attack on the mobile device occurs due to the vulnerabilities and threats that we have seen before. The attack can occur in three areas they are, in the mobile device, in the network, then finally in the database. The attacks are broadly classified into active and passive attacks. Active attacks are performed by the malicious nodes; it involves modification of data or the interruption of the communication. The passive attacks involve simply monitoring the communication and traffic analysis, it is difficult to detect the passive attack.

Attacks in Mobile Devices

Phishing Attack

The recent years have witnessed that the threats to the phishing attack have been increased in the mobile platforms. Mobile phishing is an emerging threat mainly targeting the mobile users of financial institutions, online shopping, and social networking companies. This is mainly due to the hardware limitations of mobile devices. It is the type of active attack. Phishing is an identity theft attack in online, by which the attacker steals the user's credentials resulting in a financial loss as well as a loss to the organization.

By the malicious emails, redirecting to the fake websites, impersonation, and the attacker can launch the phishing attack. As the mobile device is very compact, it provides the same functionalities that enable the user to move towards the mobile for all the transaction process. Hence the attackers targeting the mobile devices, for them it is easy to launch the phishing attack in mobile than in desktop systems due to the lack of security systems (Breiman, 2001; Wasan et al., 2013) (Peter et al., 2013).

The phishing is mainly targeting the IOS platform when compared with the android in early days. In iOS, the phishing attacks occur in the gaming applications. Hera attackers stealing the data in two different ways: by realizing knockoff games to steal the credentials and by exploiting the social elements of legitimate game applications. Then the IOS developers provide many security features to overcome this attack. Now as the number of users for Android have been increased than in blackberry and windows, due to its price and features, hence android become a major target for an attack.

Man in the Middle Attack

In earlier days it occurs in the computers and laptops but now in the mobile devices growing at a fast pace. This is a kind of active attack, in which the attacker sits between the user and the website and steals personal information by breaking the connection between them. Here the attacker impersonates himself as a legitimate user and sends the modified message to the website as it is sent by the legitimate user. This attack is possible even if the message is in an encrypted format. This problem arises when an application fails to use a proper authentication mechanism. Hence to ensure secure communication it is important to know how the mobile application performs authentication mechanisms.

The attack is targeting equally on all the platforms due to the lack of security in the application which we are downloading from the play stores. More than 75% of the applications do not meet the basic security requirements. The users of IOS think that the application is secure but it is also equally prone to the attacks.

Framing and Click Jacking Attack

Framing is a mainly caused by the web browser like internet explorer, not checking the destination of the frame. The web framing attacks occur in the browser with the malicious page loading a victim page as a frame. The common example of framing is click jacking, where the victim page is loaded which tempts the user to click on that page. This attack enables the wrapper site to execute a click jacking attack, which a real threat that has been exploited on high-profile services to steal the credentials of the user or they redirect the users to attacker-controlled sites. The goal of the framing attack is that to trick the users into clicking on something different than what they intended. This is mainly for the purpose of gathering the confidential information or take control over the affected computer through vulnerabilities. To defend against framing the entire websites use frame busting, which help to prevent the system from loading a malicious frame in the browser? The new attack called tap-jacking that uses the features of the mobile browsers to implement a strong click jacking attack on mobile phones. The tap jacking illustrates the importance of frame busting on mobile sites. The framing attack can also result in the theft of Wi-Fi passwords or WPA secrete key.

The iPhone browser supports all the basic functionality to overcome theclick jacking attack: transparency and I frames. However, the phone extra features make the attack more dangerous. in the iPhone there is possibility of an attack of hiding or faking the URL bar, in which the user cannot identify the page which is loaded as the URL is hidden, hence the user taught it as a legitimate site and share their credentials, but in the desktop systems it is somewhat difficult to hide the URL, instead they can redirect to the fake URL (similar to the original URL) and launch the attack. For other mobile browsers also the techniques we have discussed for the iPhone are applicable. For Android devices supports for IFRAMEs, opacity changes, scaling, viewport which makes them a prime target for tapjacking (Christianini & Taylor, 2000) (Jiaweihan & Kamber, 2010).

Buffer Overflow Attack

The buffer overflow is a common coding mistake by the programmer, through which the attacker could exploit to gain access to the system. It is important to understand how the buffer overflow attack occurs and what techniques the attacker uses to successfully exploit these vulnerabilities.in the mobile phones this attack occurs due to the lack of input validation, the near field communication module of Huawei mobile phones has a buffer overflow vulnerability, here the attacker may use an NFC card reader or another device to inject malicious data into a target device. Later the Huawei released an update to fix this vulnerability.

Key Concepts

1. This attack occurs when there is more data in the buffer than it can handle, thus it overwrites the data in the buffer which leads to the loss of information.
2. This attack can even crash the system and create an entry point for a cyber-attack

3.   C and C++ are more susceptible to buffer overflow when compared to other programming languages.
4.   Secure development or secure program practices should include regular testing to detect and fix the buffer overflow attack.

Data Caching

Caching is a technique of storing frequently used data in the memory, such that it could to retrieve easily within a short span of time. The attack occurs when these data is stolen by the attacker or the attacker can launch the attack by making changes to the cache data which store in random access memory. Here the attacker replaces the malicious webpage content, code or some random data he controls to steal the confidential information about the user. Many cache attacks have occurred on Intel X86 CPUs, and the powerful techniques to exploit cache side channels have been developed. However, the modern mobile phones use one or more ARM CPU that has different cache organization and instruction set than in the Intel x86 CPUs. Till now there is no attack occurs in the non-rooted android smart phones. But the attacker will try to root the Android smartphone and launch the data caching attack.

The routers implement route caching or routing tables to allow faster query. Then caching in different geographic locations can be seen as a content delivery networks (CDN). The CDN is a collection of servers that store local copies of content on servers located strategically across the internet. The each CDN server is a data caching server provides fast access for the users. Thus, in this way data caching become a major attack that even crashes the server system.

As the development of the technology increases, the possibility of the attack also increases; the data caching attack occurs frequently in the mobile devices as the number of users is larger in mobile devices than in the desktop system. But in the mobile, the size of RAM is smaller than the systems, even though the attacker targets the mobile devices. By data caching the attacker can also redirect to the different IP of the system by compromising the router

Baseband Attacks

Baseband is nothing compared to a firmware used by cellular modem manufactures in making smartphones to connect to the cellular network, make voice calls, send and receive data through this network. Cellular networks have been evolved to support high data rates and provide internet access. Here, the attacker will try to monitor a phone 's communication, place calls, and send SMS messages to the active user. By this, the attacker gathers a lot of information about the users without his/her knowledge. The attacker can even send a malware to the target a mobile device by means of SMS, email that can be hardcoded in the malware code or downloaded at runtime to avoid detection while monitoring every activity of the user. Currently, majority of the mobile malware aim at targeting financial information. Moreover, the infected mobile devices are turned into botnets for HTTP-based remote control by a bushmaster.

The mobile malware (SIM Monitor) is used for the baseband attack in android and iPhone devices. This malware has the ability to steal all the security credentials and sensitive information using the cellular technology (i.e. permanent and temporary identities, encryption keys, the location of the user, etc.). It operates in the background and it is difficult for the user to detect its existence since it would not disrupt the normal behaviors of the user's mobile device. With this malware, the attacker can entirely breach the security of the mobile devices.

Smashing Attack

This attack is also a security attack similar to the phishing attack, but refers to a fraudulent SMS (text message) rather than an email. It is a combination of terms; SMS and phishing. Similar to all attack, the attacker also tries to steal personal information. The smishers launch the attack by sending the large text messages, which is designed to capture the recipient's attention. The messages sent by the attacker provide fake information like "you have won a free gift card; visit this webpage to claim it." If the user clicks on this link, he/she will be directed to the fraudulent website, which will ask them to enter their personal detail like phone number, email id, sometimes it asks for your bank account details. In the smashing attack, the attacker masquerades as a legitimate person to get the user to reveal his/ her information. Even from the malicious application that is being downloaded from the app store can also cause smashing attack. The attacker also uses social engineering tactics to convince the user to do so.

A report shows that the number of mobile smashing attacks has been increased over the last few years on various mobile device platforms (Jiaweihan & Kamber, 2010). One of the best examples of a phishing attack in mobile devices is through the android 09Droid phishing application in the app store, which is intended to gather user's banking credentials. The IOS mobile phones and this application are also vulnerable to the smashing attack. Since mobile devices have small screens, the user is not able to view the whole URL. However, they are just attacked by clicking it and are then redirected to fake sites. Moreover, users download the application without realizing that it is a legitimate official application or not. The users should be more careful when doing any such thing in the mobile devices to prevent the device from smishing.

SUMMARY

Big data is indeed a huge number of datasets. Over the recent years, most organizations and industries have generated a lot of data. This type of data is also known as big data. For accurate analysis of datasets, some skills should be applied: programming, data warehousing, computational frameworks, quantitative aptitude and statistics, and business knowledge. Moreover, emerging technologies (such as big data analytics in the cloud, Hadoop, deep learning, no SQL, and In-memory analytics) among companies have been applied to analyse these datasets. Banking and securities, communications & media, healthcare, education, insurance, consumer trade, and the transportation sector are the top sectors applying big data analytics. However, the main challenges of big data analytics are security and privacy, which determine the data origin and access control. Consequently, big data base threats and vulnerability security should be guaranteed in an organization. These are all hot topics clarified in detail in this article.

REFERENCES

Abdullah, A. S., Gayathri, N., & Selvakumar, S. (2017). Determination of the Risk of Heart Disease using Neural Network Classifier. *Proceedings of the National Conference on Big Data Analytics and Mobile Technologies (NCBM 2017)*, Thiagarajar College of Engineering, Madurai. Academic Press.

Abdullah, A. S., Rishi, K. V., Karthickbabu, M., Prathap, D., & Selvaumar, S. (2019). Heart Disease Prediction using Data Mining. *Proceedings of the Fifth International Conference on Biosignals, Images and Instrumentation (ICBSII 2019)*, Chennai, India. Springer India.

Abdullah, A. S., & Selvakumar, S. (2018). An Improved Medical Informatic Decision Model by Hybridizing Ant colony Optimization Algorithm with Decision Trees for Type II Diabetic Prediction. *Proceedings of the International Conference on Business Analytics and Intelligence*. Academic Press.

Abdullah, A. S., Selvakumar, S., & Abirami, A. M. (2017). An Introduction to Data Analytics: Its Types and Its Applications. In *Handbook of Research on Advanced Data Mining Techniques and Applications for Business Intelligence*. Hershey, PA: IGI Global; doi:10.4018/978-1-5225-2031-3.ch001

Abdullah, A. S., Selvakumar, S., Abirami, A. M., Parkavi, R., & Suganya, R. (2018). Big data Analytics in Healthcare Sector. In *Machine Learning Techniques for Improved Business Analytics*. Hershey, PA: IGI Global; doi:10.4018/978-1-5225-3534-8.ch005

Abdullah, A. S., Selvakumar, S., Karthikeyan, P., & Venkatesh, M. (2017). Comparing the Efficacy of Decision Tree and its Variants using Medical Data. *Indian Journal of Science and Technology*, *10*(18), 1–8. doi:10.17485/ijst/2017/v10i18/111768

Abdullah, A. S., Selvakumar, S., Parkavi, R., Suganya, R., & Venkatesh, M. (2019). An Introduction to Survival Analytics, Types, and Its Applications. UK: Intech Open Publishers. doi:10.5772/intechopen.80953

Abdullah, A. S., Selvakumar, S., & Ramya, C. (2017). Descriptive Analytics. In *Applying Predictive analytics within the service sector*. Hershey, PA: IGI Global; doi:10.4018/978-1-5225-2148-8.ch006

Abdullah, A. S., Suganya, R., Selvakumar, S., & Rajaram, S. (2017). Data Classification: Its Techniques and Big data. In *Handbook of Research on Advanced Data Mining Techniques and Applications for Business Intelligence*. Hershey, PA: IGI Global; doi:10.4018/978-1-5225-2031-3.ch003

Abdullah, A. S., Varshini, R., & Niveditha, J. P. (2017). Sentiment Analysis of Movie Reviews using Twitter data. *Proceedings of the International Conference on Big data and Data Analytics*. Academic Press.

Abirami, A. M., Abdullah, A. S., & Selvakumar, S. (2017). Sentiment Analysis. In *Handbook of Research on Advanced Data Mining Techniques and Applications for Business Intelligence*. Hershey, PA: IGI Global; doi:10.4018/978-1-5225-2031-3. ch009

Austin, P. C., Tu, J. V., Ho, J. E., Levy, D., & Lee, D. S. (2013). Using methods from the data-mining and machine-learning literature for disease classification and prediction: A case study examining classification of heart failure subtypes. *Journal of Clinical Epidemiology*.

Breiman, L. (2001). Random Forests. *Machine Learning*, *45*(1), 5–32. doi:10.1023/A:1010933404324

Chang-Sik, S., Kim, Y. N., Kim, H. S., Park, H. S., & Kim, M. S. (2012). Decision-making model for early diagnosis of congestive heart failure using rough set and decision tree approaches. *Journal of Biomedical Informatics*, *45*(5), 999–1008.

Christianini, N., & Taylor, J. S. (2000). *An Introduction to support vector machines and other kernel based learning methods*. Cambridge University Press. doi:10.1017/CBO9780511801389

Han, J., Pei, J., & Kamber, M. (2010). *Data mining: concepts and techniques* (3rd ed.). Elsevier.

Harsheni, S. K., & Souganthika, S. GokulKarthik, K., Abdullah, S.A., & Selvakumar, S. (March 2019). Analysis of the Risk factors of Heart disease using Step-wise Regression with Statistical evaluation. Proceedings of the International Conference on Emerging Current Trends in Computing and Expert Technology (COMET 2019) (pp. 22-23). Springer.

Hastie, T., Tibshrani, R., & Friedman, J. (2001). *Elements of statistical learning: Data mining, Inference and prediction*. Berlin: Springer Verlag. doi:10.1007/978-0-387-21606-5

Karaolis, A., Moutiris, A., Hadjipanayi, D., & Pattichis, S. (2010, May). Assessment of the Risk Factors of Coronary Heart Events Based on Data Mining With Decision Trees. *IEEE Transactions on Information Technology in Biomedicine*, *14*(3).

Suganya, R., Rajaram, S., Abdullah, A. S., & Rajendran, V. (2016). A Novel Feature Selection method for Predicting Heart Diseases with Data mining Techniques. *Asian Journal of Information Technology*, *15*(8), 1314–1321.

Wasan, P. S., Uttamchandani, M., Moochhala, S., Yap, V. B., & Yap, P. H. (2013). Application of statistics and machine learning for risk stratification of heritable cardiac arrhythmias. *Expert Systems with Applications*, *40*(7), 2476–2486.

Chapter 4

Decoding Big Data Analytics for Emerging Business Through Data-Intensive Applications and Business Intelligence:
A Review on Analytics Applications and Theoretical Aspects

Vinay Kellengere Shankarnarayan
Dayananda Sagar College of Engineering, India

ABSTRACT

In recent years, big data have gained massive popularity among researchers, decision analysts, and data architects in any enterprise. Big data had been just another way of saying analytics. In today's world, the company's capital lies with big data. Think of worlds huge companies. The value they offer comes from their data, which they analyze for their proactive benefits. This chapter showcases the insight of big data and its tools and techniques the companies have adopted to deal with data problems. The authors also focus on framework and methodologies to handle the massive data in order to make more accurate and precise decisions. The chapter begins with the current organizational scenario and what is meant by big data. Next, it draws out various challenges faced by organizations. The authors also observe big data business models and different frameworks available and how it has been categorized and finally the conclusion discusses the challenges and what is the future perspective of this research area.

DOI: 10.4018/978-1-5225-9750-6.ch004

INTRODUCTION TO BIG WORLD

It's helpful to have some historical background on big data. Here's definition, big data are data that contains a greater variety arriving in increasing volumes and with ever-higher velocity. It is known as the three V's(Savitz, 2013). According to McAfee, &Brynjolfsson (2012), in their article mentioned Data-driven decisions are much better decisions it's as simple as that. Using big data enables managers to decide based on evidence rather than intuition. During 2012 itself, about 2.5 Exabyte of data continually are created each day, and that number is doubling every 40 months or so. More data cross the internet every second than were stored in the entire internet just 20 years ago. Although the concept of big data itself is relatively new, the origins of large data sets go back to the 1960s and '70s when the world of data was just getting started, with the first data centers and the development of the relational database.

Pal (2016) stated that, during 2005, people just began to learn the importance of data and how much data users generated through online services. Hadoop (An Open Source application as a service, created mainly to analyze bigger data sets) developed. Apparently (Alsghaier, etal., 2017) described that the big data are now mainstream, so we have to take it seriously and manage it professionally with the help of schema-less NoSQL databases to analyze unstructured data sets.

According to Chen, etal. (2014), there are opportunities that are related to data analysis in many organizations. It has generated an essential interest in business intelligence, which sometimes points to the techniques and technologies that help to produce a better understanding of the market and also make decisions wrong time, also concluded that the most significant value from big data when workers are free to explore their analyses. Establishing this type of environment leads the IT work team to change from serving into enabling models.

RESEARCH SCOPE

Big Data discipline is still evolving and not yet wholly established. Earlier RDBMS are used to store only structured data sets. However, today, nearly 80% of the data fetched is in an unstructured format, thus making it impossible to store data in RDBMS. Hadoop is used to store all structured, unstructured, and hybrid data sets, as shown in figure 2.

Polato, et.al. (2014) already conducted research studies on Apache Hadoop, Plödereder, et.al.(2014) focused mainly on Big Data in Logistics, Jamil, et.al. (2015) concentrated on Data Veracity for digital news portal, Abdellatif, et.al.

Figure 1. Hypothetical classification of big data challenges

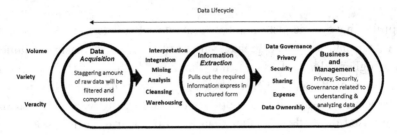

Figure 2. Types of big data

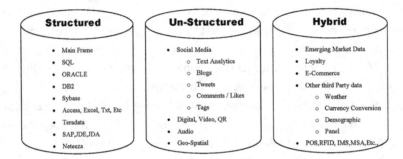

(2011) on Software analytics, this paper, we try to widen the scope of theirreviews by investigating further and assess different challenges of big data and the showcase methods used to overcome those challenges. Through this research work provides insights into Big Data, there is a lack of a methodical approach to understanding the Business intelligence and Big Data analytics in business. Thus, this article acts as a framework of reference.

Big Data Challenges

Technological improvement in business and new challenges they encounter makes companies focus on planning and directing more innovative business tactics which ensure them higher returns and lower operating expenses. (Cukier, 2010) Stated in their article that the big data revolution is in its early days, and most of the potential for value creation is still unclaimed. However, it has set the industry on a path of rapid change and discoveries; stakeholders that are committed to innovation are likely the first to reap the reward.

According to (Kumar, & Nagar, 2017) when it comes to big data, we hear a lot of it flying around it these days. There is broad recognition of the value of data, and products obtained through analyzing it. Popular news media (The Economist, 2011) in an article Drowning in numbers – Digital data floods the planet and help us understand it better, now appreciates the value of Big Data as evidenced by coverage in the Economist, (Lohr, 2012), (Noguchi, 2011) and (Manyika, et al., 2011) stated the industry is abuzz with the promise of Big Data. Government agencies have recently announced significant programs towards addressing challenges of Big Data, which can help accelerate the pace of discovery in science and engineering, strengthen national security, and transform teaching and learning[1]. However, many have an exceptionally tight translation of what that implies, and we forget about the way that there are different strides to the information investigation pipeline, regardless of whether the information is enormous or less. At each progression, there is work to be done, and there are difficulties with Big Data (Labrinidis, &Jagadish, 2012).

This Systematic Literature Review research aims to evaluate the comprehensive research published on Big Data and Big Data Analytics by employing a recognized profiling approach and analyze different Big Data challenges and Big Data Analytics technologies, techniques, methods and or approaches.

BIG DATA BUSINESS MODEL

It is anything but difficult to discover a case of an organization seen as an ideal example for enormous information. Typically, such examples of overcoming adversity include the creative utilization of enormous information to convey new items or to accomplish huge proficiency gains in some specific way. In this area, we venture once again from specific practices to take an increasingly conceptual perspective of the manners in which that information can fill in as a focal part of a plan of action and the open doors that these infer (Schroeder, 2016).

There are various new plans of action developing in the enormous information world. In our examination, we see three fundamental methodologies emerging the first spotlights on utilizing information to make separated contributions. The second includes handling this data. The third is tied in with building systems to convey information where it's required when it's required.

- **Data Differentiation**: For 10 years now, we've seen innovation and information bring new dimensions of personalization and significance. Vast information offers open doors for some more administration contributions that enhance consumer loyalty and give logical pertinence. The data can be collected from vehicles, which helps a rider to find out the nearest route from his home to the office, or If you were low on fuel and your vehicle addressed your maps application. You couldn't just discover the closest open service stations inside a 10-mile range, yet besides getting the cost per gallon or even amount of fuel required to drive to the destination.

- **Data Brokering:** (Sarkhel, &Alawadhi, 2017) stated, data brokering one obvious way to monetize proprietary first-party data is to treat it like any product and sell it to other parties. Companies such as AC Nielson, Experian, already sell raw information, provide benchmarking services, and deliver analysis and insights with structured data sources. In a big data world, though, these propriety systems may struggle to keep up. These firms collect data anonymously, including one's data. However, such information can be used for the analysis required for a specific purpose. For instance, retailers like Amazon could move raw data on the most blazing buy classifications. Extra information on climate examples and installment volumes from different accomplices could enable providers to pinpoint request flags significantly more intently. These new examinations and understanding streams could be made and kept up by data representatives who could sort by age, area, intrigue, and different classifications. With unlimited stages, intermediaries' plans of action would adjust by enterprises, topographies, and client jobs.

- **Data Delivery Networks**: this data must be conveyed under the control of the individuals who can utilize it. To additionally inspire our work, think about the generally conveyed remote LANs or info stations (Frenkiel, et al., 2000), (Goodman, et al., 1997), which can be utilized to convey notices and declarations, for example, Sale Information or remaining stock at a retail chain, accessible stopping in a parking area, and the gathering plan at a meeting room. For instance, individuals driving who needs to shop might need to inquire a few retail establishments to choose where to go; a driver may question the traffic cameras or parking area data to improve a street plan (Jing Zhao &Guohong Cao, 2008).

CATEGORIZATION OF BIG DATA MODELS

The above-mentioned big data business models can be grouped into three categories to produce a new data business model taxonomy. The first category is the so-called

Figure 3. Big data business models

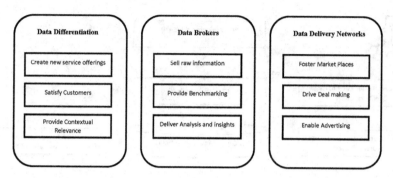

data users. These organizations use data to inform business decisions or to contribute to other products and services, such as credit reports or targeted publicity campaigns.

The second business model includes data vendors. These organizations either generate intrinsically valuable and therefore, marketable data or serve a sort of brokerage role by providing access to an aggregation of data from first and third parties.

The third business model covers the range of activities supporting third parties who lack the infrastructure or expertise. These data Coordinators provide a variety of services, including advice on how to capitalize on big data, how to provide physical infrastructure and also provision for outsourced analytical services.

Since the different types of big data business depend so closely on each other for success, any policy aimed at strengthening the data economy as a whole should adopt a relatively holistic approach to foster activities across the entire spectrum of Big Data business models and summarized in the Table 1.

Table 1. Big data model categorization

Type	Example Functions	Dependencies
Data Users	*Building data into products using data to inform strategic decisions.*	*It depends on raw data suppliers and infrastructure and skills facilitators.*
Data Vendors	*primary data collection; aggregation and packaging data for sale*	*It depends on infrastructure and skills facilitators and users both as customers and data sources.*
Data Coordinators	*Infrastructure supply; consulting; outsourced analysis;*	*It depends on customers on users and suppliers*

Figure 4. Limitations of existing data analytics architecture

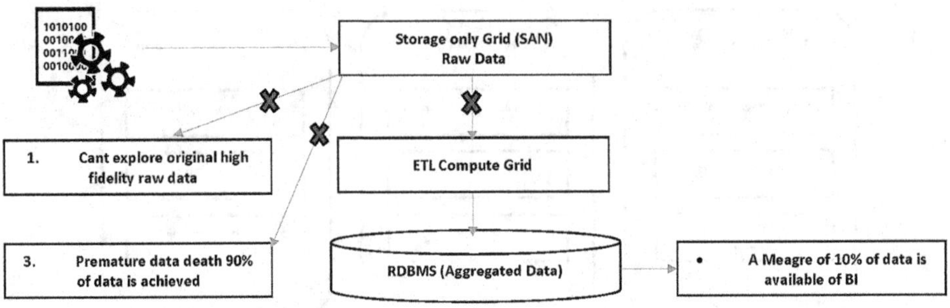

BIG DATA FRAMEWORK

We investigate four of the best open source Big Data handling structures utilized today, and the comparison made in Table 2. These aren't the main ones used, however ideally, they are viewed as a little delegate test of what is accessible, and a concise outline of what can be cultivated with the implemented devices.

Table 2. A comparative study of the big data frameworks

	Hadoop	Spark	Strom	Flink
Information format	Key-Value	RDD	Key-Value	Key-Value
Processing mode	Batch	Batch and Stream	Stream	Batch and Stream
Utilized data sources	HDFS	HDFS,DBMS,KAFKA	Spoots	Multiple
Programming model	Map and Reduce	Transformation and Action	Bolts	Transformation and Action
bolstered programming dialects	Java	Java, Scala, Python	Java	Java
Cluster Manager	Yarn	Yarn	Zookeeper	Zookeeper
Shared assets	Stores data in HDFS	API based applications	Real-time applications	Graphical Methods
iterative calculation	☒	✓	✓	✓

Figure 5. Hadoop HDFS framework

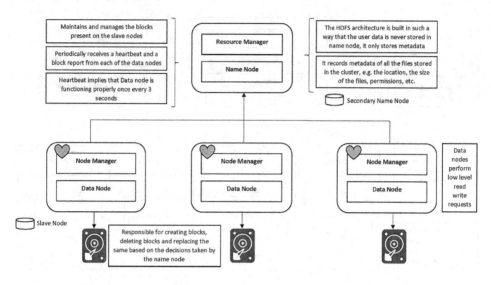

Figure 6. Apache Spark framework

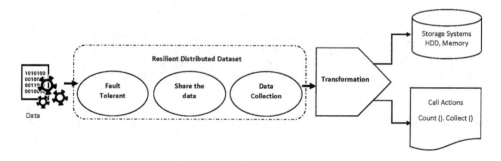

Apache Hadoop

To overcome the limitations of existing data analytics, Hadoop was developed. Hadoop is an open-source venture that was created by Apache in 2011. Hadoop is an extraordinary instrument for enormous information examination since it is exceptionally versatile, adaptable, and practical.

(Dean & Ghemawat, 2008) Introduced two segments of Hadoop: (1) Hadoop Distributed File System (HDFS) for information storage (2) Hadoop Map Reduce, execution of the Map-Reduce programming model.

Figure 7. Storm master-slave architecture

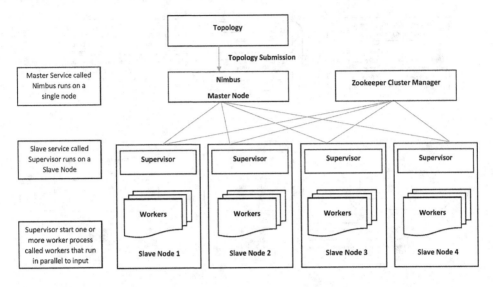

Figure 8. Apache Flink framework

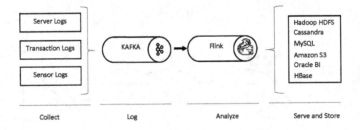

Apache Spark

Apache Spark is a fantastic handling system that gives an easy to use tool for proficient investigation of heterogeneous information. It was initially created in 2009 at UC Berkeley (Zaharia, et al., 2010). Spark differs from Hadoop and the MapReduce paradigm in that it works in-memory, speeding up processing times. Spark also circumvents the imposed linear dataflow of Hadoop's default MapReduce engine, allowing for more flexible pipeline construction.

Apache Strom

Apache Storm (Toshniwal, et al., 2014) is an open-source framework for process giant structured and unstructured knowledge in real-time. The storm could be a fault-tolerant framework that's appropriate for real-time knowledge analysis, machine learning, successive and repetitious computation. Apache Storm can run on YARN[2] and integrate into Hadoop ecosystems, providing existing implementations an answer for some time stream process.

Apache Flink

Flink is an open-source structure for handling information in both continuous mode and clump mode (Alexandrov, et al., 2014). It gives a few advantages, for example, Faults Tolerant and Large-scale calculation. The programming model of Flink is like MapReduce. By difference to Map Reduce, Flink offers extra high state capacities, for example, data joins, data filtration, and data aggregation. Flink can also be integrated with different data collection tools like Flume (Chambers, et al., 2014) and Kafka (Garg, 2013).

Table 2 is an order of the introduced systems as indicated by information format, processing mode, utilized data sources, programming model, bolstered programming dialects, cluster manager and whether the structure permits iterative calculation or not.

THE ROLE OF GOVERNMENT IN BIG DATA

Thanks to current technological advancements, government agencies are now leveraging massive information insights in a ramification of progressive approaches. With high requirements on top of flat or declining budgets, they're seeking to do greater with much less and a director of digital transformation can assist them in getting there. Alongside the manner, government agencies are modernizing their statistics warehouses, optimizing their enterprise aid planning answers, and commoditizing their storage. However, some of them don't always have the actual property for massive statistics facilities, so they desire to recall the blessings that a cloud solution can offer. In the end, maximum governments intention to store and analyze established and unstructured statistics to maximize its cost.

In a developing country like India, the number of states has set up their entries, yet the majority of these entryways are unequipped for giving a complete answer for individuals by the snap of the mouse. In the vast majority of cases, services and individual offices have separate sites to give the fundamental data. (K & K., 2017), (Chakrabarty, 2017) stated that this ought not to be the situation as the client needs to visit different sites to get essential data. In a perfect world, the official site should go about a single window to give essential data and administrations.

LIMITATIONS

The writer perceives that his examination has constraints, and peruses, what's more, future scholastics and scientists ought to know about these and in reality, decipher the material displayed in this paper inside the setting of the restrictions. By clarifying, a meta-examination lay on the current and also available research thinks about (both calculated and observational).

While the creators led exhaustive writing to seek through the Scopus database to recognize all credible critical articles, it is conceivable that some examination articles could have been missed in this audit from some other driving databases. So to maintain a strategic distance from duplication, each exertion was depleted to secure and break down all essential data fundamental, in regards to the two inquiries (i.e., Methodology and frameworks) from the articles explored from the Scopus database. Besides, the analysis and synthesis based on the interpretation of the selected articles by the authors. The author tried to avoid these problems by independently checking papers and dealing with embedded bias, but errors could have occurred, but this research is considered to be robust as the effort has been taken to avoid errors on every aspect.

SUGGESTIONS FOR FUTURE RESEARCH

Based on the rich foundation of the research findings described and the comprehensive understanding acquired in this paper, the author presents the concerns that further research deserves and anticipate that these issues may contribute to future research studies. The analysis of the selected articles shows that there is the opportunity to strengthen empirical research based on a qualitative and survey-based quantitative approach based on in-depth case studies since most of the articles analyzed followed an analytical approach. Also, a stronger infusion of generic theory into the big data and big data analysis debate is needed. Big Data is a cross-cutting theme, and there are many links to established topics across computing, engineering, mathematics, business and management, social sciences. It would be useful to broaden the scope of the subject area and to repeat this exercise to identify and link theoretical contributions made in other related areas. A publication based on this analysis would provide a precious platform for research and the community of big-data Analysts and practitioners.

REFERENCES

Abdellatif, M., Capretz, F., & Ho, D. (2015). *Software Analytics to Software Practice: A Systematic Literature Review.* Academic Press.

Alexandrov, A., Bergmann, R., Ewen, S., Freytag, J.-C., Hueske, F., Heise, A., . . . Warneke, D. (2014). *The Stratosphere platform for big data analytics.* Academic Press.

Alsghaier, H., Akour, M., Shehabat, I., & Aldiabat, S. (2017). The Importance of Big Data Analytics in Business: A Case Study. *American Journal of Software Engineering and Applications*, 6(4), 111. doi:10.11648/j.ajsea.20170604.12

Chakrabarty, T. (2017). *Towards an ideal eGovernance scenario in India.* Retrieved from Tata Consultancy Services: https://www.tcs.com/towards-an-ideal-governance-scenario-in-india

Chambers, C., Raniwala, A., Perry, F., Adams, S., Henry, R., Bradshaw, R., & Weizenbaum, N. (2010). *FlumeJava: Easy.* Efficient Data-Parallel Pipelines. doi:10.1145/1806596.1806638

Chen, H., Chiang, R., Storey, V., & Robinson, J. (2014). *Business intelligence research business intelligence and analytics: From big data to big impact.* Academic Press.

Cukier, K. (2010). *Data, data everywhere.* Retrieved from The Economist: https://www.economist.com/special-report/2010/02/27/data-data-everywhere

Dean, J., & Ghemawat, S. (2008). *MapReduce: Simplified Data Processing on Large Clusters.* Academic Press.

Drowning in numbers – Digital data will flood the planet—and help us understand it better. (2011). Retrieved from The Economist: https://www.economist.com/graphic-detail/2011/11/18/drowning-in-numbers

Frenkiel, R., Badrinath, B., Borres, J., & Yates, R. (2000). 4). The Infostations challenge: Balancing cost and ubiquity in delivering wireless data. *IEEE Personal Communications*, 7(2), 66–71. doi:10.1109/98.839333

Garg, N. (2013). *Learning Apache Kafka: start from scratch and learn how to administer Apache Kafka effectively for messaging.* Academic Press.

Goodman, D., Borras, J., Mandayam, N., & Yates, R. (2000). INFOSTATIONS: a new system model for data and messaging services. *1997 IEEE 47th Vehicular Technology Conference. Technology in Motion, 2,* 969-973.

Jamil, N., Ishak, I., Sidi, F., Affendey, L., & Mamat, A. (2015). A Systematic Review on the Profiling of Digital News Portal for Big Data Veracity. *Procedia Computer Science, 72,* 390–397. doi:10.1016/j.procs.2015.12.154

Jing Zhao, J., & Guohong Cao, G. (2008). VADD: Vehicle-Assisted Data Delivery in Vehicular <i>Ad Hoc</i> Networks. *IEEE Transactions on Vehicular Technology, 57*(3), 1910–1922. doi:10.1109/TVT.2007.901869

K., R., & K., M. (2017). e-Governance using Data Warehousing and Data Mining. *International Journal of Computer Applications, 169*(8), 28-31.

Kumar, M., & Nagar, M. (2017). Big data analytics in agriculture and distribution channel. In *2017 International Conference on Computing Methodologies and Communication (ICCMC)* (pp. 384-387). IEEE. 10.1109/ICCMC.2017.8282714

Labrinidis, A., & Jagadish, H. (2012). Challenges and opportunities with big data. *Proceedings of the VLDB Endowment International Conference on Very Large Data Bases, 5*(12), 2032–2033. doi:10.14778/2367502.2367572

Lohr, S. (2012). *Big Data's Impact in the World - The New York Times.* Retrieved from The New York Times: https://www.nytimes.com/2012/02/12/sunday-review/big-datas-impact-in-the-world.html

Manyika, J., Chui, M., Brown, B., Bughin, J., Dobbs, R., Roxburgh, C., & Hung Byers, A. (2011). *Big data: The next frontier for innovation, competition, and productivity.* Academic Press.

Mcafee, A., & Brynjolfsson, E. (2012). *HBR.ORG Spotlight on Big Data Big Data: The Management Revolution.* Academic Press.

Noguchi, Y. (2011a). *Following Digital Breadcrumbs To 'Big Data' Gold: NPR.* Retrieved from www.npr.org: https://www.npr.org/2011/11/29/142521910/the-digital-breadcrumbs-that-lead-to-big-data

Noguchi, Y. (2011b). *The Search For Analysts To Make Sense Of 'Big Data': NPR.* Retrieved from The National Public Radio: https://www.npr.org/2011/11/30/142893065/the-search-for-analysts-to-make-sense-of-big-data

Pal, K. (2016). *Why the World Is Moving Toward NoSQL Databases*. Retrieved from Techopedia: https://www.techopedia.com/2/32000/trends/big-data/why-the-world-is-moving-toward-nosql-databases

Plödereder, E., (2014). Gesellschaft für Informatik, T., Tagung der Gesellschaft für Informatik. *Informatik 2014 Big Data - Komplexität meistern ; Tagung der Gesellschaft für Informatik.*

Polato, I., Ré, R., Goldman, A., & Kon, F. (2014). A comprehensive view of Hadoop research-A systematic literature review. *Journal of Network and Computer Applications, 46*, 1–25. doi:10.1016/j.jnca.2014.07.022

Sarkhel, A., & Alawadhi, N. (2017). *Data Brokerage: How data brokers are selling all your personal info for less than a rupee to whoever wants it*. Retrieved from The Economic Times: https://economictimes.indiatimes.com/tech/internet/how-data-brokers-are-selling-all-your-personal-info-for-less-than-a-rupee-to-whoever-wants-it/articleshow/57382192.cms

Savitz, E. (2013). *Gartner: Top 10 Strategic Technology Trends For 2013*. Retrieved from https://www.forbes.com/sites/ericsavitz/2012/10/23/gartner-top-10-strategic-technology-trends-for-2013/#343d0d64b761

Schroeder, R. (2016). Big data business models: Challenges and opportunities. Cogent Social Sciences, 2(1), 1166924.

Toshniwal, A., Taneja, S., Shukla, A., Ramasamy, K., Patel, J., Kulkarni, S., . . . Ryaboy, D. (2014). *Storm @Twitter*. Academic Press.

Zaharia, M., Chowdhury, M., Franklin, M., & Shenker, S. (n.d.). Spark. *Cluster Computing with Working Sets.*

ENDNOTES

[1]   http://www.whitehouse.gov/blog/2012/03/29/big-data-big-deal
[2]   The main idea of YARN is to split functionalities of Job Scheduling and resource management in to separate background process. The idea is to have global Resource Manager (RM) and Application Master (AM)

Chapter 5
Feature Selection Algorithm Using Relative Odds for Data Mining Classification

Donald Douglas Atsa'am
Department of Mathematics, Statistics, and Computer Science, University of Agriculture, Makurdi, Nigeria

ABSTRACT

A filter feature selection algorithm is developed and its performance tested. In the initial step, the algorithm dichotomizes the dataset then separately computes the association between each predictor and the class variable using relative odds (odds ratios). The value of the odds ratios becomes the importance ranking of the corresponding explanatory variable in determining the output. Logistic regression classification is deployed to test the performance of the new algorithm in comparison with three existing feature selection algorithms: the Fisher index, Pearson's correlation, and the varImp function. A number of experimental datasets are employed, and in most cases, the subsets selected by the new algorithm produced models with higher classification accuracy than the subsets suggested by the existing feature selection algorithms. Therefore, the proposed algorithm is a reliable alternative in filter feature selection for binary classification problems.

DOI: 10.4018/978-1-5225-9750-6.ch005

INTRODUCTION

This chapter is about developing a filter algorithm that uses relative odds, also referred to as odds ratios (OR) (Vanderweele & Vansteelandt, 2010) in selecting relevant features for binary classification models. Big data consists of voluminous datasets emanating from commercial, social media, educational, health care, government, and industrial activities, etc. In most instances, these datasets comprise high-dimensional features such that some are redundant, irrelevant, duplicative and unnecessary in machine learning. When machine learning models are constructed on the entire feature space without first expunging the irrelevant features, resultant models produce poor fit and low predictive accuracies. In addition, models are complex, waste system resources and are difficult to interpret. For this reason, it is necessary to select the most important and relevant features for inclusion in classification models.

The OR is a statistical measure that evaluates the strength of association between two binary variables, where one variable is dependent on the other (Hancock & Kent, 2016). In this research, the feature selection algorithm to be developed will evaluate the OR between each predictor variable and the class variable. The result of the OR will represent how important the corresponding predictor is in determining the outcome. When comparing the importance of two predictors, the one with higher value of OR is considered the most important. Comparing computed values of all predictors in the dataset, the modeler can decide which variables are more or less important for inclusion or exclusion in predictive models. The fact that OR is usually computed on binary variables, the initial step of the proposed algorithm would be to convert the dataset to binary values. This will be achieved by rounding to 0, for each explanatory variable, all data points below 0.5, and rounding to 1 all data points from 0.5 and above. It should be pointed out that the algorithm will require a dataset that has been normalized to the scale [0, 1]. Secondly, the algorithm separately sums input/output permutations (0,0), (1,1), (0,1), and (1,0) for each predictor in all observations of the dataset. Thirdly, the OR formula is deployed for computation using the values obtained in step 2. Fourthly, the algorithm outputs the OR for each predictor variable and the name of the corresponding predictor in the order they appear in the dataset. The OR value translates to the importance rank of the corresponding predictor. As a filter method, the algorithm will work independently of any machine learning algorithm. The task is to generate variable importance ranking that should guide users in choosing the relevant subset from the variable domain that will produce better classification results. The ranking will be anchored on the strength of association between a predictor variable and the class variable. Any modeling tool at the disposal of the user can be deployed for machine learning using best subsets suggested by the proposed algorithm.

Classification is one of the techniques of data mining that is concerned about developing models that accurately distinguish the class of one data object from another (Rani, Rao, & Lakshmi, 2014). After this is done, the developed model is then used to predict the class of objects whose class is not known. Being a form of supervised learning, classification learning algorithms usually operate with predefined class labels (Mastrogiannis, Boutsinas, & Giannikos, 2009). Apart from predicting the class label of data objects, this technique is also used in predicting missing data values in a given dataset. In order to test the performance of a classification model, its classification accuracy is evaluated; which is the ratio of correctly predicted classes to total number of observations. One of the methods of evaluating classification accuracy is k-fold cross-validation, also referred to as re-sampling (Anguita, Ghelardoni, Ghio, Oneto, & Ridella, 2012). This method divides the dataset into k subsets, uses k-1 subsets to train the classifier and then tests its performance on one subset. The process is done iteratively, reshuffling subsets at every iteration, until accuracy has been evaluated on all vectors (Anguita et al., 2012; Jung & Hu, 2015). Variable selection has been identified as an important step towards constructing classification models that achieve higher accuracy (Kaushik, 2016). Inclusion of variables with little or no modeling value in machine learning negatively affects the predictive power of classifiers. The algorithm to be developed in this research is expected to offer a good alternative to existing filter methods of variable selection.

BACKGROUND

Importance of Feature Selection

Consider a dataset with predictor variables $X = \{X_1, X_2, ..., X_n\}$ in a high dimensional space $\mathbb{R}^n$; and a class variable Y. The objective of feature selection is to find a subset k of n where $k < n$, producing a classification model with high predictive accuracy (Freenay, Doquire, & Verleysen, 2013). When Y is binary, the predictive accuracy is determined as probabilities taking the form $P(Y = 1 \mid X_i)$. Usually, a decision threshold, t is set such that if $P(Y = 1 \mid X_i) > t$ then $Y = 1$, otherwise $Y = 0$. That is, if the model produced a prediction value greater than the decision boundary then the predicted class label is 1, otherwise 0.

The overall objective of feature selection is dimensionality reduction, which ultimately aims at producing a smaller subset of variables for machine learning (Chandrashekar & Sahin, 2014). With big data, the variable space is often large such that features with no classification value are equally included within the dimension (Bermejo, Ossa, Gamez, & Puerta, 2012). Limiting the number of features included in a model to only the relevant ones has several advantages: machine learning algorithms train faster, model complexity and overfitting are reduced, and predictive accuracy is enhanced (Kaushik, 2016; Frenay, Freenay, Doquire, & Verleysen, 2013; Bagherzade-Khiabani et al., 2016). Basically, there are 3 methods of feature selection: filters, wrappers, and embedded (Javed, Babri, & Saeed, 2014; Cateni, Colla, & Vannucci, 2014).

- **Filters:** The algorithms use statistical techniques to select subset of variables independent of any machine learning algorithm (Huang, Wulsin, Li, & Guo, 2009). One of the bases for selecting a feature is determined by the score of its correlation with the outcome variable. Some basic statistical tests for correlation include the Chi-square, ANOVA (Analysis of Variance), and the Pearson's correlation (Kaushik, 2016). These and many more modernized statistical approaches have been utilized in procedures for selecting relevant dataset features for machine learning tasks. Two categories of filter methods; namely, the ranker and subset selector have been identified in Bagherzade-Khiabani et al. (2016). While rankers generate numeric values indicating the importance of a predictor in determining the class, selectors are concerned about generating subsets of variables that collectively produce accurate model outcomes. It should be noted that rankers typically generate variable importance ranking without suggesting which variables to be included or excluded into a model, unlike subset selectors. It is the user's responsibility to determine a cut-off point of the variables to be included into model construction, using the ranking as guide. Performance diagnostics of the previous model determines if further exclusion or inclusion of predictors is needed until a perfect classification model is obtained. The fact that filters do not depend on any machine learning algorithm, they generally serve in the preprocessing step of data mining (Crone & Kourentzes, 2010). After the best attribute subset has been filtered out, any learning algorithm at the disposal of the modeler can be deployed for modeling (Hu, Bao, Xiong, & Chiong, 2015). Compared to other feature selection methods, filters exhibit the advantages of being computationally inexpensive and less prone to overfitting (Javed et al., 2014; Hu et al., 2015).
- **Wrappers:** In wrapper methods, the learning procedure and feature selection are done by the same algorithm (Huang et al., 2009). Subset selection is achieved by means of statistical resampling where different variable

subsets are routinely trained before arriving at a subset that produced better classification results (Bagherzade-Khiabani et al., 2016). Unlike filters, wrappers are computationally intensive due to the fact that several models with all possible subsets have to be built before arriving at the best subset (Frenay et al., 2013). Apart from the disadvantage relating to computational cost, results of wrappers lack generality since they are limited to specific machine learning algorithms. However, because features are optimized for specific training algorithm, wrappers produce models with better performance than filters (Bagherzade-Khiabani et al., 2016). Kaushik (2016) identified 3 common procedures of wrappers; namely, forward selection, backward elimination, and recursive elimination. In the forward selection procedure, the algorithm starts with a model having no feature and iteratively adds features to the model until a point when addition of a new feature does not improve model performance. Backward elimination starts with all variables and iteratively removes insignificant features until variable removal does not improve model performance. The recursive elimination procedure iteratively constructs models using different variable subsets. At each iteration, the procedure sets aside the best or worst feature then builds the next model with the remaining features. The process continues until all features may have been utilized, then the algorithm ranks the variables based on the order they were eliminated.

- **Embedded:** In this approach, the feature selection activity is integrated into the training process of the machine learning algorithm (Javed et al., 2014). The main distinctive quality of the embedded method from the wrapper method is that, while wrappers consist 2 separate procedures for subset selection and training, embedded methods perform feature selection and training within same procedure. Computational time requirement in embedded methods is smaller than that in wrappers since feature selection and training are done hand-in-hand in the former methods of feature selection (Lazar et al., 2012). Furthermore, with embedded technique, process parameters obtained during training are updated iteratively and they evolve by virtue of the efficiency of the model being constructed (Cateni, Colla, & Vannucci, 2017).

Filter Feature Selection Approaches

In this section, review of some filter feature selection approaches is conducted. Generally, filter methods are concerned about measuring the strength of the association among variables; which could be predictor-to-predictor or predictor-to-class. According to Javed et al. (2014), metrics of association are of 3 categories; correlation measures, information-theoretic measures, and probabilistic measures. The correlation-based measures evaluate the linear relationship among two variables, and predictor variables exhibiting strong correlation with the class are selected for modeling. The information-theoretic metrics evaluate the mutual information contained in two different variables. If two variables are found to exhibit similar characteristics, one of them can be eliminated from the data mining classification models in order to check redundancy. The probabilistic metrics measure the dependence between a predictor and the class using probability distributions. These metrics generate estimates ranging over [0, 1] and higher values indicate the importance of the predictor in modeling.

- **The Fisher Index:** This metric computes the importance of the i-th explanatory variable in a dataset with binary response as shown in equation (1):

$$
F_i = \left| \frac{\bar{X}_1(i) - \bar{X}_0(i)}{d_1^2(i) + d_0^2(i)} \right| \tag{1}
$$

where $\bar{X}_1(i)$ is the mean and $d_1(i)$ is the standard deviation of the i-th variable with outcome 1; $\bar{X}_0(i)$ is the mean and $d_0(i)$ is the standard deviation of the i-th variable with outcome 0 (Maldonado & Weber, 2009).

- **The t-test:** According to Rice (2007) and Cateni et al. (2014), the t-test calculates the importance of the i-th predictor variable as shown in equation (2):

$$
t_i = \frac{\left| \bar{X}_1(i) - \bar{X}_0(i) \right|}{\sqrt{\dfrac{d_1^2(i)}{n_1} + \dfrac{d_0^2(i)}{n_0}}} \tag{2}
$$

where $\bar{X}_1, \bar{X}_0, d_1, d_0$ are as defined in equation (1), n_0 and n_1 are total observations in the class 0 and 1 respectively.

- **The Kullback Liebler Distance (KL-distance):** This is a filter method that evaluates the relative entropy between predictor variables, measuring the difference in their probability distributions (Cateni et al., 2014). For $X = \{x_1, x_2, ..., x_n\}$ and $Y = \{y_1, y_2, ..., y_n\}$ both discrete, the KL-distance is defined as

$$KL(X,Y) = \sum_i X_i \log_2 \left(\frac{X_i}{Y_i} \right) \tag{3}$$

See (Kullback and Leibler, 1951). It should be pointed out that the KL-distance is not symmetric; and in situations when X and Y are continuous, an integral replaces the sum in equation (3).

The Wilcoxon Rank Sum Test: The Wilcoxon rank sum is a form of non-parametric test for two populations with no requirement for specific distributions (Li, Liu, Tung, & Wang, 2004). For a feature X, collection $C = \{A, B\}$ of classes A and B, the Wilcoxon measure $w(X, C)$ is obtained using the following steps:

- The values $v_1, v_2, ..., v_n^A + v_n^A$ of X under consideration across all samples in C are sorted in ascending order.
- To each value v_i in (i) above, assign a rank, denoted by $r(v_i)$, such that ties are taken care of by taking the average as in equation (4).

$$rank\left(v_i\right) = \begin{cases} i, & if\ v_{i-1} \neq v_i \neq v_{i+1} \\ \dfrac{\sum_{k=0}^{n} j + k}{n+1} & if\ v_{j-1} < v_j = ... = v_i = ... = v_{j+n} < v_{j+n+1} \end{cases} \tag{4}$$

- Then, the sum of the ranks for the class having fewer samples is returned as the Wilcoxon index (Li et al., 2004). That is, $w\left(X, C\right) = \sum_{v \in \arg g \min} r(v)$.

  In situations where both classes contain same number of samples, any class is chosen arbitrarily.

Signal-to-Noise Measure: Given 2 classes C_1 and C_2, in a sample dataset, the signal-to-noise measure is based on the argument that a feature that is relevant must contribute in separating data points in C_1 from those in C_2 (Li et al.,

2004). If a feature is irrelevant, it will contribute little or nothing in separating data points in C_1 from those in C_2. Specifically, this measure holds that if the values of a feature are substantially dissimilar in both samples in C_1 and C_2, then that feature is likely to be of more relevance than another feature which has similar values in both C_1 and C_2. For a feature f, the signal-to-noise concept is evaluated using the formula in equation (5) (Golub et al., 1999; Li et al., 2004).

$$S(f, C_1, C_2) = \frac{\left| \bar{X}_{C_1} - \bar{X}_{C_1} \right|}{d_{C_1} + d_{C_2}} \tag{5}$$

where $\bar{X}_{C_1}$ and $\bar{X}_{C_2}$ are the means of data points in class C_1 and C_2, respectively; d_{c_1} and d_{c_2} are standard deviations in C_1 and C_2, respectively. According to Li et al. (2004), if

$$S(f, C_1, C_2) > S(f', C_1, C_2)$$

then the feature f is considered better than the feature f'.

- **Feature Slection Based on Conditional Mutual Information:** Fleuret (2004) developed a feature selection procedure that relies on conditional mutual information. The technique, designed to operate on binary data, iteratively selects features which maximize mutual information with the class. At each iteration, features similar to the ones already selected are skipped which guarantees that selected features convey unique information and are weakly dependent on each other. Each time an iteration takes place and a feature is added to the subset, a score table is updated and the next score is calculated using equation (6).

$$S(n) = \min_{l < k} \hat{I}\left(Y; X_n \mid X_{v(l)}\right) \tag{6}$$

where $S(n)$ is the score updated at each iteration, X_n is the feature being evaluated currently, $X_{v(l)}$ is the set of features already selected.

- **Pearson Correlation:** This is one of the correlation-based filter methods, presented in equation (7) (Chandrashekar & Sahin, 2014).

$$P_i = \frac{Cov(X_i, Y)}{\sqrt{Var(X_i) * Var(Y)}}$$

(7)

where X_i is the i-th predictor variable and Y is the outcome label, $Cov()$ is the covariance and $Var()$ is the variance. The Pearson's correlation evaluates the importance of predictor variables using each predictor's individual linear dependence with the outcome.

- **Variable Ranking with Risk Ratios:** Bodur and Atsa'am (2019) developed a filter algorithm for variable ranking that uses risk ratios to evaluate the importance of a predictor in determining the response. The algorithm, designed to specifically work on datasets with binary response, is summarized in equation (8)

$$I_j = \left(\frac{\sum_{i=1,j=1}^{m,n} W_{ij}}{\sum_{i=1,j=1}^{m,n} W_{ij} + \sum_{i=1,j=1}^{m,n} X_{ij}} \right) \cdot \left(\frac{\sum_{i=1,j=1}^{m,n} Y_{ij} + \sum_{i=1,j=1}^{m,n} Z_{ij}}{\sum_{i=1,j=1}^{m,n} Y_{ij}} \right)$$

(8)

where I_j is the ranking value of the jth explanatory variable, W_{ij} is data instance with input = 1 and output = 1, X_{ij} is data instance with input = 1 and output = 0, Y_{ij} is data instance with input = 0 and output = 1, Z_{ij} is data instance with input = 0 and output = 0, m is the number of observations in the dataset, and n is the number of predictor variables. For every predictor, the algorithm sums up the total number of instances in each of these four categories then uses the formula in (8) to evaluate the importance of each predictor.

Tran, Afanador, Buydens and Blanchet (2014) examined three methods of filter variable selection, including the Variable Importance in the Projection (VIP), Beta CI, and the selectivity ratio. The VIP determines importance of variables by measuring the proportion of the explained variance of each predictor and the covariance between each predictor and the class. Usually, the average VIP equals 1, and variables that produced VIP scores greater than 1 are selected as important. The Beta CI technique evaluates the confidence interval bounding the coefficients of regression for each variable. A variable is considered important if its Beta CI does not overlap zero. In the selectivity ratio method, the sum of squares of each variable is measured by taking the ratio of the explained variance versus the residual variance, and the resultant value signifies the importance of the corresponding variable.

The Odds Ratios (OR)

The odds of an event is the probability that the event will occur (P) versus the probability that it will not occur $(1 - P)$, given by $Odds = \dfrac{P}{1 - P}$ (Enticott, Kandane-Rathnayake, & Phillips, 2012). In order to examine the extent of association between two groups, the ratio of their odds is evaluated as

$$Odds\left(Group1\right)\Big/Odds\left(Group2\right).$$

In the case of a dependence structure among two binary variables X and Y, where X is independent and Y dependent, the OR is defined as follows: Let, N00 = observations with X = 0 and Y = 0; N01 = observations with X = 0 and Y = 1; N10 = observations with X = 1 and Y = 0; N11 = observations with X = 1 and Y = 1. Then,

$$Odds\,Ratio(OR) = \frac{N00 * N11}{N01 * N10} \tag{9}$$

Possible values of odds ratios range from 0 to infinity; and if OR = 1, no relationship exists between X and Y; if OR < 1, X is negatively related to Y; and if OR > 1, X and Y are positively related (Enticott et al., 2012; Hancock & Kent, 2016).

The odds ratios have been applied in many studies. One of these is the study by Jin, Chen, and Wang (2018) who examined how OR can be used to detect Differential Item Functioning (DIF) when conducting some tests with experimental datasets. The study, which compared the performance of OR with other approaches; logistic regression and Mantel-Haenszel methods, showed that OR has better tendency to control false positive rates than the other methods when there is high percentage of DIF items in favour of particular groups within the dataset. Another research by Atsa'am and Bodur (2019) deployed the OR technique to examine the relationship between educational qualification and psychological capital among hospitality employees. The study, conducted on 329 workers in the hospitality industry, concluded that employees with higher educational qualifications are 2.6 times more likely to have positive psychological capital than employees with lower qualifications. VanderWeele and Vansteelandt (2010) used odds ratios for mediation analysis in epidemiology when the outcome is dichotomous. The role of a mediator variable between an exposure, outcome, and covariates was analysed using odds ratios. The research further proposed a technique for estimating the direct and indirect effects of a mediator in the interaction between the exposure and the outcome, using odds ratios. Odds ratios are usually estimated on binary data. If the OR technique is to be applied on continuous data, the data must first be dichotomized, which leads to information loss and reduction in precision of inference. In order to check this shortcoming, Sroka and Nagaraja (2018) proposed a method that uses the log odds link function to directly analyse continuous data without first dichotomizing same. The approach deployed three distributions for count data, namely; geometric, Poisson, and negative binomial, to prove that better precision of OR estimate could be obtained even on continuous data. Chen, Cohen, and Chen (2007) showed in their research that when age as a variable is dichotomized, a biased OR result will emerge. In the experiment, the authors reported that when age was left as a continuous variable, including it as a confounder between causes of risks and outcomes produced good OR results. However, when age was converted to categorical data, the resultant estimate was biased. The study concluded that if it is necessary that age must be dichotomized, researchers should be cautious about choosing cutpoints based on the size of empirical OR. Tamhane, Westfall, Burkholder & Cutter (2016) compared and contrasted odds ratios versus prevalence ratios (PR), both of which are measures of association between independent and dependent variables. The study examined the weaknesses and strengths of both measures and it turned out that OR usually overestimates strength of association compared to PR. However, OR has the desirable property of reciprocity, which allows for computation of the OR for group 2 by simply taking the reciprocal of the OR for group 1. The PR does not have the property of reciprocity.

Having reviewed how the OR has been applied in several studies for different purposes, this study is poised to deploy this measure as a basis for developing a feature importance ranking algorithm in the next section.

METHODOLOGY

Materials

The OR will be used as the basis for designing the proposed algorithm. After the algorithm design, the Logistic regression classification model will be deployed for testing the efficiency of the new algorithm in comparison with the Fisher score, Pearson's correlation, and varImp algorithm. The experiments would be carried out on the datasets listed below.

- **Arrests for Marijuana Possession Data (Marijuana):** The dataset, available in R package "carData", consists of information regarding individuals arrested by the Police in Toronto for being in possession of marijuana. It has a binary outcome, "released", that indicates whether the culprit was released or not (Fox, Weisberg, & Price, 2018). A total of 5226 observations with 7 predictors make up the dataset.
- **Risk Factors Associated with Low Infant Birth Weight Data (Birth Weight):** This dataset holds records regarding measurements that influence the weight of an infant at birth. Available in the R package, "MASS", the dataset has a binary outcome variable, "low", with 1 = low weight (< 2.5kg) and 0 = otherwise (Venables & Ripley, 2002). The dataset has 9 predictors and 189 observations.
- **Spam e-Mail Data (Spam):** The dataset consists of a sample of e-mails with a class attribute having two categories: "spam" or "not spam". The predictor variables are measurements relating to total length of words written in capital letters, numbers of times the "$" and "!" symbols occur within the e-mail, etc. The dataset has 6 predictors and 4601 observations, and can be accessed in the R package "DAAG" (Maindonald & Braun, 2019).
- **Beaver Body Temperature Data (Beaver):** This is a dataset consisting of observations relating to the regulation of body temperature in beavers, available in the R package, "boot". A sample of four mature female beavers were caged and their body temperature taken every 10 minutes. The dataset has a binary response that represents the activity level of the beaver, with 1 indicating the animal is outside of retreat and 0 otherwise (Davison & Hinkley, 1997; Canty & Ripley, 2017). A total of 3 predictors and 100 records make up the dataset.

Learning Algorithm

The Logistic regression classification model will be adopted as the learning algorithm to facilitate experiments in this research. Logistic regression enables the association between a categorical dependent variable and one or more independent variables to be examined in a set of observations (Liu, Li, & Liang, 2014). The foundation of this type of regression is the logistic function where values are modeled within the range 0 and 1, corresponding to binary class values. The logistic equation is given by

$$\ln\left(\frac{\pi}{1-\pi}\right) = a_0 + a_1 x_1 + \dots + a x_n,$$

where π is the probability of success, $\pi / (1-\pi)$ is the odds, a_0 is the intercept, $a_1, \dots, a_n$ are parameter estimates, and $x_1, \dots, x_n$ are raw data values; outputs probabilities that show the possibility of a vector belonging to a particular class (Enticott, Kandane-Rathnayake, & Phillips, 2012; Sperandei, 2014; Liu, Li, & Liang, 2014). The R programming language consists of a package named "caret". Within this package, the varImp (variable importance) function is utilized to rank the importance of predictor variables contained in a logistic model object (Kuhn et al., 2019).

Design of Proposed Algorithm

Consider X_i, $i = 1, \dots, n$ as a set of predictors with dimension n. When n is sufficiently large, some features are irrelevant, redundant, and have negligible modeling value. It is therefore required to reduce the features from n to $k < n$, such that k comprises of only features that are necessary in machine learning. The primary objective of the proposed algorithm is to achieve this reduction.

Now, let Data be the name of the dataset consisting of m observations $i = 1, \dots, m$, n predictors $j = 1, \dots, n$; and the outcome variable, y_i. Let DataVal[i, j] denote a data point at row i column j. The proposed algorithm will take the following steps.

Step 1: Dichotomizing the Dataset

```
1 //Listing 1. Step to convert all input to binary
2 While j <= n //counts columns
3         While i <= m //counts rows
```

```
    4                    IF DataVal[i,j] < 0.5 Then
    5                        DataVal[i,j] = 0 //round
down values to 0
    6                        ELSE DataVal[i,j] = 1 //
round up values to 1
    7                    END IF
    8                    i = i+1
    9                      j = j+1
    10          End While
    11 End While
```

Step 2: Counts N_{00}, N_{11}, N_{01}, N_{10}

```
    12 //Listing 2. This step counts N00, N11, N01, N10, for
each predictor
    13 DataVal = Array[1..m][1..n] As Integer //2-dim
array of rows/columns
    14 Class = Array[1..m] As Integer //1-dim array for
class
```

15 $A_j = 0 : B_j = 0 : C_j = 0 : D_j = 0$ As Integer //initialize
sums of N_{00}, N_{11}, N_{01}, N_{10}

```
    16 While j <= n //column index for explanatory
variables
    17      While i <= m //row index for explanatory
variables
    18              While y <= m //row index for class
variable
    19                  IF i = y THEN //compares
input and output index
    20                      If DataVal[i,j] = 0
AND Class[i,j] = 0 THEN
    21
//counts N00
    22                              ENDIF
```

$$A_j = A_j + 1$$

```
    23                              IF DataVal[i,j] = 1
AND Class[i,j] = 1 THEN
    24                                  $B_j = B_j + 1$
//counts N₁₁
    25                              ENDIF
    26                              IF DataVal[i,j] = 0
AND Class[i,j] = 1 THEN
    27                                  $C_j = C_j + 1$
//counts N₀₁
    28                              ENDIF
    29                              IF DataVal[i,j] = 1
AND Class[i,j] = 0 THEN
    30                                  $D_j = D_j + 1$
//counts N₁₀
    31                              ENDIF
    32                          ENDIF
    33                          j = j+1
    34                          i = i+1
    35                          y = y+1
    36              End While
    37          End While
    38 End While
```

Step 3: Computes OR for Each Column

```
    39 //Listing 3. This step computes Odds Ratios for
each column
    40 //temporary variables
    41 upperProduct_j, lowerProduct_j As Integer: OR_j As Real
    42 While j <= n
    43 upperProduct_j = $A_j \times B_j$
    44 lowerProduct_j = $C_j \times D_j$
    45 OR_j = $\dfrac{upperProduct_j}{lowerProduct_j}$   //computes Variable Importance
```

```
46 j = j+1
47 End While
48 Print VariableName_j + \tab OR_j +\enter
```

The importance rank of a predictor is printed when the statement on line 48 is executed. When comparing the importance of two variables for machine learning purpose, the variable with a higher OR is the most important. The formula in equation (10) summarizes the proposed algorithm.

$$
IMP_j = \left| \frac{\sum\limits_{i=1,j=1}^{m,n} A_{ij} \times \sum\limits_{i=1,j=1}^{m,n} B_{ij}}{\sum\limits_{i=1,j=1}^{m,n} C_{ij} \times \sum\limits_{i=1,j=1}^{m,n} D_{ij}} \right|
\tag{10}
$$

where, IMP_j is the importance ranking of the jth predictor $(j = 1,...,n)$, A_{ij} = data instance with input = 0 and output = 0, B_{ij} = data instance with input = 1 and output = 1, C_{ij} = data instance with input = 0 and output = 1, and D_{ij} = data instance with input = 1 and output = 0.

Experiment

- **Execution of the Proposed Algorithm:** The variables of the datasets used in this experiment are not in uniform scale. As a preprocessing activity and a requirement of the proposed algorithm, the min-max normalization procedure was applied on each dataset. According to Pandey & Jain (2017), the min-max normalization, when applied to a dataset, converts all input to the range of [0,1]; with mean 0 and standard deviation 1. It is instructive to note that this normalization procedure does not turn a dataset to binary. It only converts original values to fractions ranging between 0 and 1.

The first step of the proposed algorithm was executed on the experimental datasets and all input were dichotomized. Next, the second step was executed and all input/output occurrences of (1,1), (1,0), (0,1), and (0,0) were separately counted for each predictor and returned as four integer values. The third step used the four integers obtained in the previous step to compute the odds ratios using equation (8). The result represents the importance rank of each predictor variable; that is, the extent to which a predictor is needed in classification. Samples of variable importance ranking produced by the proposed algorithm when executed on the datasets are shown in Table 1 and Table 2.

- **Execution of Existing Ranking Algorithms:** The Fisher score, Pearson's correlation, and varImp variable selection algorithms were also executed on the experimental datasets. The output, in comparison with the ranking by the proposed algorithm, was examined as sampled in Table 1 and Table 2.

Table 1. Variable importance ranking on Birth Weight dataset

Proposed Algorithm		Fisher Score	
Variable	Importance	Variable	Importance
ht	3.3654	bwt	4.0000
ui	2.5778	ptl	0.0860
smoke	2.0219	lwt	0.0730
race	2.0046	smoke	0.0600
ftv	1.6270	ui	0.0600
ptl	1.1053	race	0.0450
lwt	0.4806	ht	0.0450
age	0.3383	age	0.0360
bwt	0.0037	ftv	0.0093

Table 2. Variable importance ranking on Marijuana dataset

Proposed Algorithm		varImp	
Variable	Importance	Variable	Importance
employed	2.9946	checks	14.0127
colour	2.1077	employed	8.9373
citizen	2.1054	citizen	5.5304
year	1.1940	colour	4.5423
sex	0.7907	age	0.4827
age	0.6688	year	0.1487
checks	0.2842	sex	0.0487

The Table 1 shows the importance ranking of the Birth Weight dataset variables according to the proposed algorithm and the Fisher score algorithm. The importance ranking of the variables in the Marijuana dataset according to the proposed algorithm and the varImp algorithm is presented in Table 2. The 'Importance' column quantifies how important the corresponding variable is in machine learning. When deciding on which variables to include in a classification model, variables with higher values of importance are selected.

- **Subset Selection, Model Construction, and Classification Accuracy Evaluation:** In order to test the performance of the proposed algorithm in comparison with existing variable selection methods, variable subsets were selected for classification modeling. One way to determine which subset to use for modeling is to select variables whose importance values are close to each other until there is a sharp decline. Another method is to keep adding variables based on their importance, one after the other, until further addition does not improve model performance. Using either of these methods, best subsets were selected from the rankings of the proposed algorithm and existing algorithms in all experimental datasets.

The Logistic regression was deployed to construct classification models with the subsets selected by the proposed algorithm, Fisher score, Pearson's and varImp methods. The classification accuracies of the classifiers were evaluated using k-fold cross validation. In this experiment, k was set to 10. This means that the dataset was split into 10 subsets and in each iteration, 9 of the subsets were used for model training while one subset retained for testing of model performance. Model performance in this context refers to the ability of the classifiers to correctly predict the response variable for vectors whose classes are unknown in advance. The validation process continued until the class of every observation in the dataset was predicted. The average classification accuracy of the model was then returned. The accuracy evaluation process was carried out on all the experimental datasets using the variables selected by the four algorithms. The classification accuracy results are presented in the next section.

RESULTS AND DISCUSSION

The Table 3 and Table 4 present classification accuracies on the datasets deployed in the experiments. These results show that the proposed algorithm performs competitively with existing methods of variable selection.

Table 3. Classification accuracy on Marijuana and Birth Weight datasets

Marijuana			Birth Weight		
Algorithm	**Subset Size**	**Accuracy (%)**	**Algorithm**	**Subset Size**	**Accuracy (%)**
Fisher score	3	72	Fisher score	4	74
Pearson's	3	72	Pearson's	5	61
varImp	4	71	varImp	4	74
Proposed	4	73	Proposed	4	61

Table 4. Classification accuracy on Spam and Beaver datasets

Spam			Beaver		
Algorithm	**Subset Size**	**Accuracy (%)**	**Algorithm**	**Subset Size**	**Accuracy (%)**
Fisher score	4	60	Fisher score	2	80
Pearson's	5	60	Pearson's	2	80
varImp	5	60	varImp	2	79
Proposed	4	61	Proposed	2	81

The subsets selected by the proposed algorithm yielded models with higher accuracies, except in the Birth Weight dataset. The classification accuracies in the experimental datasets are summarized in Figure 1.

Accuracy was determined by 10-fold cross validation. This method is considered a better means of testing for classification accuracy, compared with the traditional method of splitting the dataset into train and test sets. In the method adopted in this research, the dataset is resampled over and over, such that every vector is given the chance to be used for both training and testing. The proposed algorithm achieves variable importance ranking by first dichotomizing the dataset. After this, the four quantities needed for evaluating odds ratios are evaluated from the binary dataset. Then, the odds ratios for each predictor variable and the outcome are computed. The value of the odds ratio indicates the importance of a predictor in determining the response.

FUTURE RESEARCH DIRECTIONS

The task of the proposed algorithm ends at ranking predictor variables with values indicating their importance. There is no functionality that suggests which variables to include in a model. The most viable tactic is for the user to select variables whose

Figure 1. Classification accuracy comparison

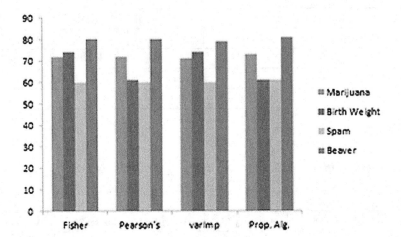

importance values follow a sequence until there is an unusual gap. The initial subset will be used for modeling and performance evaluation. The performance of the current model will determine if more variables should be added or removed from the model. The process continues until best model outcomes are achieved. It would be appropriate to extend the algorithm to be able to determine a threshold of which variables are needed for modeling computationally. This aspect is open for future research. In addition, the algorithm should be implemented and made distributable as a function in one of the open source languages such as R.

CONCLUSION

Big data comes with high-dimensional feature space such that a reasonable number of these features are duplicative, redundant and thus not necessary in modeling. Daily transactions from commercial, social media, educational, health care, government, and industrial activities, etc. generate voluminous data that is useful in machine learning for business analytics purposes. However, if irrelevant variables are not eliminated before deployment of machine learning algorithms, resultant models produce poor fit and low predictive accuracies. In addition, training of models is slow, constructed models are complex to interpret and degrees of freedom are wasted. These unwanted model outcomes would be avoided by utilizing the variable importance ranking algorithm developed in this research. As it is typical of filter methods, this algorithm will operate independently of any machine learning algorithm. This means that it will serve during preprocessing to guide modelers on selection of the most important variables for classification. One feature of the new algorithm that makes it stand out from other variable selection algorithms is the range of values available for ranking. Unlike the correlation-based variable ranking algorithms that use the interval [-1, 1] to rank the entire feature space, this algorithm has a range of 0 to infinity. This is so because the odds ratios upon which the algorithm is based takes values from 0 to infinity. When dimension is sufficiently large, limiting ranking values within a short range may not produce good visualization. The simplicity of the computations and logic involved in the new algorithm, compared with existing algorithms, is an added advantage for the new algorithm. Therefore, this algorithm is recommended for use as an alternative means of variable selection for numeric datasets with binary response.

REFERENCES

Anguita, D., Ghelardoni, L., Ghio, A., Oneto, L., & Ridella, S. (2012). The 'K' in k-fold cross validation. *Proceedings of the European Symposium on Artificial Neural Networks, Computational Intelligence and Machine Learning ESANN 2012* (pp. 441-445). i6doc.com publ.

Atsa'am, D. D., & Bodur, E. K. (2019). Knowledge mining on the association between psychological capital and educational qualifications among hospitality employees. *Current Issues in Tourism*, 1–5. doi:10.1080/13683500.2019.1597026

Bagherzade-Khiabani, F., Ramezhankani, A., Aiziz, F., Hadaegh, F., Steyerberg, E. W., & Khalili, D. (2016). A tutorial on variable selection for clinical prediction models: Feature selection methods in data mining could improve the results. *Journal of Clinical Epidemiology*, *71*, 76–85. doi:10.1016/j.jclinepi.2015.10.002 PMID:26475568

Bermejo, P., Ossa, L., Gamez, J. A., & Puerta, J. M. (2012). Fast wrapper feauture subset selection in high-dimensional datasets by means of filter re-ranking. *Knowledge-Based Systems*, *25*(1), 35–44. doi:10.1016/j.knosys.2011.01.015

Bodur, E. K., & Atsa'am, D. D. (2019). Filter variable selection algorithm using risk ratios for dimensionality reduction of healthcare data for classification. *Processes*, *7*(4), 222. doi:10.3390/pr7040222

Canty, A., & Ripley, B. (2017). *boot: Bootstrap R (S-Plus) functions. R package version 1.3-20*. Retrieved from https://cran.r-project.org/web/packages/boot/boot.pdf

Catena, S., Colla, V., & Vannucci, M. (2014). A hybrid feature selection method for classification purposes. *Proceedings of the UKSim-AMSS 8th European Modeling Symposium on Mathematical Modeling and Computer Simulation* (EMS2014), Pisa, Italy (pp. 39-44). IEEE Computer Society. 10.1109/EMS.2014.44

Catena, S., Colla, V., & Vannucci, M. (2016). A fuzzy system for combining filter features selection methods. *International Journal of Fuzzy Systems*, *19*(4), 1168–1180. doi:10.100740815-016-0208-7

Chandrashekar, G., & Sahin, F. (2014). A survey on feature selection methods. *Computers & Electrical Engineering*, *40*(1), 16–28. doi:10.1016/j.compeleceng.2013.11.024

Chen, H., Cohen, P., & Chen, S. (2007). Biased odds ratios from dichotomization of age. *Statistics in Medicine*, *26*(18), 3487–3497. doi:10.1002im.2737 PMID:17066378

Crone, S. F., & Kourentzes, N. (2010). Feature selection for time series prediction – A combined filter and wrapper approach for neural networks. *Neurocomputing*, *73*(10-12), 1923–1936. doi:10.1016/j.neucom.2010.01.017

Davison, A. C., & Hinkley, D. V. (1997). *Bootstrap Methods and their Applications*. Cambridge: Cambridge University Press. doi:10.1017/CBO9780511802843

Enticott, J. C., Kandane-Rathnayake, R. K., & Phillips, L. E. (2012). Odds ratios simplified. *Transfusion*, *52*(3), 467–469. doi:10.1111/j.1537-2995.2011.03429.x PMID:22070765

Fleuret, F. (2004). Fast binary feature selection with conditional mutual information. *Journal of Machine Learning Research*, *5*, 1531–1555.

Fox, J., Weisberg, S., & Price, B. (2018). *carData: Companion to applied regression data sets. R package version 3.0-2*. Retrieved from https://CRAN.R-project.org/package=carData

Frenay, B., Doquire, G., & Verleysen, M. (2013). Is mutual information adequate for feature selection in regression? *Neural Networks*, *48*, 1–7. doi:10.1016/j.neunet.2013.07.003 PMID:23892907

Golub, T. R., Slonim, D. K., Tamayo, P., Huard, C., Gaasenbeek, M., Mesirov, J. P., ... Lander, E. S. (1999). Molecular classification of cancer: Class discovery and class prediction by gene expression monitoring. *Science*, *286*(5439), 531–537. doi:10.1126cience.286.5439.531 PMID:10521349

Hancock, P., & Kent, P. (2016). Interpretation of dichotomous outcomes: Risk, odds, risk ratios, odds ratios and number needed to treat. *Journal of Physiotherapy*, *62*(3), 172–174. doi:10.1016/j.jphys.2016.02.016 PMID:27320830

Hu, Z., Bao, Y., Xiong, T., & Chiong, R. (2015). Hybrid filter–wrapper feature selection for short-term load forecasting. *Engineering Applications of Artificial Intelligence*, *40*, 17–27. doi:10.1016/j.engappai.2014.12.014

Huang, S. H., Wulsin, L. R., Li, H., & Guo, J. (2009). Dimensionality reduction for knowledge discovery in medical claims database: Application to antidepressant medication utilization study. *Computer Methods and Programs in Biomedicine*, *93*(2), 115–123. doi:10.1016/j.cmpb.2008.08.002 PMID:18835058

Javed, K., Babri, H. A., & Saeed, M. (2014). Impact of a metric of association between two variables on performance of filters for binary data. *Neurocomputing*, *143*, 248–260. doi:10.1016/j.neucom.2014.05.066

Jin, K., Cheng, H., & Wang, W. (2018). Using odds ratios to detect differential item functioning. *Applied Psychological Measurement*, *42*(8), 613–629. doi:10.1177/0146621618762738 PMID:30559570

Jung, Y., & Hu, J. (2015). A k-fold averaging cross-validation procedure. *Journal of Nonparametric Statistics*, *27*(2), 1–13. doi:10.1080/10485252.2015.1010532 PMID:27630515

Kaushik, S. (2016). *Introduction to feature selection methods with an example.* Analytics Vidhya. Retrieved from https://www.analyticsvidhya.com/blog/2016/12/introduction-to-feature-selection-methods-with-an-example-or-how-to-select-the-right-variables/

Kuhn, M., Wing, J., Weston, S., Williams, A., Keefer, C., Engelhardt, A., . . . Kenkel, B. (2019). *caret: Classification and regression training. R package version 6.0-82.* Retrieved from https://CRAN.R-project.org/package=caret

Kullback, S., & Leibler, R. A. (1951). On information and sufficiency. *Annals of Mathematical Statistics*, *22*(1), 79–86. doi:10.1214/aoms/1177729694

Lazar, C., Taminau, J., Meganck, S., Steenhoff, D., Coletta, A., Molter, C., ... Nowe, A. (2012). A survey on filter techniques for feature selection in gene expression microarray analysis. *IEEE/ACM Transactions on Computational Biology and Bioinformatics*, *9*(4), 1106–1119. doi:10.1109/TCBB.2012.33 PMID:22350210

Li, J., Liu, H., Tung, A., & Wong, L. (2014). The practical bioinformatician. In L. Wong (Ed.), Data mining techniques for the practical bioinformatician (pp. 35-70). 5 Toh Tuck Link, Singapore: World Scientific Publishing.

Liu, D., Li, T., & Liang, D. (2014). Incorporating logistic regression to decision-theoretic rough sets for classifications. *International Journal of Approximate Reasoning*, *55*(1), 197–210. doi:10.1016/j.ijar.2013.02.013

Maindonald, J. H., & Braun, J. W. (2019). *DAAG: Data analysis and graphics data and functions. R package version 1.22.1.* Retrieved from https://CRAN.R-project.org/package=DAAG

Maldonado, S., & Weber, R. (2009). A wrapper method for feature selection using support vector machines. *Information Sciences, 179*(13), 2208–2217. doi:10.1016/j. ins.2009.02.014

Mastrogiannis, N., Boutsinas, B., & Giannikos, I. (2009). A method for improving the accuracy of data mining classification algorithms. *Computers & Operations Research, 36*(10), 2829–2839. doi:10.1016/j.cor.2008.12.011

Pandey, A., & Jain, A. (2017). Comparative analysis of knn algorithm using various normalization techniques. *International Journal of Computer Network and Information Security, 11*(11), 36–42. doi:10.5815/ijcnis.2017.11.04

Rani, P. R. S., Rao, M. R. N., & Lakshmi, D. T. V. (2014). A study on data mining classification algorithms for medical data. *International Journal of Advanced Research in Computer Science, 5*(2), 13–16.

Rice, J. A. (2007). *Mathematical Statistics and Data Analysis* (3rd ed.). Belmont, CA: Thomson Books/Cole.

Sperandei, S. (2014). Lessons in biostatistics: Understanding logistic regression analysis. *Biochemical Medicine, 24*, 12–18. doi:10.11613/BM.2014.003

Sroka, C. J., & Nagaraja, H. N. (2018). Odds ratios from logistic, geometric, Poisson, and negative binomial regression models. *BMC Medical Research Methodology, 18*(112), 1–11. PMID:30342488

Tamhane, A. R., Westfall, A. O., Burkholder, G. A., & Cutter, G. R. (2016). Prevalence odds ratio versus prevalence ratio: Choice comes with consequences. *Statistics in Medicine, 35*(30), 5730–5735. doi:10.1002im.7059 PMID:27460748

Tran, T. N., Afanador, N. L., Buydens, L. M. C., & Blanchet, L. (2014). Interpretation of variable importance in partial least squares with significance multivariate correlation (sMC). *Chemometrics and Intelligent Laboratory Systems, 138*, 153–160. doi:10.1016/j.chemolab.2014.08.005

Vanderweele, T. J., & Vansteelandt, S. (2010). Odds ratios for mediation analysis for a dichotomous outcome. *American Journal of Epidemiology, 172*(12), 1339–1348. doi:10.1093/aje/kwq332 PMID:21036955

Venables, W. N., & Ripley, B. D. (2002). *Modern Applied Statistics with S* (4th ed.). New York: Springer. doi:10.1007/978-0-387-21706-2

KEY TERMS AND DEFINITIONS

Big Data: Very large and complex datasets that cannot be manipulated by traditional data processing methods.

Classification: In data mining, classification is a supervised learning activity concerned about developing models that can accurately predict the class labels of vectors whose classes are unknown.

Classification Accuracy: A performance measure of the ability of a classifier to predict classes of unknown vectors.

Data Mining: The process of extracting hidden but useful information from data sources.

Feature Selection: The process of assigning a numeric value, or some other form of quantifier, to individual predictors in a dataset, indicating the level of their importance in predicting the outcome.

Filter Variable Selection: The process of using statistical techniques, independent of a machine learning algorithm, to evaluate the correlation between each predictor with the outcome variable.

K-fold Validation: One of the methods of testing classification accuracy where the dataset is split into k subsets and in each iteration, k-1 of the subsets are used for model training while one subset retained for testing of model performance.

Odds Ratio: Statistical measure of the strength of association between two binary variables, where one variable is dependent on the other.

Chapter 6
Social Network Analysis

Sheik Abdullah A.
Thiagarajar College of Engineering, India

Abiramie Shree T. G. R.
Thiagarajar College of Engineering, India

ABSTRACT

Each day, 2.5 quintillion bytes of data are generated due to our daily activity. It is due to the vast amount of use of the smart mobiles, Cloud data storage, and the Internet of Things. In earlier days, these technologies were utilized by large IT companies and the private sector, but now each person has a high-end smartphone along with the cloud and IoT for the easy storage of data and backup. The analysis of the data generated by social media is a tedious process and involves a lot of techniques. Some tools for social network analysis are: Gephi, Networkx, IGraph, Pajek, Node XL, and cytoscope. Apart from these tools there are various efficient social data analysis algorithms that are far more helpful in doing analytics. The need for and use of social network analysis is very helpful in our current problem of huge data generation. In this chapter, the need for the analysis of social data along with the tools that are needed for the analysis and the techniques that are to be implemented in the field of social data analysis are covered.

DOI: 10.4018/978-1-5225-9750-6.ch006

INTRODUCTION

The social network is one of the recent trends for the analysis techniques. This is due to the advancement of the World Wide Web and the network users. All users make use of the smartphones supported by 3G and 4G networks. This makes each individual person is generating a wide amount of social data. These collaboration and communication of users through social network is increasing in a rapid manner. With this trustworthiness, each person is posting and updating their day to day activities in the form of posts and status updates along with the geographical location tags in them.

Another cause for this amount of the use of social network is that the cost of the network usage is dramatically low when it is compared with few years back. It leads to the invention of the 5G network which is very much faster when compared to our current network speed. Social data are also generated apart from the social networks such as online shopping, Online education and even emergency services. Due to these number of advantages after the wide spread of social networks, the data shared among the users in the public forum becomes valid and even these data are taken as an evidence at the time of judgement. So, this implies the importance of the data shared in social networks such as Twitter, Facebook, YouTube and even in Gmail. These data can be used effectively to produce the sentimental analysis or even these data are used for the wrong purpose and it leads to affect the person's privacy and security.

So, in this book chapter section 2 covers the ways the social data gets generated followed by types of the social networks and the types of data. In the section 3 the paper covers the data analytics tools on the social network data. Section 4 covers the algorithms that efficiently classify the social network data. Section 5 covers the pros and cons present in this type of social data analytics and the recent trends in the social network analysis part and the section 6 concludes the social network analysis method.

SOCIAL NETWORK ANALYSIS

Social Network Analysis (SNA) is an analysis method in which the analysis process is done on the socially available data (Bifet & Frank, 2010). Here, the analysis method consists of nodes and edges of a graph. The node (Vertices V) which represents an individual user or customer or employee or company which varies depends on the data and the edges (E) which represents the relationship or association or intimacy of friendship between them. This type of analysis behavior is also known as sociograms or graph analysis or even graphical structure analysis of social data.

Figure 1. Sociogram representation data

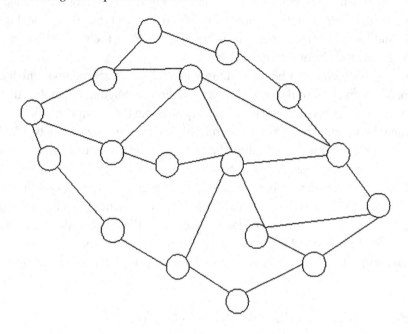

This type of analysis is used for the finding of the network structure of the social data which highlights the association of the social data between them. Community detection is one of the major uses of sociograms. In this method, the sociogram helps to identity how these people are connected to one another and can be helpful to justify them. This community detection method is widely used in the social media such as Twitter and Facebook. These types of representation are effective only if the social data is presented for a small group or for small analysis whereas for a large data analysis the use of the matrix representation of data is more useful. It represents the data in a matrix format where the columns and rows of the data are in vector format. Mostly all type of analysis on the social data helps to extract the relationship between the data and predict the association and justifies that cause of the connection between them.

TYPES OF SOCIAL NETWORK ANALYSIS

There are basically two methods for the analysis of the social data. They are, the researchers stated that Ego network analysis is associated with the analysis is done only on the nodes of the network (Akhtar, 2014). The possible answers from the nodes such as why they connected together? What the association of connection between them? These are the common findings from this type analysis and help to find the individuals persons network in the social site or their way of connection and communication between the people.

This approach can also be used along with the statistical method which eases the process of analysis of the data. Another method is called the complete network analysis method. This is method is completely all about the relationship between the nodes and their connections among them. This method justifies the networks from the edges point of view. This analysis helps to find the metrices from the network graph. They are closeness, degree, and betweenness among them (Godfrey, 2014). The Closeness is nothing but the measure of how these nodes are closely associated between them. Degree is the measure of the number of vertices that are leaving and adding to a node in the graph. The last metric is that the shortest distance between any to nodes in the given network where the no of nodes and links are counted between them. This is the process of complete analysis of the given sociogram.

TYPES OF SOCIAL MEDIA AND ITS DATA

There are varieties of social media network which are increasing day by day due to the advancements of technology in this century (J Travers S Milgram, 1969).

- **Social Network Facebook, Twitter and LinkedIn:** The first category is the Social Networks with includes Facebook, Twitter and LinkedIn. In this type of social media which are used to connect with people and make relationship with them through the process of friend request or follow. The process of sharing our data with others these social media works well. The benefits of these analysis are that it is used to interact through online. The data stored in the form of graph API's (Albert et al., 1999). These API are used for the analysis of data from the social data and produce a meaning information or relation from them.
- **Sharing Media social Networks Instagram, Snapchat and YouTube:** In this category, the user can share audio, videos and images. These helps to make reputation in the social network by the user. Live streaming of sharing media to the small groups of audiences and convert into monopoly from them. This is possible in the YouTube medium where the subscribers and likes and the trending of videos matters more. High number of videos are uploaded into the social network sites.

- **Discussion Forums: Reddit, Quora, Digg** This type of category is used for sharing and posting out ideas, opinions and news into the social networks. Before the advancement of Facebook this becomes more popular type of forum where people help to connect with the people and socialize with them. The forums are also used for the advertising also.

- **Bookmarking and content curation networks: Pinterest, Flipboard** Here, the social media helps to share and discuss a variety of content images which are in current trend as well. In Pinterest, the image can be also searched with the help of the scanning the images using the application. The Flipboard helps to create a customized magazine using the application and post it to the audiences. Both applications are famous to host the images and videos which are linked to the actual site or web page.

- **Consumer Review networks: Yelp, Zomato, TripAdvisor:** In this category, which is called the consumer review networks help to sale the products at their doorstep. It also helps to ease the work of the customers by reducing the burden (R Dunbar 1998). Here, the customer sends review to the respective pages who provide service to the customers. It also provides location-based service to the customers which helps to locate the customer. These type of social media networks are growing fast and have lot of companies getting profit from this type of service.

- **Blog and Publish Network: WordPress, Tumblr:** It is similar to the Twitter where we post our opinion and ideas in the form of a blog but these detailed (Watts, 2003). These blogs attract the reader to view the blog pages and helps to indulge in their favorite blogs. From this blog we can perform content-based analysis. It helps to recover the content of the blog in a short form.

- **Social Shopping Networks: Amazon, Flipkart:** Here, the customer can buy their need of things through online framework. It is the most important and trending analysis method nowadays. This analysis method is called sentimental analysis where the customers emotions helps to sell the products which are most buyable product by the customer. It helps the companies to do online marketing and getting product from them.

- **Interest-based Network: Goodreads:** Here, the users can connect with the persons who are all having similar behaviors and hobbies and common interests in them. The analysis of this type of data provide what are the social behaviors of the common people when they met a people like them.

Here, all these types of social networks provide data of different formats and the analysis method for these social data varies from each other. These data are more important today because even the US election uses the data from the Facebook to predict the result of the election process (S. Poria 2014). So, the analysis method is far more different from the previous methods. The data are not easily accessible as in early days. For each if the sematic analysis has been done on a Twitter data then the person has to have a verified developer account and has to answer the Twitter for which reason the Twitter API is needed by the user. All these constraints are considered and the disclosure of the private data without the concern of the user to a violation of law itself.

SOCIAL DATA ANALYSIS TOOLS

Social data which are generated due to the usage of the social media sites are used for the analysis where the various tools and packages are available for the easy handling of those data. The tools help to visualize the data and analyze it with the help of the user interface after the successful prediction of results from them. As the known Analysis libraries and package are available at the International Network for Social Network Analysis (INSNA) as mentioned in the paper (Ahktar, 2014). There are various analysis tools which are of open source and paid packages along with online social media analysis tool. The famous and most precise tools are NetworkX, IGraph, Gephi and Pajeck which are high end tools for better classification data. Other than these tools there are tools such as Sprout Social, Snaplytics, Iconosquare, Buzzsumo, Tailwind, Google analytics and Shortstack.

MOST COMMON SOCIAL NETWORK ANALYSIS TOOLS

NETWORKX

This tool uses the language called Python where the creation and analysis of the social data structure and functions of the complex network upon the social data. Using this tool, the user can load the data and frame a network model of the data and analyze the network model with some other network model and finding the relationship and correlation between the two models are all possible in this tool. The network model is nothing but a graph structure which consists of two important things. The node which represents the customers and users and the edges which corporates the relation between them. The graphs are all in various formats they are DI-Graphs and Multi-Graphs.

GEPHI

Another tool for the analysis of the social data which helps to view the data in the form of graphs. It is supported in all the Operation systems with its functions. Same as the previous tool the user can analyze the graph of our data and helps to predict the result from them. These graph formats also help to identify the data relationship with each other. It reveals the data which are buried inside the graphs.

PAJEK

A software tool which helps to analyze the data of the user and compute the metrics which are related to our process extraction of the data from them. In addition, this graph helps to find the centrality of the graphs which helps to know which node has high centrality than the other and can able to justify why this node alone is having a high centrality than the other.

IGRAPH

It is an open source software which helps us to form a graph from the given dataset. It uses the algorithms such as graph theory, minimum spanning tree and network flow algorithm. Here, the community detection from the graph can be done even for a very large graph structure. This graph analysis requires time to compute and are high in prediction of result from the graph.

SPROUT SOCIAL

This tool helps to measure the performance across the Facebook, Twitter, Instagram and LinkedIn which are all in this tool. These analysis process helps to track and also to compare the results of all the data in a single tool.

SNAPLYTICS

This tool helps to compare the performance of each person's data in the social data. The tool is a new released product where the current advantages of auto prediction and analysis of the text present in the data (Clauset, 2004). The social network analysis using this tool is much more efficient for current graph which includes complex graphs.

ICONOSQUARE

This tool is specially designed for the analysis of social data present in Instagram. It helps to analyze the photos and videos of our profile. It also helps to insight the Instagram which proves the Instagram stories from them.

BUZZSUMO

This tool is nothing but not differ from another analytics tool. This helps to predict the content which are shared in the websites. It provides the shares and posts received in our profiles and helps to predict the future of our posts.

TAILWIND

Apart from the use of Instagram and Snapchat there is a large increase of the use of Pinterest. Using this tool, the analysis of images and videos on the Pinterest in done with this tool.

GOOGLE ANALYTICS

This tool helps to measure the campaigns in the social media which also helps to measure the social ROI. It also helps to track the traffic and monitor the social data. This process is easily done in this tool and also helps to do in the google free platform.

SHORTSTACK

It does the performance analysis on the social data quickly than the other tools. It produces graph representation of the social data with nodes and edges.

SOCIAL ANALYTICS ALGORITHM

Social analysis is also referred as web content analysis where the mining of the data is done on the social data. This process is also called as Graph mining, rule mining and link mining and also as clustering analysis or classification findings. It initially starts with the network dynamic process. Here, it is nothing but understanding of the network model and the presence of the nodes and edges between them (Poojawadhwa

& MP Sbhatia 2017). Next, the Organizational structure discovering process where the activity of the graph along with the pattern of how well the graph is formed due to the interaction between them. After this comes the community detection where the users and their close related community is easily findable (S Fortunato2010). This type of community detection is based on various process.

- **Density Based:** It shows the connection between the different groups of nodes where the edges run between them.
- **Vertex Based:** This process is compared with the group of vertices which are all similar to each other process.
- **Action Based:** This process is done with the help of action that performed by the nodes.

The algorithms of the community-based detection are,

1. Hierarchical Clustering Algorithm: It classifies the graph in a hierarchical manner. Here, the similarity is found between the algorithm vertices. It is further classified into two types. They are the agglomerative algorithm and the divisive algorithm. In agglomerative algorithm, all the small clusters are combined to merge them into a single cluster at the end of the execution of the algorithm. In the divisive algorithm, a large single cluster is split up into a small and each individual cluster.
2. Partitional Clustering Algorithm: Here, the given graph is made up into k clusters. The k clusters help to minimize the diameter of the cluster. It is done with the help of the intra-cluster distance between them.
3. Modularity-based Algorithm: The modularity values are added to each cluster which is nothing but the good quality of the cluster. This improves the optimization of the cluster where the clusters are more efficient.

RECENT TRENDS IN SOCIAL NETWORK ANALYSIS

The social network analysis of social data is the new advancement of the analytics process. Using these analytics, we can predict the current nature of the social data and liking of the people. In recent survey, the analysis helps to predict that the social media are mostly used for the entertainment and also for the knowing of current trends in the society. All age groups especially youths tend to use the social media for the current update of news and information along with entertainment. Here, the attackers or the eavesdroppers use this period of time to manipulate the original data and spread rumors. These rumors are spreading and overtaking the true information. These and all can be found with the help of the analysis of the social data which distinguish the true information and the rumors. All these uses of the analytics will also helps the future generation to do analyze of the data in a more efficient manner.

CONCLUSION

Apart from all these techniques and algorithms for the analysis of data due to advancement of technology there are lots of advantages in many ways for the users. This helps to find the communication and collaboration between the users in the social site. Using this further we can improve the utilization of the social media where the better connection and collaboration is made. With this we further improve the analysis method which in future helps to improve the benefit for the companies, organizations or even governments. This shows the direct view and opinion of the real people which is better in the world of fake opinions.

REFERENCES

Akhtar, N. (2014, April). Social network analysis tools. *Proceedings of the 2014 Fourth International Conference on Communication Systems and Network Technologies* (pp. 388-392). IEEE.

Albert, R., Jeong, H., & Barabasi, A. (1999). Diameter of the World Wide Web. *Nature*, *401*(6749), 130–131. doi:10.1038/43601

Bifet, A., & Frank, E. (2010, October). Sentiment knowledge discovery in twitter streaming data. *Proceedings of the International conference on discovery science* (pp. 1-15). Berlin: Springer.

Clauset, A., Newman, M., & Moore, C. (2004). Finding community structure in very large networks. *Physical Review. E, 70*(6), 066111. doi:10.1103/PhysRevE.70.066111 PMID:15697438

Dunbar, R. (1998). *Grooming, gossip, and the evolution of language.* Harvard University Press.

Fortunato, S. (2010). Community detection in graphs. *Physics Reports*, *486*(3-5), 75–174. doi:10.1016/j.physrep.2009.11.002

Godfrey, D., Johns, C., Meyer, C. D., Race, S., & Sadek, C. (2014). *A case study in text mining: Interpreting twitter data from world cup tweets.*

Poria, S., Cambria, E., Winterstein, G., & Huang, G.-B. (2014). Sentic patterns: Dependency-based rules for concept-level sentiment analysis. *Knowledge-Based Systems*, *69*, 45–63. doi:10.1016/j.knosys.2014.05.005

Travers, J., & Milgram, S. (1969). An experimental study small world problem, (1969). *Sociometry*, *32*(4), 425–443. doi:10.2307/2786545

Wadhwa, P., & Bhatia, M. P. S. (2012). Social networks analysis: trends, techniques and future prospects. *Springer open journal, 455*, 19-32.

Watts, D. J. (2004). *Six degrees: The science of a connected age.* WW Norton & Company.

Chapter 7
Role of Machine Intelligence and Big Data in Remote Sensing

Suriya Murugan
KPR Institute of Engineering and Technology, India

Anandakumar Haldorai
iD https://orcid.org/0000-0001-9975-6462
Sri Eshwar College of Engineering, India

ABSTRACT

Technological advances in computing, data storage, networks, and sensors have dramatically increased our ability to access, store, and process huge amounts of data. "Big data" as a term has been the biggest trends of the last few years, leading to an elevation in research, as well as industry and government applications. The problem with current big data analysis faces any one of the following challenges: heterogeneity and incompleteness, scale, timeliness, privacy, and human collaboration. It's an undeniable fact that "data" forms the basis for geospatial industry. With technological advances in the collection, distribution, management, and access of data, there is an exponential increase in the amount of geospatial information. Computational intelligence techniques such as machine learning optimization and advanced data analytics can help make faster decisions. This chapter analyses how geospatial data is driving software and services market as a "big data challenge" and how biologically inspired techniques are effective in analyzing remote sensing data.

DOI: 10.4018/978-1-5225-9750-6.ch007

INTRODUCTION

Human knowledge competes' technology and hence thrust to process and store voluminous data creates challenges. Researchers from various communities like Computer Intelligence, Data Intelligence, Data Mining and Data Security need to analyze emerging optimization techniques to handle growth in data processing. The process of handling big data encompasses collection, storage, transportation and exploitation of data through data analytics, which is the core of big data processing.

A sensor is used to measure the energy reflected from the earth. This information can be displayed as a digital image or as a photograph. Sensors can be mounted on a satellite orbiting the earth, or on a plane or other airborne structure. As Lary, D. J., Alavi, A. H., Gandomi, A. H., & Walker, A. L. (2016) states the amount of remote sensing and other geographic data keeps getting bigger every day, the traditional GIS (Graphical Information Systems) are often insufficient for meaningful interpretation. Mapping and analysis become further complicated with the explosion of disruptive technologies like the cloud, embedded sensors, mobile and social media. Nature provides space for every living organism in spite of its numerous growth, similarly Nature Inspired Algorithms can help compute huge amount of data through its optimization techniques. Bio Inspired Algorithms (BIAs) like Evolutionary Computation based, Swarm Intelligence based or Ecology based are increasingly becoming popular in system identification, modeling, processing, and data mining.

In order to take advantage and make good use of remote sensing data, we must be able to extract meaningful information from the imagery. Geeta R. Gupta and Prof. S. M. Kamalapur, (2014) Interpretation and analysis of remote sensing imagery involve the identification and/or measurement of various targets in an image in order to extract useful information about them. Soft computing methods for this kind of big data can be used in many applications and in many modules of remote sensing systems. Fig [1] depicts the process involved in remote sensing using IS tools and the data obtained from GIS will be only of two types' spatial or temporal data. This data is categorized as Big Data and specifies some machine learning algorithms applicable for analyzing remote sensing data efficiently.

This paper is organized as follows Section II provides an detailed review of Challenges and Myths in GIS for Bigdata; Section III the Modeling using BigData tools is described, Section IV describes the Role of Bio Inspired algorithms for GIS Data analytics, Section V provides further Discussion. Section VI concluded with further enhancement.

Figure 1. Application of big data and machine learning tools for GIS

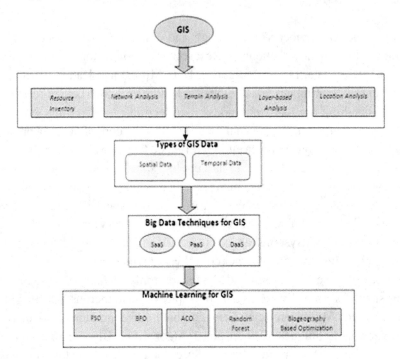

LITERATURE SURVEY

Big Data: Challenges and Myths

Big Data has been one of the current and future research frontiers. It is right to say that Big Data will revolutionize many fields, including business, the scientific research, public administration, and so on. It is generally defined by the four V's — Volume, Velocity, Veracity, and Variety. It is assumed that either all or any one of the characteristics needs to be met for the classification of a problem as a Big Data problem. Analyzing big data allows analysts, researchers, and business users to make better and faster decisions Goel, L., Gupta, D., Panchal, V. K., & Abraham, A. (2012) using data that was previously inaccessible or unusable. More commonly, Big Data is a collection of very huge data sets with a great diversity of types so that it becomes difficult to process by using state-of-the-art data processing approaches or traditional data processing platforms.

Challenges in Big Data analysis include data inconsistence and incompleteness, scalability, timeliness and data security Heterogeneity, scale, timeliness, complexity, and privacy problems with Big Data impede progress at all phases of the pipeline that can create value from data.Much data today is not natively in structured format; for example, tweets and blogs are weakly structured pieces of text, while images and video are structured for storage and display, but not for semantic content and search: transforming such content into a structured format for later analysis is a major challenge. Data analysis, organization, retrieval, and modeling are other foundational challenges.

As the sizes of data set are often very huge, sometimes several gigabytes or more, and their origin from heterogeneous sources, current real-world databases are severely susceptible to inconsistent, incomplete, and noisy data. Therefore, a number of data preprocessing techniques, including data cleaning, data integration, data transformation and date reduction, can be applied Daya Gupta, Bidisha Das, and V. K. Panchal, (2011) to remove noise and correct inconsistencies. Different challenges arise in each sub-process when it comes to data-driven applications. As Big Data technology is able to process large quantities of data in the shortest curve, it has emerged as a new frontier for geospatial analysis. For instance, NASA has made inroads into climate research integrating Big Data (past and current global climate data) with geographies. This has enabled a synergized approach to climate modeling, analysis and resilience building.

Empowering GIS with Big Data

GIS data is today the fastest growing segment of geospatial business. Geospatial data and content are referring to any geo-referenced information. There are Shelly Bansal, Daya Gupta, V.K. Panchal, Shashi Kumar,(2009) various types of spatial data - maps (raster and vector), imagery, derived data, publicly crowd sourced data, open sourced data, tagged data, temporal, metadata, classified, non classified, video, sensors, etc . As more and more geospatial data becomes available to more than the typical geospatial professional, it is finding its place within the larger community of published content. Geospatial data is evolving from data to what most people refer to as content which by definition is more about the logical organization and improved accessibility of various types of structured and unstructured electronic information. There are a couple of elements that makes our industry very unique.

One is geospatial data or geospatial referenced content and the other comprises the theories and algorithms inherent in extracting, managing, processing, analyzing and visualizing spatial data. The spatial analysis segment of our industry has been core to the definition of our industry and has supported solid historical growth. In other words, the advent of massive amounts of new content creates challenges for both the technology companies and the consumers. For example, each mile of road driven with terrestrial LiDAR and digital video can produce terabytes of data. This large content output must be managed, processed, stored and displayed, all of which requires different technologies. A critical aspect of this vast amount of content is that is often more accurate than most of the existing content. Geospatial analysis Dong, W., & Xiang-bin, W. (2008) has always approached the development of geospatial databases with a layered approach. The idea was to divide the existing maps into data layers so that the information could be more easily managed by allowing better interpreting the spatial relationship between the features and layers on the map and/or the earth's surface. This situation has occurred due to the 'stovepipe' data acquisition process. Each of the layers of GIS data was collected separately and with varying degrees of spatial accuracy and attribution. However, Bonabeau, E., Dorigo, M. and Theraulaz, G., (1999) in more recent times, the concepts of object oriented data- bases have been implemented.

MODELING USING BIG DATA TOOLS

The Big Data approach to GIS allows analysis and decision making from huge datasets, by using algorithms, query processing and spatiotemporal data mining. It's the process of extracting information from maximum possible sources using established procedures and computational techniques.

Areas where geospatial technology has applied Big Data for enhanced analysis:

- Climate modeling and analysis
- Location analytics
- Retail and E-commerce
- Intelligence gathering
- Terrorist financing
- Aviation industry
- Disease surveillance
- Disaster response

GIS tools search, sift and sieve data from multiple and disparate databases to organize it for better workflows and spatial analysis. They run operations that aggregate terabytes and more of spatial information, run analysis, and visualize results as maps. All this Lavika Goel, Daya Gupta, V.K. Panchal,(2011) occurs in real-time, with multiple data streaming into the existing GIS for better understanding of spatial trends and relationships. The availability of more accurate content is definitely driving the GIS software companies to provide tools and methods for their users to incorporate this new content into legacy geospatial databases. One challenge geospatial industry has been addressing for years is to integrate new and better content with existing geospatial datasets that are older, less detailed and in some cases, much less accurate. Big data supports remote sensing data processing using following features:

- *Taps huge datasets for policy measures* – GIS tools for Big Data processing facilitate deep insights and predictive modeling for policy making in health care, crime detection, disaster response and more.
- *Supports spatial analysis of unstructured data in real-time* – Maps integrate unstructured data (sensor data, meteorological data, driving times, etc.) in real-time. This is useful for location analysis in retail, finance and insurance.
- *Integrates multiple data layers for a complete picture* – Huge amount of data is pulled from different formats, devices or systems and given a geographic context for a complete picture or analysis.
- *Enables spatiotemporal queries over big geospatial data* – Case-by-case query processing and data mining of huge spatiotemporal data is possible for different projects.

GIS Tools for Hadoop works with big spatial data (big data with location) and provides complete spatial analysis using the power of distributed processing in Hadoop. GIS Tools for Hadoop is an open source toolkit that brings spatial analysis to your big data. Some of the popular tools are:

- Esri Geometry API for Java
- Spatial Framework for Hadoop
- Geoprocessing Tools for Hadoop
- GIS Tools for Hadoop

ROLE OF BIO INSPIRED ALGORITHMS FOR GIS DATA ANALYTICS

One big problem faced by engineers, public works departments, and facilities is that they have lots of old maps (scanned paper copies and/or CAD files) without known coordinate/projection systems. Machine learning could be used to automatically line up building outlines of old maps to known base maps or aerial images using elements of computer vision/object recognition.

Soft computing methods are valuable assets in intelligent data analysis. The most obvious characteristic of machine learning is to discover knowledge and make intelligent decisions automatically. When Big Data is concerned, Demetrics Stathakis and Anthanassios Vasilakos, (2006) it is necessary to scale up machine learning algorithms, both supervised learning and unsupervised learning, to cope with it. The types of the ML algorithms commonly used are artificial neural networks (ANN), support vector machines (SVM), self-organizing map (SOM), decision trees (DT), Naïve Bayes classifier, random forests, case-based reasoning, neuro-fuzzy (NF), genetic algorithm (GA), multi-variate adaptive regression splines (MARS), etc. Artificial neural network (ANN) is a mature techniques and has a wide range of application coverage. Its successful applications can be found in pattern recognition, image analysis, adaptive control, and other areas.

Figure 2 gives an overall classification of various Bio-inspired techniques and its respective algorithms popularly used and a brief discussion on each is given below.

Based on Evolutionary Algorithm

Evolutionary algorithms (EAs) are computational methods inspired by the process and mechanisms of biological evolution. According to Darwin's natural selection theory of evolution, in nature the competition among individuals for scarce resources results in the fittest individuals dominating over the weaker ones (i.e. survival of the fittest). The process of evolution by means of natural selection helps to account for the variety of life and its suitability for the environment. The mechanisms of evolution describe how evolution actually takes place through the modification and propagation of genetic material (proteins). EAs provide solutions to many real-world, complex, optimization problems that are difficult to tackle using the conventional methods, due to their nature that implies discontinuities of the search space, non-differentiable objective functions, imprecise arguments and function values. EAs can be applied to many types of problems, viz. continuous, mixed-integer, combinatory, etc. Furthermore, these algorithms can be easily combined with the existing techniques such as local search and other exact methods.

Figure 2. Taxonomy of bio-inspired algorithms

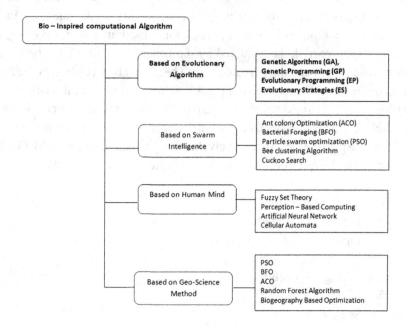

Most of the present implementations of EA come from any of these three basic types: Genetic Algorithms (GA), Evolutionary Programming (EP) and Evolutionary Strategies (ES). Two groups of EA have became very important, Genetic Programming (GP) with a lot of real problems and Classifier Systems (CS) used for machine learning and for discovering rules in rules based systems (RBS).

Based on Swarm Intelligence

Particle swarm optimization (PSO) is a population based stochastic optimization technique developed by swarm is used for the assembling of animals such as fish schools, bird flocks and insect colonies (such as ants, termites and honey bees) performing collective activities. Simple local rules, without any relation to the global pattern, and interactions between systematic or self-organized agents led to the emergence of collective intelligence called Swarm Intelligence (SI). Swarms use their environment and resources effectively by collective intelligence. Self organization is the key characteristic of a swarm system, which results in global-level response by means of local level interactions. The main paradigms of biologically inspired SI algorithms include ant colony optimization (ACO), particle swarm optimization (PSO), artificial bee colony (ABC), honey-bee mating optimization (HBMO) algorithms, etc.

In the PSO algorithm, Murugan, S., & Sumithra M. G. (2019) each particle is associated with a position in the search space and velocity for its trajectory. Particle is initialized with a random swarm of particles and random velocity vectors. Then the fitness of each particle is evaluated by the fitness function. Two 'best' values are defined, the global and the personal best. The global best (GBest) is the highest fitness value in the entire population (best solution so far), and the personal best (PBest) is the highest fitness value achieved by a specific particle over the iterations. Each particle is attracted towards the location of the 'best fitness achieved so far' across the whole population. Accordingly the, Suriya, M., & Sumithra, M. G. (2018) nature inspired techniques proposed under this category is listed below.

- Ant Colony Optimization
- Particle Swarm Optimization
- Biogeography Based Optimization
- Bacterial Foraging Optimization
- Bee Clustering Algorithm
- Artificial Swarm fish
- Cuckoo Search
- River Formation Dynamics
- Gravitational Search
- Charged System Search
- Intelligent Water Drop
- Firefly Optimization
- Stochastic Diffusion Search

Based on Human Mind

To provide a solution to the problems posed by classical AI techniques, computational intelligence techniques based on the modelization of human mind were introduced. In effect, the role model for these techniques is the human mind. The above-mentioned computational intelligence techniques differ from the conventional (hard) computing techniques in that, unlike hard computing, they are tolerant of tolerance for imprecision, uncertainty and partial truth to achieve tractability, robustness and low solution cost. Computational models require a mathematically and logically formal representation of a problem. All the approaches based on the modelization of human mind tend to be generalized to the form of integrated computational models of synthetic / abstract intelligence, in order to be applied to the explanation and improvement of individual and social / organizational decision-making and reasoning. The computational techniques proposed to be under this category are listed below.

- Fuzzy set theory
- Perception – based computing
- Artificial Neural Network
- Cellular Automata
- DNA computing

Based on Geo-Science Method

Earth science (also known as geo-science) is an all embracing term for the sciences related to the planet Earth. It is arguably a special case in planetary science, the Earth being the only known life-bearing planet. The formal discipline of Earth sciences may include the study of the atmosphere, hydrosphere, oceans and biosphere, as well as the solid earth. Typically Earth scientists will use tools from physics, chemistry, biology, chronology and mathematics to build a quantitative understanding of how the Earth system works, and how it evolved to its current state. The following nature inspired techniques that can be categorized under geo-sciences as listed below:

- Plate Tectonics
- Big bang Crunching
- Oceanic currents
- Tidal waves
- Volcanic eruptions
- Earth's Electromagnetism
- Earthquakes

DISCUSSION

With the satellite remote sensing, it has become feasible to observe a vast area of the terrain and knowledge extracted out of these images. Earth Observation Satellite-based (EOS) sensors have emerged into a rapid source of multi-sensor, multi-resolution and multispectral geospatial information for decision making in varying application domains. In order to encounter with the inherent uncertainty in geo-spatial data, our observation is that Nature-Inspired Computing mechanism is aptly fit into the problem-solving framework. A new wide range of nature-inspired computational algorithms is proposed which have emerged from evolutionary algorithms and geo-sciences based natural phenomenon. These nature inspired intelligent techniques can form the basis of building an optimization algorithm, which can adapt itself to suit our purpose of feature extraction and prove to be better by giving more accurate results than the other existing optimization techniques Table 1below presents the proposed general taxonomy of the existing nature inspired computational intelligence techniques that have been used for geo-spatial feature extraction application till date.

CONCLUSION

As the geospatial industry matures, the demand for better and more accurate geospatial content will grow rapidly. From the study it is analyzed that most of the recent Nature- inspired algorithms like swarm intelligence, Fuzzy Networks and Neural Networks are highly applicable to feature extraction problems and other traditional methods are well- suited for resource inventory and network analysis problems. These techniques with lower cost and higher degree of classification accuracy will be able to replace high resolution high cost satellite imageries. The taxonomy of nature inspired CI techniques for various Remote sensing problems was analyzed in this chapter. This analysis helps conclude that the nature inspired techniques of cuckoo search, firefly optimization, stochastic diffusion search, geo-sciences based techniques of plate tectonics, big bang crunching etc. have never been used to suite

Table 1. Taxonomy of GIS problems and respective bio-inspired Geo-Science algorithm

Remote Sensing Problems	Type of Data	Computational Algorithm in Geo-Science
Resource Inventory	Spatial Data	k-Neigh roust neighbor
Network Analysis	Spatial Data	Support Vector Machine
Terrain Analysis	Spatial Data	Artificial Neural Network
Layer-based Analysis	Spatial Data	PSO
Location Analysis	Spatial Data	PSO
Feature extraction	Temporal Data	Fuzzy Logic Rough set theory Artificial Neural Network Swarm Intelligence

the land cover feature extraction applications. Finally this chapter concludes that certain nature inspired techniques when integrated with the existing optimization techniques can drastically improve their optimization capability hence leading to better terrain classification.

REFERENCES

Bansal, S., & Gupta, D. (2009). Remote Sensing Image Classification by Improved Swarm Inspired Techniques. *International Conference on Artificial Intelligence and Pattern Recognition (AIPR-09).*

Bonabeau, E., Dorigo, M., & Theraulaz, G. (1999). *Swarm Intelligence from Natural to Artificial System* (1st ed.). Oxford University Press.

Dong, W., & Xiang-bin, W. (2008). Particle Swarm Intelligence Classification Algorithm for Remote Sensing Images. *IEEE Pacific-Asia Workshop on Computational Intelligence and Industrial Application.* 10.1109/PACIIA.2008.26

Goel, Gupta, & Panchal. (2011). Hybrid bioinspired techniques for land cover feature extraction: A remote sensing perspective. *Applied Soft Computing, 12*(2), 832-849.

Goel, L., Gupta, D., Panchal, V. K., & Abraham, A. (2012). Taxonomy of nature inspired computational intelligence: A remote sensing perspective. *Fourth World Congress on Nature and Biologically Inspired Computing (NaBIC).* 10.1109/NaBIC.2012.6402262

Gupta, D., Das, B., & Panchal, V. K. (2011). *A Methodical Study for the Extraction of Landscape Traits Using Membrane Computing technique, GEM.* WORLDCOMP.

Gupta & Kamalapur. (2014). Study of Classification of Remote Sensing Images using Particle Swarm Optimization based approach. *International Journal of Application or Innovation in Engineering & Management, 3*(10).

Lary, D. J., Alavi, A. H., Gandomi, A. H., & Walker, A. L. (2016). Machine learning in geosciences and remote sensing. *Geoscience Frontiers, 7*(1), 3–10. doi:10.1016/j.gsf.2015.07.003

Murugan, S., & Sumithra M. G. (2019). Efficient Space Communication and Management (SCOaM) Using Cognitive Radio Networks Based on Deep Learning Techniques. *Cognitive Social Mining Applications in Data Analytics and Forensics,* 65–76. doi:10.4018/978-1-5225-7522-1.ch004

Stathakis & Vasilakos. (2006). *Comparison of computational Intelligence based Classification Techniques for Remotely Sensed optical Image Classification* (Vol. 44). IEEE Transactions on and Remote Sensing.

Suriya, M., & Sumithra, M. G. (2018). Efficient Evolutionary Techniques for Wireless Body Area Using Cognitive Radio Networks. *EAI/Springer Innovations in Communication and Computing,* 61–70. doi:10.1007/978-3-030-02674-5_4

Chapter 8
Provisioning System for Application Virtualization Environments

Tolga Büyüktanır
Yildiz Technical University, Turkey

Hakan Tüzün
Link Bilgisayar R&D Office, Turkey

Mehmet S. Aktaş
Yildiz Technical University, Turkey

ABSTRACT

Monitoring application virtualization environments for auto-scaling purposes have become an important requirement in today's computing world. In this chapter, the authors introduce the design and implementation of resource monitoring and management software architecture for application virtualization environments. They also present a prototype application of the proposed architectures with details. They discuss the performance evaluation of prototype implementation. All the results were observed to be successful.

DOI: 10.4018/978-1-5225-9750-6.ch008

INTRODUCTION

Micro-services are widely used in distributed programming. They provide independent deployable small services. A micro-service can be developed to perform less comprehensive business logic. It communicates with simple data representation models like JSON to use less network bandwidth in inter-service communication. Micro-services can have different programming interfaces and be written in different programming languages. Micro-service architecture is inspired by service-oriented architecture, which runs faster and consumes fewer resources such as network bandwidth and CPU cycles. With these perspectives, micro-service architecture has found a wide usage area in recent years compared to traditional monolithic web service architectures.

While the micro-service runs on the application virtualization platform, its resource needs can change instantly and periodically. For example; let us consider a service that is used by a hotel, which is mostly open in summer months. The application will be used more often in summer months and will decrease usage frequency in winter months. Another example; Stock Exchange Market's daily-closure data web service may run under different workloads. Following the closing of the stock market, the workload of this service will increase. By looking at these examples; it can be seen that for periodic and instant usages, application virtualization environments should be managed in a way that they can use resources (CPU, bandwidth, memory) in an optimal and fair manner. Optimal resource usage can only be possible by allocating resources to containers running on the application visualization environment based on the usage patterns.

In this book chapter, we focus on software architectures, which include resource usage monitoring for application virtualization environments. In particular, we propose a software architecture, which dynamically monitors and manages the application virtualization environments according to instantly changing resource needs. The proposed real-time resource management methodology analyzes the streaming performance data for auto-scaling purposes. We apply complex event processing on performance data collected from application virtualization environment. This approach is able to detect potential failures in application virtualization environments by continuously monitoring performance data. We also introduce details of a prototype application of the proposed software architectures and discuss its performance evaluation from the perspective of scalability and performance. The results of the evaluation are promising.

The rest of the chapter is organized as follows: In Section 2, we define the problem. Some superficial background information is given about distributed messaging platforms and containerization technologies in Section 3. The basic concepts and literature review are shared in Section 4. In Section 5, we represent resource provisioning application architecture for application virtualization environments and in Section 6, explain a prototype of the proposed architecture in details. The tests performed on the prototype application are explained in Section 7. Section 8 includes results and future studies.

PROBLEM DEFINITION

Theoretically, when allocating resources for a virtualization environment, there is no limitation. To this end, the virtualization environment can use all of the resources allocated from host to it. Considering multi-tenant architecture, multiple users and multiple applications can run on the same host. In these cases, it is necessary to use host resources effectively. CPU resource usage of application virtualization environments can be limited, but application virtualization environments spent CPU resource according to predefined rules in most cases. For example; predefined resource usage rules are usually identified by a Scheduler. CPU scheduling and prioritization are advance kernel properties. If the Scheduler is not performed correctly, the system will become unstable or even unusable (Limit a container's resources, 2019).

An application virtualization environment needs memory resource. However, memory resource neither should be allocated to it more than its needs nor should be allocated less than its needs. On one hand, if the memory resource is allocated more than necessary, the resources of the cloud computing environment will be wasted. On the other hand, if memory resource is allocated less than necessary, when an important task is running, "out of memory exception" will be thrown. This error may cause interruption of the running process. The memory requirements of application virtualization environments can change instantly in most cases. Therefore, the memory should be allocated to the virtualization environment in real-time. When memory usage increases, the new resource should be supplemented and when memory usage decreases, allocated resources should be released (Nardelli, 2017; Hoenisch, Weber, Schulte, Zhu, & Fekete, 2015).

Response time to a request is critical. In addition, the failure of a system is expensive. Fast and accurate reaction to resource needs and to failures is necessary for system reliability. Because of this, in order to create a pattern of resource usage and detect failures, it is vital to collect the log files from virtualization environments and analyze in real-time.

Within the scope of this chapter, it is envisaged that the proposed real-time resource management application will be able to detect potential failures by analyzing log files. Thus, it will help to prevent possible failures of the application hosted in the virtualization environment.

BACKGROUND

In this section, some superficial background information is given about distributed messaging platforms and containerization technologies.

Distributed Messaging Platforms

Real-time data is continuously generated from applications such as social media, iot devices, business or any other data generating application. This data stream multiple location independent sources. It typically includes primitive events as clicks, click positions, pageviews, statistical information, temperature, humidity and so on. It is essential to store lossless this streaming data and to route quickly and reliably to multiple receivers. Apache Kafka, Amazon Kinesis, Microsoft Azure Event Hubs, and Google Pub/Sub are the distributed messaging platforms work with low latency and scalability. In this study, we proper Apache Kafka due to ease of use and suitability to our problem.

Apache Kafka: Apache Kafka is horizontally scalable, fault-tolerant and fast real-time data streaming application. It also is open-source, distributed pub/sub messaging system developed by LinkedIn. Apache Kafka spends O(1) constant-time to write data to disk even very large volume. It can use commodity hardware, and supports to write million of messages to disk per second. Apache Kafka also support multiple client such as python, java, .net, php, ruby etc.

Apache Kafka can get data from multiple source without blocking data, and can send data to multiple consumers. Apache Kafka categorizes message feeds. Each category is called topic. The processes publish messages from data sources to Apache Kafka topics are called producers. Apache Kafka runs as a cluster consists of one or more server. The processes reads published messages from topics are called consumers (Thein, 2014; Kreps, Narkhede, & Rao, 2011).

Containerization Technologies

Before talking about containers, it is necessary touch upon the subject of virtual machines. One physical server is used to create multiple operating system with virtualization technologies, aka virtual machines. Each virtual machine contains the entire operating system and the applications runs on it. The physical server has a hypervisor to run multiple machines at the same time. Although, there is a lot of overhead because of a single hypervisor, and there is a lot of storage requirements because of replicated operating system files. Therefore, the number of hosted virtual machines on a single server is limited.

Due to these problems, container technology has emerged as an alternative solution. The physical server runs an operating system with the containerization technology. The single operating system is hosted on server and each container shares operating system with other containers. To avoid any interference, the permission of the shared files are set read-only. Each container is a light-weight computing environment. Compared with the virtual machines, containers require fewer resources (memory, CPU, storage, etc.) of the physical server, and are more efficient. In contrast to virtual machines, a lot of containers can be hosted on a single server. There are a lot of containerization technologies such as Docker, rkt, Apache Mesos, LXL Linux, Nanobox, Singularity Container and etc., but we have chosen to use Docker in this study because of documentation and developer communities.

Docker: Docker images are light-weight, standalone, executable packages including everything needed to run an application. Docker images are transformed into Docker container at runtime, and they run by the Docker Engine. Docker containers run on Docker Engine are portable, light-weight and isolated. Docker containers can run platform independent. It's mean that Docker Containers are available on Linux, Windows, Data Centers, Cloud and Serverless platforms (Bernstein, 2014).

LITERATURE REVIEW

Micro-services divide software into small services that can be deployed independently of each other and allows service-based development. The micro-service a widely used distributed programming technique. Micro-services should be written as functional according to their domains. All services are autonomous and full-stack. So, changes to any service do not affect other services unless there is a change in the communication interface. In this way, loosely coupled (usually with REST interface), high cohesion, flexibility, agility, and scalability are provided (Lewis & Fowler, 2014; Aderaldo, Mendonça, Pahl, & Jamshidi, 2017).

Micro-services can be described as small, autonomous services that work together. These services are developed as part of functionality according to the limits of the work. All communication between the services is done via the network. Even if the services are changed, the services are designed independently from each other so that no other changes are needed. Micro-services are widely used on application virtualization platforms and cloud computing infrastructures (Newman, 2015).

Cloud technologies are built on virtualization. There are basically three types of virtualization. Type 1 and Type 2 require a lot of time to install and boot the virtual machine. In addition, these virtualization methods use a lot of CPU, memory, and storage. The other virtualization method is light-weight virtualization, which is the application virtualization. This virtualization method is faster than others and resource consumption is small enough to be neglected. Virtual machine creation and boot time are very low (Gupta, Kaur, & Kaur, 2017).

Application virtualization is the most suitable for micro-service architectures. Web applications like the PayPal web site and its services use this method of virtualization with micro-services. In order to serve 218 million active users, PayPal runs 700 micro-services on the Docker. A total of 150 million application virtualization environments work for these applications. Application virtualization with PayPal, developer productivity has increased by 50%. In some applications, 10-20 percentage increase in efficiency has been achieved (Armstrong, 2017).

DevOps and DevOps practices are widely used in IT departments. In these practices, the changes in the services running in the application virtualization environment and the re-publication of the new version are made in a short time. Also, it is easier to perform performance-related feedback and anomaly detection by providing continuous monitoring with DevOps tools (Aderaldo, Mendonça, Pahl, & Jamshidi, 2017; Newman2015; Dragoni, Giallorenzo, Lafuente, Mazzara, Montesi, Mustafin, & Safina, 2017; Merkel, 2014).

Application virtualization environments provide convenience in terms of scalability. However, as the number of application virtualization environments increases, the amount of scientific resources used increases. In cases where resources are insufficient, the following two situations can be made: a) Resources of all application virtualization environments need to be updated. b) If the resource requirement of the application virtualization environment increases, the amount of resources should be increased. Considering these two situations, resource planning should be done independently of the virtualization environment. In this way, either application performance can be increased or optimum results can be found for current needs (Nardelli, 2017; Hoenisch, Weber, Schulte, Zhu, & Fekete, 2015).

Service-based architectures have been studied extensively in different fields (Aktas, Fox, & Pierce, 2007; Nacar, Aktas, Pierce, Lu, Erlebacher, Kigelman, ... Yuen, 2007; Pierce, Fox, Aktas, Aydin, Gadgil, Qi, & Sayar, 2008; Aydin, Pierce, Fox, Aktas, & Sayar, 2004; Aktas, Aydin, Donnellan, Fox, Granat, Lyzenga, ... Rundle, 2005; Aktas, Fox, & Pierce, 2005; Aydin, Aktas, Fox, Gadgil, Pierce, & Saya, 2005; Aktas, Fox, Pierce, & Oh, 2008; Aktas, & Pierce, 2010; Aktas, Aydin, Fox, Gadgil, Pierce, & Sayar, 2005). However, we see that these studies focus on monolithic services. The study we presented here is a case study for developing a service-based system using micro-services. There exist some studies on the monitoring of the resources by analyzing the events obtained from the virtualization environments (Aktas, &Astekin, 2019; Aktas, 2018; Fox, Aktas, Aydin, Bulut, Pallickara, Pierce, ... &Zhai, 2006; Fox, Aktas, Aydin, Gadgil, Pallickara, Pierce, & Sayar, 2009). By conducting data analyzes on the event data, different applications were implemented providing information about the resources (Chen, Plale, & Aktas, 2014; Chen, Plale, & Aktas, 2014). This chapter focuses on the management of resources by analyzing the measurement data received from the application virtualization environments. In this chapter, information is extracted from measurement data and decisions are made on the use of resources.

PROPOSED SOFTWARE ARCHITECTURE

Our proposed distributed software architecture is shown in Figure 1. According to proposed architecture, resource management of multiple application virtualization environments can be done. In Figure 1, we depict the application virtualization environments (i.e. containerization platform host) in blue rectangles and containers in the colored pentagon.

As it can be seen in Figure 1, while micro-services run in virtualization environments, we collect some metadata, which includes resource usage data, via topic-based pub-sub messaging system. The metadata is collected through a dedicated topic in the pub-sub system. The Stats Monitoring Module, which is responsible for metadata collection, is depicted in green dotted rectangles. Resource Provisioning Module, shown with the red dashed rectangle, receives messages from the Stats Monitoring Module.

As soon as any virtualization environment's memory usage exceeds a certain threshold, Resource Provisioner decides to increase allocated memory for it. This decision is sent out within a message via pub-sub messaging service to another topic, called the "Action Topic". When memory usage decreases under a certain threshold, Resource Provisioner produces another message to decrease the allocated memory and again publishes it to the "Action Topic". In Figure 1, Action Consumer Module is depicted in green dotted rectangles. It performs the action command received via the Action Topic. In this way, resource allocation/deallocation can be done location independently. Resource Provisioner Module may receive metadata on CPU usage as well.

With this architecture, our aim in this study is to provide a tool that can prove the management of resources effectively. We argue that resource usage can change instantly or periodically. Estimation of periodic change and the implementation of a pay-as-you-go business model may be possible by analyzing log files of applications hosted in application virtualization environments.

Figure 1. Application software architecture

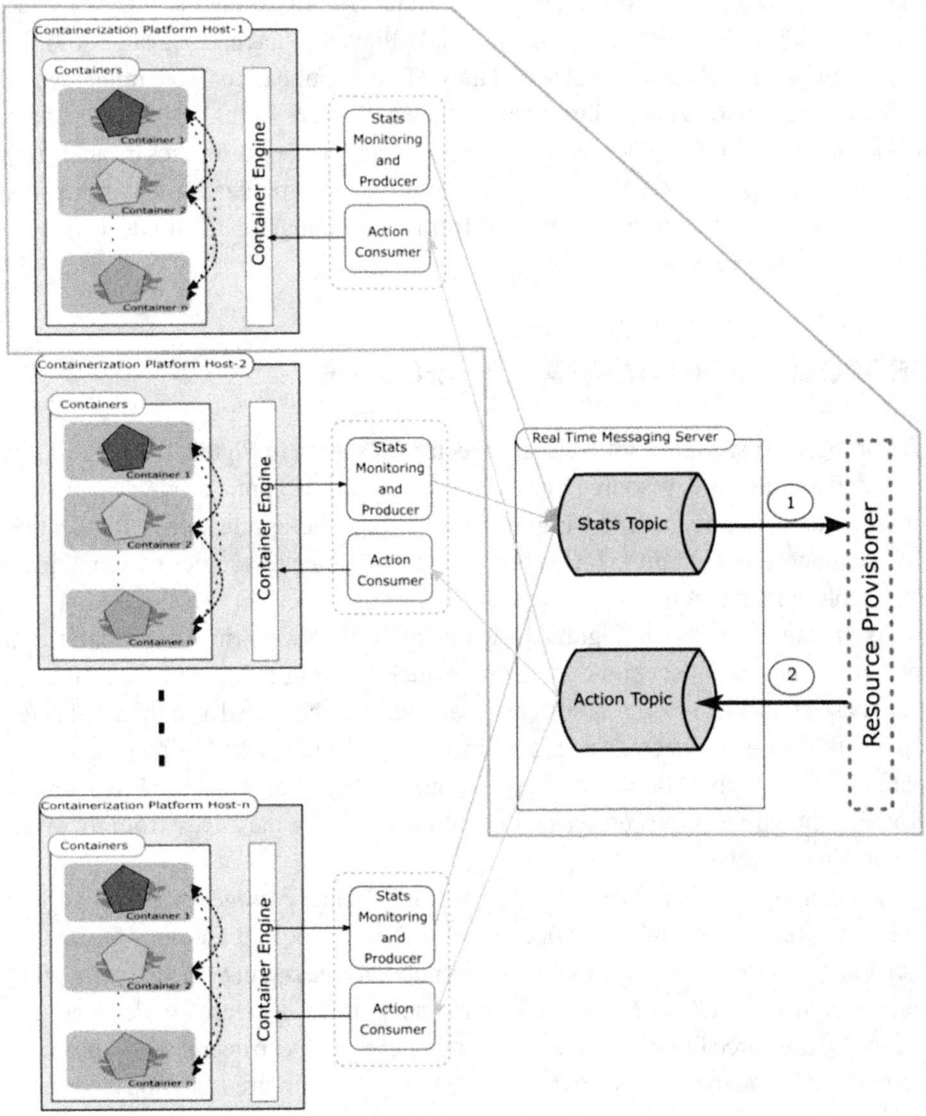

PROTOTYPE APPLICATION

The prototype application of the proposed architecture is discussed in this section. We show the Technologies used in the prototype application in Figure 2. As it is seen in Figure 2, Docker is preferred as an application virtualization environment.

Figure 2. Prototype application architecture

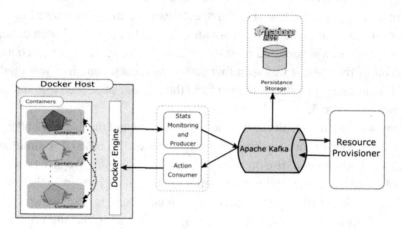

In order to provide communication, Apache Kafka is used as a pub-sub messaging service. Our application is run on Docker Containers which are hosted on Linux Operating System.

The prototype application provides a real-time provisioning system. To this end, performance measurement data (CPU usage, memory usage, band width usage, etc.) are collected from Docker containers; wrapped within JSON objects and sent to the Apache Kafka Server. The Resource Provisioner Module receives the messages via a topic on the Kafka Server. The Resource Provisioner Module decides on the auto-scaling action based on predefined rules and threshold values. In order to an auto-scale action to take place, a message is published to the corresponding topic on the Apache Kafka Server. Performance measurement data (Stats data) and auto-scaling action messages are published via two different Apache Kafka topic: Stats topic and Action topic, respectively. The stored messages on Apache Kafka are also stored on the Hadoop Distributed File System (HDFS).

PERFORMANCE EVALUATION

In this section, the performance tests of the prototype application and tests results are explained. The tests were done with hardware consists of 4-core CPU and 10 GB memory on a virtual machine running Linux Ubuntu 16.04 LTS operating system. Docker 18.03 version is used in the performance evaluation tests. The application running in the Docker container consumed 5 MB memory at the beginning of the test. If the running application inside Docker needed extra memory, Resource Provisioner requested 4 times (up to 80 MB) auto-scaling action to increase allocated memory. The same process was repeated by starting 2, 4, 8, 16 and 32 different containers. As a result of the tests, it was seen that on average, each container was updated 4 times. The number of started containers and the number of needed resource update are shown in Figure 3.

Figure 4 shows the results of the total update time and the average update time, when the number of auto-scaling updates increased. In case of 4 simultaneous updates; each resource update on average takes 0.21 seconds. We also observe that it takes 4.21 seconds to fully satisfy the amount of memory needed by the container. These results indicate that the times required for auto-scaling actions are negligible.

Figure 5 shows the results of a test where we investigated the effects of the resource requirements of containers. In the first test, the containers were started with insufficient memory (5MB) and the "Resource Provisioner" was not run. This test is shown with a gray curve in the graph presented in Figure 5. In the second test, as in the first test, containers were started with an in sufficient amount of memory (5MB) but this time Resource Provisioner test was run. This test result is presented in Figure 5 with the orange curve. Finally, the containers were started with a sufficient amount of memory (80MB). The final test is available in Figure 5 with a blue-colored curve. Consequently, as the number of containers working in the system and the

Figure 3. The number of started containers and the number of required resource update for container is illustrated

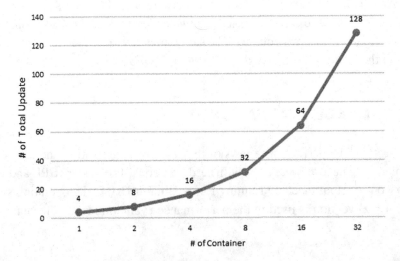

Figure 4. The number of started containers in the same time and total execution time is showed

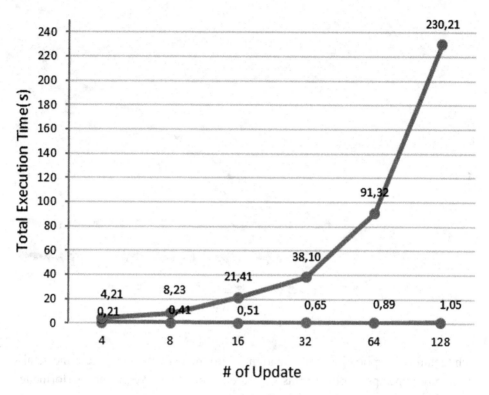

number of containers whose resources need to be updated increases, it is observed that the operation time of the Docker commands increased slightly. However, when container resources are insufficient and there is no resource provisioning system, the Docker commands run very slowly. Therefore, the resource provisioning system is not just for optimal utilization of resources. It is also necessary to prevent the Docker commands from slowing down.

CONCLUSION AND FUTURE STUDIES

Monitoring application virtualization environments for auto-scaling purposes have become an important requirement in today's computing world. In this book chapter, we introduce a design of a resource monitoring and management software

Figure 5. The effects of the source requirements of containers on the start time of new containers are presented

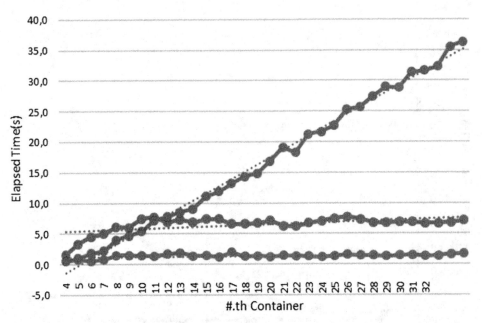

architecture for application virtualization environments. We also discuss the details of the prototype application of this software architecture. We present performance evaluations that were conducted to demonstrate the usability of the prototype application. As a result of these evaluations, we observe that auto-scaling functionality can be achieved with minimal processing overheads. Furthermore, we conclude that the most ideal approach for running the application virtualization environments is used pre-estimated threshold values for resource usages. In our future work, we plan to predict initial resource size allocated to application virtualization environment by analyzing log files by utilizing machine learning algorithms.

REFERENCES

Aderaldo, C. M., Mendonça, N. C., Pahl, C., & Jamshidi, P. (2017, May). Benchmark requirements for microservices architecture research. *Proceedings of the 1st International Workshop on Establishing the Community-Wide Infrastructure for Architecture-Based Software Engineering* (pp. 8-13). IEEE Press.

Aktas, M., Aydin, G., Donnellan, A., Fox, G., Granat, R., Lyzenga, G., & Rundle, J. (2005, June). Implementing geographical information system grid services to support computational geophysics in a service-oriented environment. Proceedings of the *NASA Earth-Sun System Technology Conference*. Adelphi, MD: University of Maryland.

Aktas, M. S. (2018). Hybrid cloud computing monitoring software architecture. Concurrency and Computation. *Practice and Experience, 30*(21), e4694.

Aktas, M. S., & Astekin, M. (2019). Provenance aware run-time verification of things for self-healing Internet of Things applications. *Concurrency and Computation, Practice and Experience, 31*(3), e4263.

Aktas, M. S., Aydin, G., Fox, G. C., Gadgil, H., Pierce, M., & Sayar, A. (2005, June). Information servicesforgrid/web service orientedarchitecture (soa) basedgeospatialapplications. *Proceedings of the 1st International Conference*, Beijing, China (pp. 27-29). Academic Press.

Aktas, M. S., Fox, G. C., & Pierce, M. (2005, November). Information services for dynamically assembled semantic grids. *Proceedings of the 2005 First International Conference on Semantics, Knowledge and Grid* (pp. 10-10). IEEE. 10.1109/SKG.2005.83

Aktas, M. S., Fox, G. C., & Pierce, M. (2007). Fault tolerant high performance Information Services for dynamic collections of Grid and Web services. *Future Generation Computer Systems, 23*(3), 317–337. doi:10.1016/j.future.2006.05.009

Aktas, M. S., Fox, G. C., Pierce, M., & Oh, S. (2008). Xml metadata services. Concurrency and Computation. *Practice and Experience, 20*(7), 801–823.

Aktas, M. S., & Pierce, M. (2010). High-performancehybridinformation service architecture. ConcurrencyandComputation. *PracticeandExperience, 22*(15), 2095–2123.

Armstrong, J. (2017, December 4). The Journey to 150,000 Containers at PayPal. Docker. Retrieved from https://blog.docker.com/2017/12/containers-at-paypal

Aydin, G., Aktas, M. S., Fox, G. C., Gadgil, H., Pierce, M., & Saya, A. (2005, November). SERVO Grid complexity computational environments (CCE) integrated performance analysis. *Proceedings of the 6th IEEE/ACM International Workshop on Grid Computing.* IEEE.

Aydin, G., Pierce, M., Fox, G., Aktas, M., & Sayar, A. (2004). Implementing GIS Grid Services for the International Solid Earth Research Virtual Observatory. *Pure and Applied Geophysics.*

Bernstein, D. (2014). Containers and cloud: From lxc to docker to kubernetes. *IEEE Cloud Computing, 1*(3), 81–84. doi:10.1109/MCC.2014.51

Chen, P., Plale, B., & Aktas, M. S. (2014). Temporal representation for mining scientific data provenance. *Future Generation Computer Systems, 36*, 363–378. doi:10.1016/j.future.2013.09.032

Dpkp. (2019). Dpkp/kafka-python. Retrieved from https://github.com/dpkp/kafka-python

Dragoni, N., Giallorenzo, S., Lafuente, A. L., Mazzara, M., Montesi, F., Mustafin, R., & Safina, L. (2017). Microservices: yesterday, today, and tomorrow. In *Present and ulterior software engineering* (pp. 195–216). Cham: Springer.

Dragoni, N., Lanese, I., Larsen, S. T., Mazzara, M., Mustafin, R., & Safina, L. (2017, June). Microservices: How to make your application scale. *Proceedings of the International Andrei Ershov Memorial Conference on Perspectives of System Informatics* (pp. 95-104). Springer, Cham.

Fox, G. C., Aktas, M. S., Aydin, G., Bulut, H., Pallickara, S., Pierce, M., & Zhai, G. (2006). Real time streamingdatagridapplications. In *Distributed Cooperative Laboratories: Networking, Instrumentation, and Measurements* (pp. 253–267). Boston, MA: Springer. doi:10.1007/0-387-30394-4_17

Fox, G. C., Aktas, M. S., Aydin, G., Gadgil, H., Pallickara, S., Pierce, M. E., & Sayar, A. (2009). Algorithms and the Grid. *Computing and visualization in science, 12*(3), 115-124.

Gupta, V., Kaur, K., & Kaur, S. (2017). Performance comparison between lightweight virtualization using docker and heavy weight virtualization. *Mar, 2*, 211-216.

Hoenisch, P., Weber, I., Schulte, S., Zhu, L., & Fekete, A. (2015, November). Four-foldauto-scaling on a contemporary deployment platform using docker containers. *Proceedings of the International Conference on Service-Oriented Computing* (pp. 316-323). Springer. 10.1007/978-3-662-48616-0_20

Kreps, J., Narkhede, N., & Rao, J. (2011, June). Kafka: A distributed messaging system for log processing. *Proceedings of the NetDB* (pp. 1-7). Academic Press.

Lewis, J., & Fowler, M. (2014). Microservices. Retrieved from https://martinfowler.com/-articles/microservices.html

Limit a container's resources. (2019, May 25). Docker. Retrieved from https://docs.docker.com/config/containers/resource_constraints

Merkel, D. (2014). Docker: lightweight linux containers for consistent development and deployment. *Linux Journal*, (239), 2.

Nacar, M. A., Aktas, M. S., Pierce, M., Lu, Z., Erlebacher, G., Kigelman, D., ... Yuen, D. A. (2007). VLab: collaborative Grid services and portals to support computational material science. Concurrency and Computation. *Practice and Experience*, *19*(12), 1717–1728.

Nardelli, M. (2017). Elastic Allocation of Docker Containers in Cloud Environments. In ZEUS (pp. 59-66). Academic Press.

Newman, S. (2015). *Building micro services: designing fine-grained systems*. O'Reilly Media, Inc.

Pierce, M. E., Fox, G. C., Aktas, M. S., Aydin, G., Gadgil, H., Qi, Z., & Sayar, A. (2008). The Quake Sim project: Web services for managing geophysical data and applications. In Earthquakes: Simulations, Sources and Tsunamis (pp. 635-651). Birkhäuser Basel.

Thein, K. M. M. (2014). Apache kafka: Next generation distributed messaging system. *International Journal of Scientific Engineering and Technology Research*, *3*(47), 9478–9483.

Chapter 9
Big Data–Based Spectrum Sensing for Cognitive Radio Networks Using Artificial Intelligence

Suriya Murugan
KPR Institute of Engineering and Technology, India

Sumithra M. G.
KPR Institute of Engineering and Technology, India

ABSTRACT

Cognitive radio has emerged as a promising candidate solution to improve spectrum utilization in next generation wireless networks. Spectrum sensing is one of the main challenges encountered by cognitive radio and the application of big data is a powerful way to solve various problems. However, for the increasingly tense spectrum resources, the prediction of cognitive radio based on big data is an inevitable trend. The signal data from various sources is analyzed using the big data cognitive radio framework and efficient data analytics can be performed using different types of machine learning techniques. This chapter analyses the process of spectrum sensing in cognitive radio, the challenges to process spectrum data and need for dynamic machine learning algorithms in decision making process.

DOI: 10.4018/978-1-5225-9750-6.ch009

INTRODUCTION

The radio spectrum is a valuable and strictly regulated resource for wireless communications. With the proliferation of wireless services, the demand for the radio spectrum is constantly increasing, leading to contention of spectrum resources. Recently, standardization activities have concerned the re-use of the spectrum unused or underutilized by digital TV signals, the so-called TV white space, by exploiting it to extend the coverage of Wi-Fi signals with the IEEE 802.11af standard. A fundamental task in the development of cognitive radio is the spectrum sensing, which allows individuating specific usage patterns in the various dimensions (time, frequency, space, angle, etc.), useful to exploit free spectrum.

Since continuous spectrum sensing is a very demanding task for a wireless device, we propose the introduction of a monitoring platform that makes spectrum sensing available as a service. This service consists of a number of geographically distributed spectrum sensors, implemented through software defined radio (SDR), which carry out the sensing operation and report results to a storage and computing platform, whose task is to disseminate its available data to any requesting device. Although this service cannot completely eliminate the need of spectrum sensing by the wireless terminals, it can be extremely effective for instructing mobile devices to carry out the sensing only where it is expected to find unused radio bands, thus achieving improvements in terms of energy consumption and stand-by times extension.

A cognitive radio has the potential to learn and adapt to its operating environment without intervention from human operators. Current space networks are manually configured. The Cognitive networks and cognitive radios have received a lot of attention due to their promised feature of autonomy, cost, and scalability. Adaptive radio software could circumvent the harmful effects of space weather, increasing science and exploration data returns. A cognitive radio network could also suggest alternate data paths to the ground. These processes could prioritise and route data through multiple paths simultaneously to avoid interference. The cognitive radio's artificial intelligence could also allocate ground station downlinks just hours in advance, as opposed to weeks, leading to more efficient scheduling. Cognitive radio may make communications network operations more efficient by decreasing the need for human intervention. An intelligent radio could adapt to new electromagnetic landscapes without human help and predict common operational settings for different environments, automating time-consuming processes previously handled by humans.

Traditional radio spectrum sensing technologies usually detect the target channel through certain sensor devices in real time or sends inquiring information to the target channel to obtain the target channel state by obtaining the feedback. When it is detected that the channel is free, the secondary user is allowed to access at this moment, otherwise, keeping detection and not accessed. On the one hand, the shortcomings of these technologies are not good enough at real time which will affect the communication rate; on the other hand, when the secondary users are accessing which detect the access of the primary users, signals, the exit of the secondary users may be inevitably collide with the primary users which will interfere with primary users signals. Using the spectrum sensing prediction based on big data can look for a certain regularity of the access of primary users to make full preparation before the access and exit of secondary users and combine with the traditional detection methods to make full use of the channels, free state in the spectrum sensing process and it will be not easy to cause interference for the primary users signals.

LITERATURE SURVEY

In Huang, Wang, Bai et al. (2018) describe the standardization process of the fifth generation (5G) of wireless communications has recently been accelerated. The increasing of enormous smartphones, new complex scenarios, large frequency bands, massive antenna elements, and dense small cells will generate big datasets and bring 5G communications to the era of big data. Authors investigated various applications of big data analytics, especially machine learning algorithms in wireless communications and channel modelling and proposed a big data and machine learning enabled wireless channel model framework.

Omar (2015) explained at the time of interruption, sensing the nearby free channels and switching to them will take some time, hence the ongoing data will be interrupted, which will delay the data transmission. To minimize this delay, creating cache of the SU signal at multiple nodes in a cluster has shown significant improvement in reducing the transmission delay if cache placement is done systematically. This systematic and accurate placement of cache is possible if the data accumulated is accessed and processed quickly. Taking into account the vastness of cluster networks, a huge amount of data will be required to be accessed and processed. Cognitive Radio networks are very complex structures when it comes to the information sharing amongst the secondary users and with the cluster head. Taking into account, whether unlicensed users share their information with other secondary users, and in case if they do, how much proportion of it they allow the fusion center to process, several big data scenarios exist. Author proposed the possible information sharing scenarios in cognitive radio network systems and their possible Big Data solutions.

Du, Wang, Xia et al. (2018) suggested with the popularity of smart devices and the widespread use of machine learning methods, edge computing have become the mainstream of dealing with wireless big data. When smart edge nodes use machine learning models to analyze wireless big data, nevertheless, some models may unintentionally store a small portion of the training data with sensitive records. Thus, intruders can expose sensitive information by careful analysis of this model. To solve this issue, they proposed and implemented a machine learning strategy for smart edge nodes using differential privacy. And they focused on privacy protection in training datasets in wireless big data scenario.

Baruffa, Femminella, Pergolesi et al. (2018) proposed that a crucial requirement for future cognitive radio networks is the wideband spectrum sensing, which allows detecting spectral opportunities across a wide frequency range. On the other hand, the Internet of Things concept has revolutionized the usage of sensors and of the relevant data. Connecting sensors to cloud computing infrastructure enables the so-called paradigm of Sensing as a Service (S2aaS). They suggested an S2aaS architecture to offer the Spectrum Sensing as a Service (S3aaS), by exploiting the flexibility of software defined radio. They analyze the connectivity requirements between the sensors and the processing platform, and evaluate the trade-offs between required bandwidth and target service delay.

Zhang, Yang, Chen et al. (2019) explains that Big Data feature learning is a crucial issue for the service management for Internet of Things. However, big data collected from Internet of Things is of dynamic nature at a high speed, which poses an important challenge on wireless big data learning models, especially the deep computation model. In this paper, an incremental deep computation model is proposed for wireless big data feature learning in Internet of Things. They presented a model that can modify the network in an incremental manner for new arriving data learning efficiently with preserving the prior knowledge for the previous data learning, proving its potential for dynamic wireless big data learning in Internet of Things.

MACHINE LEARNING APPROACHES FOR CR BASED ON BIG DATA

Regarding spectrum detection and allocation, many different approaches have been utilized such as machine learning, artificial intelligence, model prediction, fuzzy logic reasoning, greedy search, and dynamic programming. As for machine learning, the system first learns the pattern of the object through the training samples, then the system can perform the operation on the data which is not encountered before.

A contemporary technique is to combine machine learning and game-theoretic methods. Since the over complexity of the selected model may lead to overfitting, there is a need to adaptively learn the situation when other users try to access the system. In the scenario of opportunistic spectrum access, it is aimed to find the spectrum holes to transmit the signal without interference the primary users.

The cognitive radio based on big data refers to building a radio environment map based this large radio database and looking for effective information to complete the forecast target. The main methods are related analysis, classification analysis, cluster analysis and anomaly detection, etc.

Based on the survey it is observed that, some common machine learning algorithms are used widely for big data wireless computing use cases and they are:

1. **Linear Regression** is a statistical method to regress the data with dependent variable having continuous values whereas independent variables can have either continuous or categorical values. In other words, "Linear Regression" is a method to predict dependent variable (Y) based on values of independent variables (X). It can be used for the cases where we want to predict some continuous quantity.

2. *K*-**means** clustering is a type of unsupervised learning, which is used when you have unlabeled data (i.e., data without defined categories or groups). The goal of this algorithm is to find groups in the data, with the number of groups represented by the variable K. The algorithm works iteratively to assign each data point to one of K groups based on the features that are provided. Data points are clustered based on feature similarity.

3. **K-Neighrest Neighbour (k-NN)** is non-parametric, which means that it does not make any assumptions about the probability distribution of the input. This is useful for applications with input properties that are unknown and therefore makes k-NN more robust than algorithms that are parametric. The contrast is that parametric machine learning algorithms tend to produce fewer errors than non-parametric ones, since taking input probabilities into account can influence decision making. k-nearest neighbors can be used in classification or regression machine learning tasks.

4. **Naive Bayesian classifier** is based on Bayes' theorem with the independence assumptions between predictors. A Naive Bayesian model is easy to build, with no complicated iterative parameter estimation which makes it particularly useful for very large datasets. Despite its simplicity, the Naive Bayesian classifier often does surprisingly well and is widely used because it often outperforms more sophisticated classification methods.

5. A **Support Vector Machine (SVM)** is a supervised machine learning algorithm that can be employed for both classification and regression purposes. Each data item is plotted as a point in n-dimensional space (where n is number of features you have) with the value of each feature being the value of a particular coordinate. Then classification is performed by finding the hyper-plane that differentiate the two classes.

6. **Neural Networks (NN)** are parallel and distributed information processing systems that are inspired and derived from biological learning systems such as human brains. The architecture of neural networks consists of a network of nonlinear information processing elements that are normally arranged in layers and executed in parallel. This supervised learning algorithm is often referred to as a back-propagation algorithm, which is useful for training multiple-layer preceptron neural networks (MLPs).

7. **Anomaly detection** is referred to the identification of items or events that do not conform to an expected pattern or to other items present in a dataset. Anomaly detection can be a key for solving intrusions, as while detecting anomalies, perturbations of normal behaviour indicate a presence of intended or unintended induced attacks, defects, faults, and so on. Machine learning for anomaly detection includes techniques that provide a promising alternative for detection and classification of anomalies based on an initially large set of features.

BIG DATA SPECTRUM

Big Spectrum Data refers to massive and complex spectrum data that can't be processed or analyzed using traditional systems and tools. It Sun, H., Chen, C., Ling, Y., Huang, J., & Lin, X. (2018) refers to all the data that are related to radio environment awareness, mainly including:

- Radio spectrum state data (idle or busy, signal energy levels, signal features, etc) in the time, space and frequency dimensions.
- User or device data, e.g., device ID, device capability, user spectrum requirement and user feedback, etc.
- Environment side information, e.g., terrain data, meteorologic and hydrographic data, etc.

It's characterized by six keywords: volume, variety, velocity, veracity, viability and value.

Volume

It refers to the mass quantities of spectrum data that are used to improve decision-making for better radio spectrum utilization. The sheer volume of spectrum data being stored and processed is exploding at an unprecedented rate, which is mainly driven by the need to gain a full understanding of radio spectrum dynamics. The volume of spectrum state data grows with the time duration, the frequency range, and the spatial scale of interest, as well as the corresponding resolution in each dimension.

Value

The value of Big Spectrum Data covers following aspects:

1. **Spectrum modelling**: This depends highly on extensive spectrum measurement data, reflects spectrum usage patterns in the time, space and frequency dimensions, and serves as the cornerstone for the analysis, design and simulation of cognitive wireless networks.

2. **Spectrum prediction**: It infers unknown spectrum state from known spectrum data, by effectively exploiting the statistical correlations extracted from Big Spectrum Data. Accurate spectrum prediction can enable efficient spectrum usage by looking into the future. Just as Amazon has used huge records of consumers' historical behaviours to successfully predict their future preferences, accurate spectrum prediction is also possible since many real world spectrum measurements have revealed that radio spectrum usage is not completely random, actually, correlations exists across time slots, frequency bands, and locations.

3. **Spectrum management**: It is known that the current radio spectrum scarcity problem actually results from static and inflexible spectrum licensing and allocation policies, rather than the physical scarcity of usable radio frequencies. With Big Spectrum Data, both real time and statistical information on spectrum usage in a much finer granularity can be obtained, which makes spectrum management much more flexible by performing dynamic spectrum assignment and smart interference management to improve spectrum utilization.

Variety

Spectrum data are also of heterogeneous types. Besides the traditional structured data suitable for database systems, the emergence of semi-structured and unstructured spectrum data create new challenges. For example, spectrum data are generally labeled with geo-spatial and temporal lags, creating challenges in maintaining coherence across spatial scales and time.

Veracity

Veracity refers to quality of spectrum data. We include veracity as the fourth key characteristic of Big Spectrum Data to emphasize the importance of addressing and managing the uncertainty on spectrum data quality. The key idea is that no spectrum data exists in isolation, and there are correlations between each data and its neighbours in time, frequency, and space dimensions. By properly exploiting these correlations, either explicitly or implicitly, the uncertainty can be reduced or the quality of spectrum data can be improved. One way to achieve this is through data fusion, where combining multiple spectrum data from less reliable sources creates a more accurate and useful data. Another way is through data filtering, where abnormal spectrum data are filtered out by comparing the differences or divergences among Big Spectrum Data. Other ways include data cleansing, data completion, and data recovery, etc.

Viability

Viability guides the selection of the attributes and factors that are most likely to predict outcomes that matter most to the value of Big Spectrum Data. For instance, to build a radio propagation predictive model from Big Spectrum Data, we're not simply collecting a large number of records, actually, we're collecting multidimensional data that spans a broadening array of variables.

Velocity

Velocity impacts latency is the lag time between when spectrum data are captured and when decisions based on them are made. Today, spectrum data is continually being generated at such a speed that it is more and more difficult for traditional systems to handle in time. Some delay tolerant tasks, such as statistical spectrum modeling of radio spectrum usage, can possibly be performed in an off-line manner using batch algorithms. However, for time-sensitive processes such as spectrum prediction, the shelf life of spectrum data is short, which must be analyzed in real-time to be of value for decision-making, in which case online or incremental processing techniques on Big Spectrum Data are urgently needed.

ML BASED SENSING FOR COGNITIVE BIG SPECTRUM DATA

The area of spectrum sensing Lu, Li, Chen et al. (2017) has become progressively significant as CR is being used in applications. In many areas CR systems coexist with other radio systems without causing undue interference to existing systems. When spectrum sensing occupancy is considered, the cognitive radio system must accommodate a range of considerations:

- **Continuous Spectrum Sensing:** It is mandatory for the CR system to constantly sense the spectrum occupancy. Normally PU in a CR network on a non-interference basis and sensing of the spectrum when PU returns during spectrum sensing.
- **Monitor for Alternative Empty Spectrum:** if the PU returns to the spectrum being used, then an alternative space needs to be allocated for existing SU.
- **Monitor Type of Transmission:** The CR system should find the PU transmission type and sense the received signal. When this is done, the false transmissions and intrusion are ignored.

The Baruffa, Femminella, Pergolesi et al. (2018) cognitive big data spectrum sensing environment is illustrated in Figure 1, where each node can conduct its own spectrum sensing. As a sequence of signal is achieved, the fog node conducts feature extraction, anomaly detection, and decision making. The feature extraction includes waveform-based sensing, energy sensing, radio identification, cyclostationarity based sensing, and match filtering. All extracted features are used to determine the existence of spectrum and allocate the spectrum for the transmitting signals. Based on the computation capability of each node, different types of machine learning methods stated above can be incorporated.

Energy Detector

Energy detector-based sensing is the most widely used spectrum sensing algorithm due to its low computational complexity. Another advantage of energy assessment is that the energy detector is developed based on the assumption that receivers need no prior information of the primary user signals, which makes this sensing technique much more practical as compared to other existing approaches.

Basic assumptions used in energy detection are noise is statistically stationary and detector is aware of noise power. Energy detector though it is simple has limitation in detection performance compared to other detectors.

Bayesian detector can be also utilized for detection. The received signal is assumed as in equ [1]

$$(n) = hx(n) + w(n) \tag{1}$$

where $y(n)$ is the received signal, h is the channel coefficient, $x(n)$ is the primary user's signal to be detected, $w(n)$ is the additive white Gaussian noise (AWGN), and n is the sample index.

The performance of the energy detector (probability of false alarm and detection) depends on noise power, signal power and detection time. Under ideal operating conditions, the energy detector can achieve arbitrary detection performance by increasing the detection time. The output of the detector is compared to a decision threshold to achieve different detection performance reflecting different design approaches.

Waveform-Based Sensing

In waveform based detectors, correlation is performed to detect a prior known signal or sequence expected within the PU signal. In Murugan, S., & Sumithra M. G. (2019) communication systems pre-known patterns are used for synchronization, signal detection and other purposes. Sensing can is performed by correlating the observed signal with the known pattern/sequence to detect the presence of a PU signal exhibiting this pattern.

In general, waveform detectors have better detection performance. Also they require lesser detection time over the energy detector. Synchronization errors can severely degrade detection performance as synchronization between the PU signal and detector is required.

The waveform-based sensing metric is written as in Equation 2.

$$M = \left[\sum_{n=1}^{N} y\left(n\right) x * \left(n\right)\right] \tag{2}$$

where $*$ denotes the conjugate operation.

When primary user signal presents on the spectrum then it is denoted as in Equation 3

$$M = h\sum_{n=1}^{N} \left|x\left(n\right)\right|^{2} + \sum_{n=1}^{N} w\left(n\right) x * \left(n\right) \tag{3}$$

When primary user signal is absent then it is denoted as in equ[4]

$$M = \sum_{n=1}^{N} w\left(n\right) x * \left(n\right) \tag{4}$$

Similarly, a threshold value needs to be set in the system to make spectrum occupancy decision.

Cyclostationarity-Based Sensing

Cyclostationary-based detectors detect the cyclostationary signatures and features that are unique in PU signal. A signal is said to be cyclostationary if the signal's statistics such as the mean and autocorrelation are periodic with time. Communication systems signals typically have induced cyclostationary features because information data is often modulated onto periodic carriers which are cyclostationary in nature. Cyclostationary features Suriya, M., & Sumithra, M. G. (2018). can also be artificially introduced to assist signal detection. The detection is based on the cyclic spectral density and is able to separate PU signal from noise due to the fact that while noise has little correlation hence its cyclic spectral density is weak.

The cyclic spectral density function of a received signal is written as

$$S\left(f,\alpha\right) = \sum_{\tau=-\infty}^{\infty} R_{y}^{\alpha}\left(\tau\right) e^{-j^{2}\pi a n} \tag{5}$$

where α is the cyclic frequency, and R_{y}^{α} is the cyclic autocorrelation function, which can be written as

$$R_y^\alpha\left(\tau\right) = E\left[y\left(n+\tau\right)y*\left(n-\tau\right)e^{j^2\pi\alpha n}\right] \tag{6}$$

When the cyclic frequency α equals the frequency of transmitted signal (n), the output of (5) reaches the peak value.

Feature Detection Sensing

Since primary user signal usually has its unique transmission pattern such as modulation scheme, carrier frequency, bandwidth, etc.; feature detection and machine learning algorithms can also be applied for spectrum sensing. This category of sensing techniques usually uses data-driven model rather than physical model to differentiate the primary user signal from the secondary user signal and noise. In this work, all types of features extracted by feature detection sensing are sent to the machine learning engine to make the decision on spectrum access.

MACHINE LEARNING PROCESS FROM BIG SPECTRUM DATA

Intelligence capabilities will be of paramount importance in the development of future wireless communication systems to allow them observe, learn and respond to its complex and dynamic operating environment. For wireless networks ML algorithms may play a key role in automatically classifying wireless signals as a step towards intelligent spectrum access and management schemes and its cycle of processing is illustrated in Figure 1.

- **Data Acquisition**: Data is a key asset in the design of future intelligent wireless networks. In order to obtain spectrum data, the radio first senses its environment by collecting raw data from various spectrum bands. The raw data consist of n samples, stacked into data vectors rk which represent

Figure 1. Application of Machine Learning to Big spectrum data

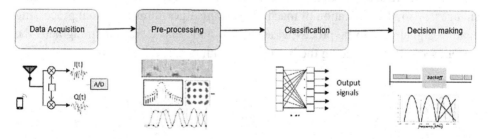

the complex envelope of the received wireless signal. These data vectors are the input for end-to-end learning to obtain models that can reason about the presence of wireless signals.

- **Data Pre-processing**: Data pre-processing is concerned with the analysis and manipulation of the collected spectrum data with the aim to arrive at potentially good wireless data representations. The raw samples organized into data vectors rk in the previous block are pipelined as input for signal processing (SP) tools that analyze, process and transform the data to arrive at simple data representations such as frequency, amplitude, phase and spectrum, or more complex features xk such as e.g. cyclostationary features. In addition, feature learning such as deep learning may be utilized to automatically extract more low-level and high-level features. In many ML applications the choice of features is just as important, if not more important than the choice of the ML algorithm.

- **Classification:** The "Classification" processing block enables intelligence capabilities to assess the environmental radio context by detecting the presence of wireless signals. This may be the type of the emitters that are utilizing the spectrum (spectrum access scheme, modulation format, wireless technology, etc.), type of interference, detecting an available spectrum band, etc. This process as spectrum learning.

- **Decision**: The predictions calculated by the ML model are used as input for the decision module. In a CR application, a decision may be related to the best transmission strategy (e.g. frequency band or transmission power) that will maximize the data rate without causing interference to other users. This process is called spectrum decision.

CONCLUSION

This chapter proposed that depending on the computational capabilities of the cognitive intelligent nodes, different features and machine learning techniques can be applied to optimize the process of spectrum allocation. Big data analytics makes the system more adaptive to the local environment and robust to dynamic spectrum changes. Also, the utilization of machine learning algorithms for signal processing enables signal data to be processed at the CR node and it further strengthens the system security by reducing the burden of communications network.

REFERENCES

Baruffa, G., Femminella, M., Pergolesi, M., & Reali, G. (2018). A Big Data architecture for spectrum monitoring in cognitive radio applications. *Annales des Télécommunications*, *73*(7-8), 451–461. doi:10.100712243-018-0642-7

Baruffa, G., Femminella, M., Pergolesi, M., & Reali, G. (2018). A Big Data architecture for spectrum monitoring in cognitive radio applications. *Annales des Télécommunications*, *73*(7-8), 451–461. doi:10.100712243-018-0642-7

Du, M., Wang, K., Xia, Z., & Zhang, Y. (2018). Differential privacy preserving of training model in wireless Big Data with edge computing. *IEEE Transactions on Big Data*. doi:10.1109/tbdata.2018.2829886

Huang, J., Wang, C.-X., Bai, L., Sun, J., Yang, Y., Li, J., Zhou, M. (2018). A Big Data Enabled Channel Model for 5G Wireless Communication Systems. *IEEE Transactions on Big Data*. doi:10.1109/tbdata.2018.2884489

Lu, J., Li, L., Chen, G., Shen, D., Pham, K., & Blasch, E. (2017). Machine learning based Intelligent cognitive network using fog computing. *Sensors and Systems for Space Applications*, *X*. doi:10.1117/12.2266563

Murugan, S., & Sumithra M. G. (2019). Efficient Space Communication and Management (SCOaM) Using Cognitive Radio Networks Based on Deep Learning Techniques. In *Cognitive Social Mining Applications in Data Analytics and Forensics* (pp. 65–76). Hershey, PA: IGI Global. doi:. doi:10.4018/978-1-5225-7522-1.ch004

Omar, A. (2015). Improving Data Extraction Efficiency of Cache Nodes in Cognitive Radio Networks Using Big Data Analysis. *Proceedings of the 9th International Conference on Next Generation Mobile Applications, Services and Technologies*. Academic Press. 10.1109/NGMAST.2015.15

Sun, H., Chen, C., Ling, Y., Huang, J., & Lin, X. (2018). The Study of Cognitive Radio Prediction Based on Big Data. *Proceedings of the 2018 International Conference on Mechanical, Electronic, Control and Automation Engineering (MECAE 2018)*. Academic Press. 10.2991/mecae-18.2018.70

Suriya, M., & Sumithra, M. G. (2019). Efficient Evolutionary Techniques for Wireless Body Area Using Cognitive Radio Networks. In *Computational Intelligence and Sustainable Systems* (pp. 61–70). Springer.

Zhang, Q., Yang, L. T., Chen, Z., & Li, P. (2019). Incremental Deep Computation Model for Wireless Big Data Feature Learning. *IEEE Transactions on Big Data*. doi:10.1109/tbdata.2019.2903092

Chapter 10
Big Data Analytics in the Healthcare Industry:
An Analysis of Healthcare Applications in Machine Learning With Big Data Analytics

Arulkumar Varatharajan
Computer Science and Engineering, Sri Krishna College of Engineering and Technology, Coimbatore, India

Selvan C.
National Institute of Technology, Tiruchirappalli, India

Vimalkumar Varatharajan
Cognizant Technology Solutions, Coimbatore, India

ABSTRACT

Big Data has changed the way we manage, analyze and impact the data information in any industry. A champion among the most promising zones where it will, in general, be associated with takeoff progress is therapeutic medicinal administrations. Administration examinations can diminish costs of treatment, foresee flare-ups of pestilences, keep up a key separation from preventable diseases and improve individual fulfillment overall. The chapter depicts the beginning field of a huge information investigation in human services, talks about the advantages, diagrams a design structure and approach, portrays models revealed in the writing, quickly examines the difficulties, and offers ends. A continuous examination which targets the utilization of tremendous volumes of remedial data information while combining multimodal data information from various sources is discussed. Potential locales of research inside this field which can give noteworthy impact on medicinal administrations movement are in like manner dissected.

DOI: 10.4018/978-1-5225-9750-6.ch010

INTRODUCTION

The idea of Big Data is no longer new and it continues to advance progressively. Various activities that describe the big data information depict that it as a collection of data information segments whose measure, speed, type, or potentially multifaceted nature anticipate that one should search for, embrace, and devise new gear and programming frameworks to successfully store, separate, and conceive the data information (Yang, Li, & Wang, 2015). These models for redid, perceptive, participatory and preventive remedy rely upon the use of electronic wellbeing records (EHRs) and huge proportions of complex biomedical data information and high bore – omics data information (Yang, Li, & Wang, 2015).

Contemporarily genomics and post-genomics improvements define significant proportions of big data information about complex biochemical and authoritative methodologies in the living structures (Kankanhalli et al., 2016). This genomics data information are heterogeneous, and as often as possible, they are secured in different data information groups. Like these genomics data information, the EHRs data information are also in form of various heterogeneous designs. The EHRs data information can be sorted out, semi-composed or unstructured; discrete or continuous.

Human managements are a prime instance of how the three data information, (speed and age of data information), variety, and volume (Wang et al., 2017), form a characteristic piece of the data information produced. This data information is spread among different human administrations systems, prosperity wellbeing net suppliers, masters, government components, and so on. Moreover, all of these data information vaults are soloed and inherently unequipped to define the phase of the overall data information truthfulness.

Welfare contexts that would like to exploit ongoing advances in information investigation, for example, the blossoming capacities of AI, should begin considering building up a center guide that will turn into an information first association, the group said. To add to the three Vs, the veracity of healthcare data information is likewise basic for its important use towards creating translational research. 66% of the data would be achieved by reducing US restorative administrations utilization (Li & Liang, 2017). Obvious approaches to manage restorative researches have generally revolved around the examination of disease states subject to the alterations in physiology, which is a key point of view around the specific procedure of data information (Desjardins, Crawford, & Good, 2009). Nevertheless, managing and understanding ailments is essential whereby investigation at this measurement calms the assortment and interconnectedness that portray the authentic concealed remedial instruments (Chen, Sha & Zhang, 2015).

In reference to the resourceful sloth, the field of medicine has begun to conform to the present propelled data information age. New advances make it possible to get massive proportions of data information about each individual patient over a huge timescale. Nevertheless, regardless of the methodology of therapeutic devices, the data information got from these patients has remained perpetually underutilized. The social protection industry evidently has made a ton of data information, driven by record keeping, consistence and authoritative requirements, including the patient's thought. While most data information is secured in printed edition structure, the present example is toward quick digitization of these great deals of data information (Jin, Deyu & Yi, 2011). Driven by mandatory necessities and the likelihood to improve the idea of social protection movement while decreasing the costs, these immense measures of data information (known as 'large data information') hold the assurance of supporting a wide extent of restorative and therapeutic administrations limits, including other clinical decision help, affliction perception, and aspects related to the prosperity of people.

In this paper, three domains of big data examination in medicine are analyzed (Arulkumar & Vivekanandan, 2014). These three areas do not totally reflect on the use of big data examination in prescription; rather, they are intended to give a perspective of an understood zone of research where the thoughts of big data examination are presently being connected. The rest of the paper is created as follows. Related work is portrayed in the second section. Section 3 depicts the traits of huge data, while huge data examination is portrayed in the subsequent sections. The accompanying portion explains some potential issues about big data analysis and methodologies, while big data assurance and security are delineated in Section 6. The last section wraps up this paper with discourse for further research.

IMAGE PROCESSING DIAGNOSIS AND THERAPY ASSESSMENT AND PLANNING

Medicinal images form a critical wellspring of data information used for examination, treatment evaluation and orchestrating (Hou, et al., 2016). Figured tomography (CT), fascinating resonation imaging (MRI), X-beam, atomic imaging, ultrasound, photograph acoustic imaging, fluoroscopy, positron discharge tomography-registered tomography (PET-CT), and mammography, include the cases of imaging strategies that are settled in clinical settings.

MEDICAL SIGNAL PROCESSING

The medical signal presents volume and speed deterrents especially for relentless and high objectives in establishing countless screens related with each patient. Regardless of the data information size issues, the medical signal presents unconventionality of a spatiotemporal sort. Examination of the physiological sign is continuously noteworthy when evaluating nearby situational settings, which ought to be embedded into the improvement of constant insightful systems to ensure its practicality and quality.

Presently, social insurance frameworks utilize various unique and nonstop observing gadgets that use particular physiological waveform information or discredited essential data to provide potential instruments in case of an occurrence of unmistakable occasions (Adil, Kar & Jangir, 2015). Nonetheless, such uncompounded philosophies towards progress and execution of alert structures will when all is said in done be conflicting and their sheer numbers could cause "ready exhaustion" for both parental figures and patients.

NEED FOR BIG DATA ANALYTICS IN HEALTHCARE

Huge prerequisite for big data in social protection likewise, on account of expanding costs in nations like the United States. As a McKinsey report states, "After more than 20 years of suffering extends, medicinal administrations costs by and by address

Figure 1. Medical Image processing hierarchies

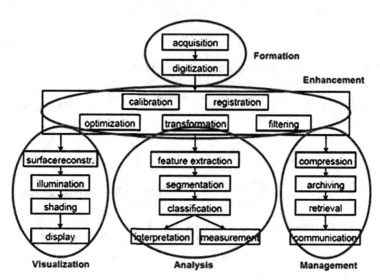

17.6 percent of GDP — nearly $600 billion more than the ordinary benchmark for a nation of the United States' size and riches (Jangade & Chauhan, 2016). "Obviously, we need some keen, data information driven thinking around there. Additionally, current driving forces are evolving as well: various protection organizations are changing from charge for-organization plans (which reward using expensive and all over unnecessary meds and treating a great deal of patients quickly) to plans that sort out calm results Wellbeing data information volume is depended upon to grow definitely in the years ahead.

Moreover, social protection reimbursement models are changing; noteworthy use and pay for implementation are acting as fundamental new factors in the present human administrations condition. Nevertheless, the way in which an advantage is not fundamentally flash makes it importantly huge for social protection relationships to pick up the available instruments, structure, and frameworks to utilize enormous data information effectively or risk the danger of losing countless dollars in salary and advantages.

Advantages to Healthcare

- Research and advancement
- Public wellbeing
- Clinical activities
- Evidence-based medication
- Genomic examination
- Pre-mediation extortion investigation
- Device/remote checking

Figure 2. Big Data Analytics in healthcare ecosystem

Figure 3. Measures of Big Data Challenges

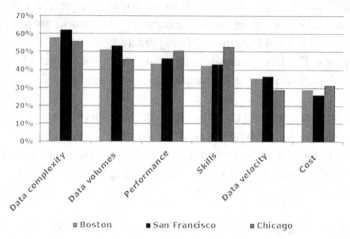

What are the Biggest Challenges in Big Data Analytics?

BIG DATA ANALYTICS CHALLENGES

Some troublesome issues should be considered. Gaining high-throughput – omics data information is appended to the cost of preliminary estimations. Concerning heterogeneity of the data information sources, the confusion of the preliminary – omics data information and the variety of the exploratory methodology, environmental conditions, and organic nature should be considered, before the joining of this heterogeneous data information and before using of the data mining methods (Hussain & Lee, 2015). Different data mining methods can be associated on these heterogeneous biomedical instructive files, for instance, irregularity disclosure, clustering, grouping; connection administers simply like rundown and portrayal of those enormous enlightening accumulations.

The clearest test related with huge data information is essentially securing and researching such information. In its Digital Universe report, IDC checks that the proportion of information set away on the planet's IT systems is increasing about at ordinary interims. By 2020, the total aggregate will be adequate to fill a heap of tablets that ranges from the earth to the moon 6.6 events. Also, adventures have obligation or hazard for around 85 percent of that data information. On the administration and investigation side, undertakings are utilizing devices like NoSQL databases, Hadoop, Spark, big information examination programming, business knowledge applications, computerized reasoning and AI to enable them to go over their big information stores to discover the experiences their organizations need (Arulkumar & Selvayinayagam, 2012).

Here is a short rundown of difficulties and openings in Big Data Analytics-

Moderate framework advancement: There is a gigantic interest supply hole in light of the fact that the rate of increment in information is route quicker than the handling frameworks that are set up. These capacity frameworks are not competent enough to store the kind of information being created.

Time confines: The Big Data expert needs to process the information in a given timeframe on the grounds that after certain time the estimation of the information diminishes.

In order to make, direct and run those applications that produce bits of learning, affiliations need specialists with enormous data information aptitudes. That has driven up enthusiasm for enormous data information masters — and huge data pay rates have extended definitely accordingly (Liu, Wang & Chen, 2015).

PRIVACY AND SECURITY IN BIG DATA ANALYTICS

Two critical issues towards huge data in human administrations and drug are security and assurance of the general population/patients.

A scenario: While the snowball of big information is surging down a mountain picking up speed and volume, organizations are endeavoring to stay aware of it. What's more, down they go, totally neglecting to put on veils, head protectors, gloves and once in a while even skis. Without these, it's horrendously simple to never make it down in one piece. What's more, putting on all the safeguard measures at a fast can be past the point of no return or excessively troublesome (Rallapalli & Gondkar, 2016).

Furthermore, shown in the figure 4, as 'astounding' for what it's worth, practically all security difficulties of big information originate from the way that it is big. Extremely big.

Issues with security present genuine dangers to any framework, which is the reason it's pivotal to know your holes. Here, our big information counseling specialists spread the most horrible security challenges that big information has available. Considering Big Data there is a ton of peril zones that ought to be considered. These fuse the data information lifecycle (provenance, ownership, and request of data information), the data information creation and social affair process, and the nonappearance of security frameworks. Finally, the Big Data security objectives are equivalent to some other data information types – to ensure its protection, uprightness, and availability (Jee & Kim, 2013).

Figure 4. Security challenges of big data scenario

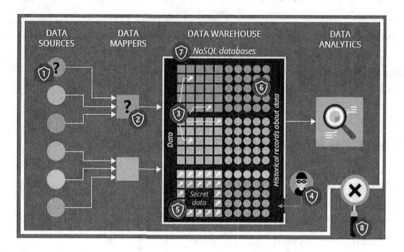

Figure 5. Big Data's 5 V's – Privacy and security

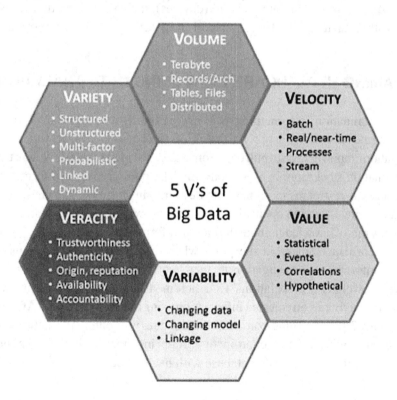

INFORMATION PRIVACY

- Information Analysis through Data Mining Preserving Data Privacy
- Cryptographic Solutions for Data Security
- Granular Access Control

INFORMATION MANAGEMENT AND INTEGRITY

- Secure Data Storage and Transaction Logs
- Granular Audits
- Information Provenance
- Overseeing the Security Level in Real-Time

These security and assurance troubles spread the entire scope of the Big Data lifecycle (Figure 6): wellsprings of data creation (devices), the data information itself, data dealing with, data storing, and data transport and data usage on different contraptions.

STREAMING HEALTHCARE DATA USING DATA ANALYTICS

Spilling examination is something contrary to bunch investigation. Rather than gathering and dissecting huge measures of information at one time, spilling investigation empowers you to pull data from each bit of information traveling through the information stockroom in close constant. The final product is information can be expended as it streams in, rather than devoured in enormous bunches.

Steaming investigation opens the open door for wellbeing frameworks to make noteworthy bits of knowledge about the patient information, empowering customized persistent correspondence. At the point when the social insurance industry can associate information investigation to their work processes, tolerant results will improve and wellbeing associations' ROI increments. Stream preparing investigates and performs activities on constant information using nonstop questions (Afendi, Ono & Nakamura, 2013). Gushing examination associates with outer information sources, empowering applications to coordinate certain information into the application stream, or to refresh an outside database with handled data.

Figure 6. Big Data ecosystem Security and Privacy challenges

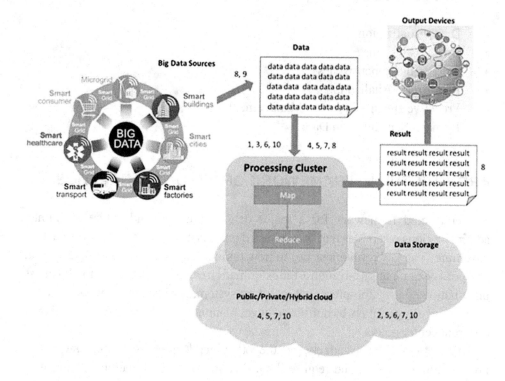

Figure 7. Generalized healthcare data streaming

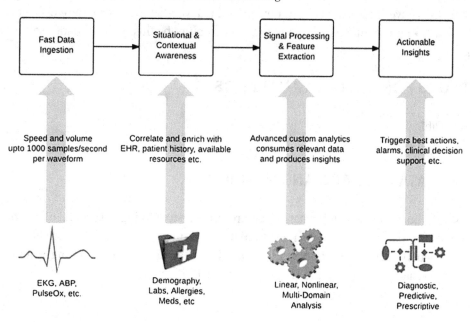

Advantages of Streaming

- Data visualization
- Business insights
- Increased competitiveness
- Real-time Visualization
- Proactive Business Process Management
- Demand Sensing from Data

ARCHITECTURAL FRAMEWORK OF BIG DATA ANALYTICS

The connected framework for a major data examination adventure in human administrations resembles that of a standard prosperity informatics or examination adventure. The key refinement lies in how taking care of is executed. In a typical prosperity examination adventure, the examination can be performed with a business information contraption presented on a free system, for instance, a work territory or PC. Since huge data is by definition huge, planning is isolated and executed over different center points.

Big Data Analytics gadgets, on the other hand, are staggeringly awesome, programming genuine, and require the utilization of a combination of capacities (Nambiar & Bhardwaj, 2013). They have ascended in an uncommonly designated way generally as open-source improvement contraptions and stages, and therefore they don't have the assistance and convenience that vendor driven prohibitive gadgets have. As Figure 8 illustrates, the multifaceted nature begins with the data itself.

TOOLS FOR BIG DATA ANALYTICS

See Table 1.

BIG DATA STORAGE AND RETRIEVAL

As for the rising big information environment, stockpiling suppliers offer the framework on which every single systematic instrument run, and by a long shot the most widely recognized framework for putting away and cluster handling venture big information is HDFS, the Hadoop dispersed File method.

Figure 8. Architectural framework of Big Data Analytics and concepts

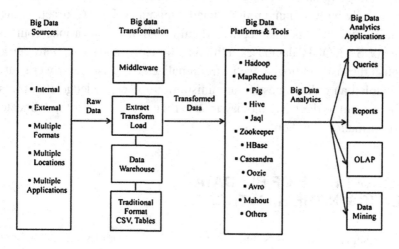

Table 1.

Platform/Tool	Descriptions
The Hadoop Distributed File System (HDFS)	HDFS enables the underlying storage for the Hadoop cluster. It divided the data into smaller parts and distributes it across the various servers/nodes.
MapReduce	MapReduce provides the interface for the distribution of sub-tasks and the gathering of outputs. When tasks are executed, MapReduce tracks the processing of each sever/node.
PIG and PIG Latin (Pig and PigLatin)	Pig programming language is configured to assimilate all types of data (structured/unstructured, etc). It is comprised of two key modules; the language itself, called PigLatin, and the runtime version in which the PigLatin is executed.
Hive	Hive is a runtime Hadoop system architecture that leverages Structure Query Language (SQL) with the Hadoop platform. It permits SQL programmers to develop Hive Query Language (HQL) statements akin to typical SQL statements.

"Hadoop is a getting together component for individuals utilizing big information since it is a standard to store and recover enormous informational collections. It resembles a big information parking garage," said Abe Usher, boss advancement officer of the HumanGEO Group, where he works with resistance and insight offices (Jangade & Chauhan, 2016).

The innovative aspect of our diagnostic information distribution center concentrated on amassing the majority of information in one spot just as streamlining information gets to. For the previous, we chose to utilize Vertica as our information stockroom programming due to its quick, adaptable, and section arranged plan. We additionally built up numerous specially appointed ETL (Extract, Transform, and Load) employments that replicated information from various sources (for example AWS S3, OLTP databases, administration logs, and so on.) into Vertica. To accomplish the last mentioned, we institutionalized SQL as our answer's interface and assembled an online question administration to acknowledge client inquiries and submit them to the basic inquiry motor. Figure 9, underneath, delineates this logical information storehouse.

IMPORTANT ROLE OF BIG DATA ANALYTICS IN THE HEALTHCARE

Healthcare services, expenses and inconveniences frequently emerge when loads of patients serves for emergency care. While greater expenses rise, those patients are still not profiting by better results, so executing an adjustment in this office can upset the manner in which medical clinics really work. Keeping an eye on patients with (Jin, Deyu & Yi, 2011) high-chance issues and guaranteeing an increasingly compelling, modified treatment approach would thus be able to be encouraged. Absence of data makes the formation of patient-driven consideration programs increasingly troublesome, so one can obviously grasp why utilizing big data exercises can be so very huge in the business.

Figure 9. Storage and retrieval using big data concepts

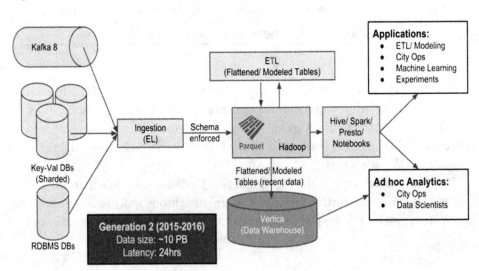

Figure 10. Importance of Big Data in Healthcare

Some of the major important role of big data analytics plays in area:

- High-risk patient care
- Cost reduction
- Personal injuries
- Tracking Patient health
- Patient engagement could be enhanced

Big data investigation empowers the relationship to burden their data information and use it to perceive new shots. That, in this manner, prompts progressively smart business moves, progressively viable undertakings, higher advantages and increasingly euphoric clients. There's no single advancement that incorporates big data investigation. Clearly, there's bleeding edge investigation that can be associated with big data, yet truth be told, a couple of sorts of advancement coordinate to empower you to get the most impetus from your data information.

CONCLUSION AND FUTURE WORK

Big data analytics in medication and human administrations is the promising strategy of consolidating, exploring and separating tremendous entirety, complex and heterogeneous data information with different natures: biomedical data, test data, electronic prosperity records data and online life data information. As big data analytics becoming famous as time passes, it is vital for organizations to know about the big data examination forecasts and remain side by side with all the most recent patterns. The scene is continuously changing hence organizations must be on the toes to recognize the future prospect of big data investigation since the volume of information are just expanding constantly. Taking into account that individuals' inclinations and requirements change at regular intervals, it is vital to mention that there would be many cases about the utilization of big data investigation by organizations to measure various market patterns and examples.

As more organizations receive big data analytics, more advances will be created to provide progressively precise expectations. This resembles a chain where one factor influences the other, and if every one of the elements are just expanding and holding hands and helping the market, big data analytics is just going to develop and think of more varieties. It is proficient and predicts the greater part of the data right and spares time and cost. As we finish up with the help of Hadoop and MongoDB, achieving practical information driven organizations to patients by strategies for conjectures has been made possible. Later on, every single restorative administration affiliations will be benefitted by achievements of human administrations examination. The gadgets that are used by this paper for directing big data has been discussed and moreover would have gotten a kick out of the chance to give a prevalent response for face difficulties in future needs. Diabetes issue is picked as our application in view of its mind boggling standard volume and datasets.

FUTURE RESEARCH RECOMMENDATIONS

Future analytics is firmly identified with AI; truth be told, ML frameworks regularly give the basis to futuristic analytics programming. Toward the start of big data analytics, affiliations were looking back at their data information to see what happened and a short time later, later they started using their investigation gadgets to investigate why those things happened. Farsighted examination goes well beyond, using big data examination to predict what will happen thereafter.

The Internet of Things (IoTs) is also obliged to sizably influence the big data. According to a September 2016 report from IDC, "31.4 percent of affiliations contemplated have impelled IoT plans, with an additional 43 percent planning to pass on in the accompanying a year." With all of those new contraptions and applications going ahead the web, affiliations are going to encounter a lot speedier data information improvement than they have experienced already. Many will require new progressions and structures in order to have the alternative to manage and comprehend the flood of big data starting from their IoT associations.

The most recent Hadoop strategy has just been confirmed in a paltry group utilizing some medicinal dataset measurements. Therefore, extra examination is mandatory to check whether this technique would survive through scaling as the bunch size is enhanced. The ongoing equipment developments in processor innovation, more state-of-the-art sorts of memories/arrange building will restrain the time spent in moving the data information from the facility to the processor in a circulated setting.

REFERENCES

Adil, A., Kar, H. A., Jangir, R., & Sofi, S. A. (2015, December). Analysis of multi-diseases using big data for improvement in healthcare. *Proceedings of the 2015 IEEE UP Section Conference on Electrical Computer and Electronics (UPCON)* (pp. 1-6). IEEE.

Afendi, F. M., Ono, N., Nakamura, Y., Nakamura, K., Darusman, L. K., Kibinge, N., ... Kanaya, S. (2013). Data mining methods for omics and knowledge of crude medicinal plants toward big data biology. *Computational and Structural Biotechnology Journal*, *4*(5), 1–14. doi:10.5936/csbj.201301010 PMID:24688691

Arulkumar, C. V., Selvayinayagam, G., & Vasuki, J. (2012). Enhancement in face recognition using PFS using Matlab. *International Journal of Computer Science & Management Research*, *1*(1), 282–288.

Arulkumar, C. V., & Vivekanandan, P. (2015). Multi-feature based automatic face identification on kernel eigen spaces (KES) under unstable lighting conditions. *Proceedings of the 2015 International Conference on Advanced Computing and Communication Systems*. IEEE.

Arulkumar, V., & Vivekanandan, P. (2018). An Intelligent Technique for Uniquely Recognizing Face and Finger Image Using Learning Vector Quantisation (LVQ)-based Template Key Generation. *International Journal of Biomedical Engineering and Technology*, *26*(3/4), 237–249. doi:10.1504/IJBET.2018.089951

Chen, N. J. Y., Sha, J., & Zhang, M. (2015). Hadoop-based Distributed Computing Algorithms for Healthcare and Clinic Data Processing. *Proceedings of the Eighth International Conference on Internet Computing for Science and Engineering*. Academic Press.

Desjardins, B., Crawford, T., Good, E., Oral, H., Chugh, A., Pelosi, F., ... Bogun, F. (2009). Infarct architecture and characteristics on delayed enhanced magnetic resonance imaging and electro anatomic mapping in patients with post infarction ventricular arrhythmia. *Heart Rhythm*, *6*(5), 644–651. doi:10.1016/j.hrthm.2009.02.018 PMID:19389653

Gu, D., Li, J., Li, X., & Liang, C. (2017). Visualizing the knowledge structure and evolution of big data research in healthcare informatics. *International Journal of Medical Informatics*, *98*, 22–32. doi:10.1016/j.ijmedinf.2016.11.006 PMID:28034409

Hou, B., Li, K. L., Shi, Y., Tao, L., & Liu, J. (2016). MongoDB NoSQL Injection Analysis and Detection. *Proceedings of the International Conference on Cyber Security and Cloud Computing*. Academic Press.

Hussain, S., & Lee, S. (2015). Semantic transformation model for clinical documents in big data to support healthcare analytics. *Proceedings of the Tenth International Conference on Digital Information Management*. Academic Press.

Jangade, R., & Chauhan, R. (2016). Big Data with Integrated Cloud Computing For Healthcare Analytics. *Proceedings of the International Conference on Computing for Sustainable Global Development*. Academic Press.

Jee, K., & Kim, G. H. (2013). Potentiality of big data in the medical sector: Focus on how to reshape the healthcare system. *Healthcare Informatics Research*, *19*(2), 79–85. doi:10.4258/hir.2013.19.2.79 PMID:23882412

Jin, Y., Deyu, T., & Yi, Z. (2011). A Distributed Storage Model for HER Based on HBase. *Proceedings of the International Conference on Information Management, Innovation Management and Industrial Engineering*. Academic Press.

Kankanhalli, A., Hahn, J., Tan, S., & Gao, G. (2016). Big data and analytics in healthcare: Introduction to the special section. *Information Systems Frontiers*, *18*(2), 233–235.

Liu, Y., Wang, Q., & Chen, H. Q. (2015). Research on IT Architecture of Heterogeneous Big Data. *J. Appl. Sci. Eng.*, *18*, 135–142.

Nambiar, R., Bhardwaj, R., Sethi, A., & Vargheese, R. (2013). A look at challenges and opportunities of Big Data analytics in healthcare. *Proc. of the 2013 IEEE Int. Conf. Big Data* (pp. 17–22). IEEE. 10.1109/BigData.2013.6691753

Raghupathi, W., & Raghupathi, V. (2014). Big data analytics in healthcare: Promise and potential. *Health Inform. Sci. Syst.*, *2*(1), 3. doi:10.1186/2047-2501-2-3 PMID:25825667

Rallapalli, S., Gondkar, R. R., & Kumar, U. P. (2016). Impact of processing and analyzing healthcare big data on cloud computing environment by implementing Hadoop Cluster. *Procedia Computer Science*, *85*, 16–22. doi:10.1016/j.procs.2016.05.171

Wang, Y., Kung, L. A., Wang, W. Y., & Cegielski, C. G. (2017). An integrated big data analytics-enabled transformation model: Application to health care. Information & Management, 55(1), 64–79.

Wicks, P., Massagli, M., Frost, J., Brownstein, C., Okun, S., Vaughan, T., ... Heywood, J. (2010). Sharing health data for better outcomes on PatientsLikeMe. *Journal of Medical Internet Research*, *12*(2), e19. doi:10.2196/jmir.1549 PMID:20542858

Yang, C., Li, C., Wang, Q., Chung, D., & Zhao, H. (2015). Implications of pleiotropy: Challenges and opportunities for mining big data in biomedicine. *Frontiers in Genetics*, *6*, 229. doi:10.3389/fgene.2015.00229 PMID:26175753

Chapter 11

Big Data Analytics and Visualization for Food Health Status Determination Using Bigmart Data

Sumit Arun Hirve
VIT-AP University, India

Pradeep Reddy C. H.
VIT-AP University, India

ABSTRACT

Being premature, the traditional data visualization techniques suffer from several challenges and lack the ability to handle a huge amount of data, particularly in gigabytes and terabytes. In this research, we propose an R-tool and data analytics framework for handling a huge amount of commercial market stored data and discover knowledge patterns from the dataset for conveying the derived conclusion. In this chapter, we elaborate on pre-processing a commercial market dataset using the R tool and its packages for information and visual analytics. We suggest a recommendation system based on the data which identifies if the food entry inserted into the database is hygienic or non-hygienic based on the quality preserved attributes. For a precise recommendation system with strong predictive accuracy, we will put emphasis on Algorithms such as J48 or Naive Bayes and utilize the one who outclasses the comparison based on accuracy. Such a system, when combined with R language, can be potentially used for enhanced decision making.

DOI: 10.4018/978-1-5225-9750-6.ch011

INTRODUCTION

Classes of 'Big Data'

Big Data could be found in three structures: structured, unstructured, semi-structured.

Structured

Any information that can be put away got to and prepared as the settled configuration is named as a 'Structured' information. Over the timeframe, ability in software engineering has made more noteworthy progress in creating methods (Li, Wang, Lian et al., 2018) for working with such information (where the organization is outstanding ahead of time) and furthermore inferring an incentive out of it. In any case, presently days, we are predicting issues when the size of such information develops to an immense degree, normal sizes are being in the fury of a various zettabyte.

Unstructured

Any information with the obscure frame or the structure is delegated unstructured information. Notwithstanding the size being tremendous, un-organized information represents various difficulties as far as its preparing for inferring an incentive out of it. The regular case of unstructured information is a heterogeneous information source containing a blend of basic content records, pictures, recordings and so on (Anandakumar & Umamaheswari, 2018). Presently, multi-day associations have an abundance of information accessible with them yet sadly they don't realize how to determine an incentive out of it since this information is in its crude shape or unstructured arrangement.

Semi-structured

Semi-organized information can contain both types of information. We can see semi-organized information as a structured in frame however it is not characterized with for example a table definition in social DBMS. A case of semi-organized information is information spoken to in XML document.

Qualities of 'Big Data'

Volume

The name Big Data itself is identified with a size which is tremendous. Size of information assumes the extremely vital job in deciding an incentive out of information (Ahmed, 2019). Likewise, regardless of whether a specific information can be considered as a Big Data or not, it is an endless supply of information. Henceforth, 'Volume' is one trademark which should be considered while managing Big Data.

Variety

The following part of Big Data is its assortment (Lee, 2019). Assortment alludes to heterogeneous sources and the idea of information, both organized and unstructured. Amid prior days, spreadsheets and databases were the main wellsprings of information considered by the vast majority of the applications. Presently days, information as messages, photographs, recordings, checking gadgets, PDFs, sound, and so forth is additionally being considered in the examination applications. This assortment of unstructured information represents certain issues for capacity, mining and dissecting information.

Velocity

The term 'speed' alludes to the speed of age of information. How quick the information is created and handled to meet the requests, decides genuine potential in the information.

Enormous Data Velocity manages the speed at which information streams in from sources like business forms, application logs, systems, and web-based life locales, sensors, Mobile gadgets, and so on. The stream of information is huge and ceaseless (Anandakumar & Umamaheswari, 2017).

Variability

This alludes to the irregularity which can be appeared by the information on occasion, subsequently hampering the way toward having the capacity to deal with and deal with the info viably.

Advantages of Big Data Processing

Capacity to process 'Big Data' acquires numerous advantages, for example,

1.   Businesses can use outside knowledge while taking choices
2.   Access to social information from web crawlers and locales like Facebook and Twitter are empowering associations to calibrate their business systems.
3.   Improved client benefit
4.   Conventional client input frameworks are getting supplanted by new frameworks planned with Big Data advances. In these new frameworks, Big Data and normal dialect preparing innovations are being utilized to peruse and assess shopper reactions.
5.   Early recognizable proof of hazard to the item/administrations, assuming any better operational effectiveness.
6.   'Big Data' innovations can be utilized for making organizing zone (Lv, Zhu, & Liu, 2019) or landing zone for new information before recognizing what information ought to be moved to the information stockroom. Such coordination of Big Data advances and information distribution center causes the association to offload inconsistently gotten to information.

Visualization of Big Data Analytics

Visualization has led to a rapid increase in the growth of innovations. The display can be categorized into analytical visualization and Information Visualization. When data is not directly processed and conveyed as information, then information Visualization is similar to Data Visualization. Information Visualization is used for visual analysis of public and private repositories such as business datasets, student datasets, medical datasets (Haldorai & Ramu, 2019) in their research article mentioned the use of visual analytics for information age-solving problems. People who access Social media sites such as YouTube, Facebook, and Google leave their traces on social media and help other investigators to track them via social media datasets. Chen et al. mentioned the process of analytics of geo-sampled social media data along with the movement patterns and Visual Analytics of sampled trajectories.

What Is Business Intelligence?

The amazing quality the universe of information examination has seen is stunning, developing from spreadsheets to OLTP and OLAP frameworks and after that digging device for the procedure of choice making (Harerimana, Jang, Kim et al., 2018).

"Business knowledge is intended to help the procedure of basic leadership." Arnott and Gibson characterize the job of business insight "to remove the data esteemed vital to the business, and to display or control that information into data that is helpful for administrative choice help." The authors noticed that business insight is "utilized to comprehend the capacities accessible in the firm; the condition of the workmanship, patterns, and future headings in the business sectors, the advances, and the administrative condition in which the firm contends; and the activities of contenders and the suggestions of these activities". Along these lines, Business knowledge (BI) is an umbrella term used to envelop the procedures, techniques, and estimations to effectively see, dissect and get it data significant to the history, current execution or future projections for a business.

What Is Business Intelligence?

The transcendence the world of data analysis has seen is staggering, growing from spreadsheets to OLTP and OLAP systems and then mining tools for the process of decision making. "Business intelligence is designed to support the process of decision-making." Arnott and Gibson define the role of business intelligence "to extract the information deemed central to the business, and to present or manipulate that data into information that is useful for managerial decision support." (Haldorai & Kandaswamy, 2019) notes that business intelligence is "used to understand the capabilities available in the firm; the state of the art, trends, and future directions in the markets, the technologies, and the regulatory environment in which the firm competes; and the actions of competitors and the implications of these actions." Thus, business intelligence (BI) is an umbrella term used to encompass the processes, methods, and measurements to easily view, analyze and understand information relevant to the history, current performance or future projections for a business.

Big Data

Data nowadays is flowing in from all directions be it a multimedia website, a sensor or RFID panel to support the internet of things or mobile applications the term Big Data is ominously causing the most turbulences. According to McKinsey, Big Data refers to datasets whose size are beyond the ability of typical database software tools to capture, store, manage and analyze. The exact grain size of the data set in case of big data cannot be defined explicitly (Mokhtari, Anvari-Moghaddam, & Zhang, 2019). Thus, big data forms the basis of data analysis of larger size that may be structured, semi structured or unstructured. According to O'Reilly, "Big data is data that exceeds the processing capacity of conventional database systems. The data is too big, moves too fast, or does not fit the structures of existing database architectures. To gain value from these data, there must be an alternative way to process it."

Business Intelligence Tools

Business intelligence tools (BI tools) act as a mechanism for companies to monitor data and generate business insights that are necessary components in making smarter, better decisions that drive results. But once research into BI is done a realization is observed that there are many types, from analytics and big data statistics to reporting tools and dashboards that offer at-a-glance information across indicators. When choosing the right business intelligence tools for an organization, consideration is given to the company, its employees, departments and teams – and the success factors that drive the process of decision-making. What isn't working currently, and what factors would benefit from improvement (Salloum, Huang, He, & Chen, 2019).

The goal thus is to make fact-based and insightful decisions that will improve company performance. BI Tools can range from simple MS-Excel spreadsheets to querying and reporting software, OLAP as well as data mining tools. But it may be conclusively reported that business intelligence tools can be categorized into generalized or tools that function on normal data sets, of smaller size, in structured or semi-structured format and big data-specific tools that utilize the big data, i.e., data large enough but of no explicit size and that too in any structural format be it structured, semi-structured or unstructured.

PHASES OF DATA ANALYTICS

The sort of systematic process picked is reliant on the client's utility and mastery. The client may shift from business examiners, engineers, end-client, researcher that require to work upon data, separated from information (Xiao, Li, Zhang, Liu, & Bergmann, 2018). The undertaking which is performed on information can be from basic information questions to information mining, algorithmic preparing, content recovery, and information explanation.

Planning Phase

In the readiness stage the information is being arranged, gathered, what's more, chose for further preparing or examination — the planning stage experiences following advances viz information arranging, information accumulation, highlight age, information determination. Here accumulation of information should be possible either by the review of information or utilizing existing information, and consequently, the information is chosen for the second stage preparing.

Pre-Processing Phase

The pre-handling stage bargains for the most part with sentence structure examination and remedy of information. After the readiness of information, the information is prepared for starting handling. This stage incorporates the information cleaning process, separating of information, the fruition of information, information revision, institutionalization, and change (Jang, Park, Lee, & Hahn, 2018).

Investigation Phase

After the pre-preparing stage, there is the investigation stage where the characterization and gathering of information are done in a way that information with comparative examples is united. The examination stages experience the accompanying advances viz representation, connection, relapse, estimating, arrangement and bunching.

Post-Processing Phase

The post handling stage is the last phase of information investigation. The post preparing stage incorporates the information understanding, documentation of information and assessment of information.

TYPES OF DATA ANALYTICS

Prescriptive analytics is valuable, but largely not used. Where big data analytics in general sheds light on a subject, prescriptive analytics gives you a laser-like focus to answer specific questions. For example, in the health care industry, you can better manage the patient population by using prescriptive analytics to measure the number of patients who are clinically obese, then add filters for factors like diabetes and LDL cholesterol levels to determine where to focus treatment (Haldorai & Kandaswamy, 2019).

The same prescriptive model can be applied to almost any industry target group or problem. Predictive analytics use big data to identify past patterns to predict the future. For example, some companies are using predictive analytics for sales lead scoring. Some companies have gone one step further use predictive analytics for the entire sales process, analyzing lead source, number of communications, types of communications, social media, documents, CRM data, etc. Properly tuned predictive analytics can be used to support sales, marketing, or for other types of complex forecasts. Demonstrative investigation is utilized for disclosure or to decide why something occurred. For instance, for a web-based life promoting the effort, you can utilize distinct investigation to survey the number of posts, specifies, supporters, fans, online visits, audits, pins, and so forth. There can be a great many online notices that can be refined into a solitary view to perceive what worked in your past crusades and what didn't. Spellbinding investigation or information mining is at the base of the huge information esteem chain, yet they can be significant for revealing examples that offer knowledge. A straightforward case of spellbinding examination would evaluate credit hazard; utilizing past budgetary execution to anticipate a client's imaginable money related execution. The expressive investigation can be valuable in the business cycle, for instance, to order clients by their presumable item inclinations and deals cycle (She, Liu, Wan, Xiong, & Fan, 2019).

Illustrative Analytics

As the name infers, elucidating investigation or insights can outline crude information and convert it into a frame that can be effectively comprehended by people. They can depict in insight concerning an occasion that has happened previously. This sort of investigation is useful in inferring any example if any from past occasions or drawing translations from them so better techniques for the future can be encircled. This is the most much of the time utilized kind of examination crosswise over associations. It's essential in uncovering the key measurements and measures inside any business.

illustrative analytics examines "what has occurred?" This is a straight forward methodology way to deal with assessing and that reduce the huge information into confined or little scale accommodating information chunks. The dominant part of the ventures keeps an eye on this application. As it's the perfect or plain procedure, a large portion of the online life patterns are found through this office. The brilliant component of this system is that it considers constant information gathering with vital information understanding which advantages to orchestrate approaches to the future (Haldorai & Kandaswamy, 2019).

Symptomatic Analytics

The conspicuous successor to elucidating examination is a symptomatic investigation. Indicative logical instruments help an expert to dive further into an issue within reach so they can touch base at the wellspring of an issue. In an organized business condition, devices for both distinct and indicative examination go connected at the hip!

Prescient Analytics

Any business that is seeking after progress ought to have a premonition. Prescient investigation causes organizations to gauge patterns dependent on recent developments. Regardless of whether it's foreseeing the likelihood of an occasion occurring in future or assessing the precise time it will happen would all be able to be resolved with the assistance of prescient systematic models. Generally, various yet mutually dependent factors are broken down to foresee a pattern in this kind of investigation. For instance, in the human services area, planned wellbeing dangers can be anticipated dependent on a person's propensities/diet/hereditary piece. In this way, these models are the most essential crosswise over different fields.

Prescriptive Analytics

This sort of examination clarifies the well-ordered process in a circumstance. For example, a prescriptive investigation is a thing that becomes possibly the most important factor when your Uber driver gets the less demanding course from G-maps. The best course was picked by considering the separation of each accessible course from your get course to the goal and the traffic imperatives on every street. An information expert would need to apply at least one of the above examination forms as an aspect of his responsibilities. In the wake of perusing the above post, are you left considering how to end up an information examiner, at that point If you are pondering about the extent of information examination in India, If you are excited about seeking after a profession in the field of information investigation, you can apply for these courses offered by Availed. On fruition of these courses, you would be qualified for probably the most difficult jobs in the area. A prescriptive examination can be named as a mix of upsurge reproduction which is the main methodology. It additionally benefits in producing the FICO rating to reason business establishments. By prescriptive investigation, Aurora Health Care spared $6 million yearly to lessen readmission rates by 10%.

Figure 1. Phases of Data Analytics

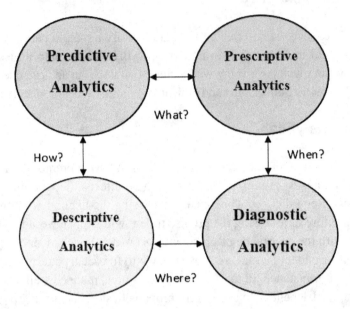

METHODOLOGY

The examination system of the investigation comprised of a contextual analysis of 5 associations in the wellbeing division, browsed Big Data Analytics pioneers headquartered in New York City and featured in driving professional distributions in the July – December 2014 period. The wellbeing segment was picked by the creators as the segment connected to the main division of concentrate in their fixation educational modules for Big Data Analytics at the Seidenberg School of Computer Science and Information Systems of Pace University–vitality, stimulation, monetary and retailing areas will be contemplated in the 2016 – 2019 period. The activities in the five associations in the wellbeing area were assessed by the first and third creators from an agenda definition instrument of the overview of the 41 previously mentioned Big Data Analytics components of the system program, in January – April 2015 period. The variables were assessed on proof of commitment to Big Data Analytics venture achievement, on a 6-point Likert-like rating scale: - (5) Very High in Contribution to Project Success; - (4) High in Contribution; - (3) Intermediate in Contribution; - (2) Low in Contribution; - (1) Very Low in Contribution; and - (0) No Contribution to Success. The assessments were established on inside and out perception of mid-administration venture individuals in the associations, averaging 3 – 5 staff in the associations; educated impression of perception basis by the third creator, a specialist of 35+ years; and research audits of optional investigations by the principal creator. The agenda instrument of the examination was checked with regards to develop, substance and face legitimacy and substance legitimacy, estimated in test legitimacy, continuously creator. The strategy was predictable in respectability and demonstrated unwavering quality with before concentrates by the creators on distributed computing and benefit arranged design (SOA) innovation. The information from the assessments was deciphered in the MATLAB 7.10.0 Statistics Toolbox continuously creator, in the May – June 2015 period, for the accompanying segment and the tables in the Appendix.

Approach and Solution to break in Top 20 of Big Mart Sales expectation

Hypothesis Generation

This is an essential advance during the time spent dissecting information. This includes understanding the issue and making some theory about what could conceivably goodly affect the result. This is done BEFORE taking a gander at the information, and we end up making a clothing rundown of the distinctive analysis which we can perform if the information is accessible.

Store Level Hypotheses:

- **City Type**: Stores situated in urban or Tier 1 urban communities ought to have higher deals due to the higher salary dimensions of individuals there.
- **Populace Density**: Stores situated in thickly populated zones ought to have higher deals on account of more interest.
- **Store Capacity:** Stores which are huge ought to have higher deals as they act as one-stop-shops and individuals would lean toward getting everything from one place
- **Contenders**: Stores were having comparative foundations close-by should have fewer deals on account of more challenge.
- **Showcasing**: Stores which have a decent promoting division ought to have higher deals as it will probably pull in clients through the correct offers and publicizing.
- **Area**: Stores situated inside well-known commercial centers ought to have higher sales because of better access to clients.

- **Client Behavior**: Stores keeping the correct arrangement of products to meet the neighborhood needs of clients will have higher deals.
- **Vibe**: Stores which are very much kept up and overseen by respectful and humble individuals are relied upon to have higher footfall and in this manner higher deals.

Product Level Hypotheses

Brand: Branded products should have higher deals given higher trust in the client.

- **Bundling**: Products with great bundling can pull in clients and move more.
- **Utility**: Daily use items ought to have a higher inclination to offer when contrasted with the particular use items.
- **Show Area**: Products which are given greater retires in the store are probably going to get consideration first and move more.
- **Visibility in Store:** The area of item in a store will affect deals. Ones which are comfortable will grab the attention of client first as opposed to the ones toward the rear.
- **Promoting**: Better publicizing of items in the store will should higher sales much of the time.
- **Limited Time Offers:** Products went with appealing offers and limits will move more.

These are only some essential 15 speculations I have made. However, you can think further and make your very own portion. Keep in mind that the information probably won't be adequate to test these, however, framing these gives us a superior comprehension of the problem and we can even search for open source data if accessible.

Data Exploration

We will be playing out some essential information investigation here and think of a few deductions about the information. We will endeavor to make sense of a few inconsistencies and address them in the following segment.

The initial step is to take a gander at the information and endeavor to distinguish the data which we conjectured versus the accessible information. An examination between the information lexicon on the challenge page and out speculations appears as follows:

Table 1. Data Exploration Values

	Item_MRP	Item_Outlet_Sales	Item_Visibility	Item_Weight	Outlet_Establishment_Year
count	14204.000000	8523.000000	14204.000000	11765.000000	14204.000000
mean	141.004977	2181.288914	0.065953	12.792854	1997.830681
std	62.086938	1706.499616	0.051459	4.652502	8.371664
min	31.290000	33.290000	0.000000	4.555000	1985.000000
25%	94.012000	834.247400	0.027036	8.710000	1987.000000
50%	142.247000	1794.331000	0.054021	12.600000	1999.000000
75%	185.855600	3101.296400	0.094037	16.750000	2004.000000
max	266.888400	13086.964800	0.328391	21.350000	2009.000000

Data Cleaning

This progression normally includes crediting missing qualities and treating exceptions. Even though anomaly evacuation is critical in relapse methods, propelled tree based calculations are impenetrable to anomalies.

PROPOSED SYSTEM

The proposed framework will defeat the constraints of the current frameworks. This framework will foresee the wellbeing remainder of the client dependent on the way of life he/she lives for example how much solid an individual is as of now and what the illnesses he/she can get are in not so distant future if the client keeps on carrying on with a similar kind of way of life. A portion of the explanations behind any client falling sick is the way of life the individual lives, the sustenance and the planning of having nourishment, not doing any activity, not taking enough rest and not taking breaks from work for unwinding. This framework will likewise recommend maintaining a strategic distance from those maladies. Recommendations of sustenance to have and way of life to adjust to have a sound existence. This framework will likewise give proposals of specialists whenever required. This framework will likewise demonstrate its client's late headways in the field of medicinal sciences.

Information Analysis Module will comprise of the expectation module planned in R. The model is planned to utilize Naive Bayes characterization algorithm. The characterization calculation is connected to the information present in the database.

COMPARISON OF VISUALIZATION TOOLS

The visualization tools have been analyzed and assessed on the premise of their highlights, support, attributes, and offices gave. A few datasets with size fluctuating Densities were tried on every one of these devices, and Google Charts and Apache Zeppelin were considered on needs as they outflanked the examination test. Scene: As examined in the writing review, Tableau is a Visualization device which is utilized in numerous corporate ventures and territories of the building. Its primary reason for existing is utilized to make outlines, pie charts and maps for graphical examination. Discussing cost, Tableau is available for $200 every year for a solitary client get to. Combination Charts XL is the new e-outlines created utilizing JavaScript for web and portable by Infosoft Global private constrained offer an incredible component of similarity with web programs (Mozilla Firefox, Google Chrome, and Safari).

Additionally, this enables the delicate mapped code to prepare methods, for example, outlines, line charts, pie diagrams, and others. Numerous social associations, for example, Facebook, Twitter, and other colossal associations use Data Wrapper apparatuses for reportage and Analytics. It has an intuitive GUI and is Easy to utilize, requires right around zero Coding. Google Charts is an API made by Google which is anything but difficult to learn and envision information. Takes a shot at all cutting-edge programs and can peruse information from MySQL, Big Data's HDFS and exceed expectations spreadsheet. The main drawback of Google graphs is that it re-quires a system association with showcase the pictured substance. This representation technique would be a perfect skill to use in the proposed idea as the API is suitable to coordinate with an incorporated advancement Environment (IDE, for example, Eclipse. The information created in SQL can be transported into Eclipse utilizing modules and .container records availability strategies. The information can be installed in the API code and displayed on the web interface in the 2D frame. Ying Zhu in the year 2012 featured the ideas of Google maps and instruments utilized for Visualization. The proposed hypothesis turned out to be entirely noteworthy for understudies seeking after investigations of significance.

NOURISHMENT QUALITY

Quality incorporates positive and negative traits that impact an item's incentive to the purchaser. Positive properties that show great quality might be the inception, shading, flavor, surface and handling strategy for the sustenance, while negative traits might be unmistakable deterioration, sullying with foulness, discoloration, or terrible smells or tastes. Anyway, not every perilous nourishment may show terrible quality, that is, hazardous sustenance may have all the earmarks of being of good quality, for example, spoiled meat camouflaged utilizing dye or solid flavors. This qualification among security and quality has suggestions for open arrangement and impacts the nature and substance of the sustenance control framework most suited to meet foreordained national destinations.

How Is Nourishment Quality Assessed?

Customarily, characteristics of sustenance are assessed by our tactile organs – our eyes, nose or mouth or, all the more as of late, by the utilization of instruments. Tangible assessment is normally drilled by sustenance administrative specialists who comprise of deciding the nature of nourishment by a board of judges. The assessment manages to estimate, assessing, dissecting and deciphering the characteristics of sustenance as they are seen by the faculties of sight, taste, contact, and hearing.

Watchful inspecting of the nourishment is important for tangible assessment. It is not constantly conceivable to recognize with tactile strategies alone the defilement of sustenance by pesticides, veterinary medication deposits and contaminated. Target assessment is done which incorporates compound, physiochemical, microbial and physical techniques for examination. Compound techniques incorporate the assurance of nutritive estimation of nourishments when cooking, and to distinguish the results of disintegration and adulterants in sustenance's. The most generally utilized target assessment is the estimation of physical properties by the utilization of instruments. Estimations of the appearance and volume of nourishments are additionally vital.

What Is Sustenance Wellbeing?

Sustenance wellbeing alludes to constraining the nearness of those perils whether endless or intense, that may make nourishment harmful to the soundness of the purchaser. Sustenance wellbeing is tied in with creating, taking care of, putting away and planning nourishment to anticipate disease and defilement in the sustenance generation chain and to help guarantee that nourishment quality and healthiness are kept up to advance great wellbeing.

How Protected Is Natural or Privately Created Nourishment?

Natural and privately created sustenance's may have ecological advantages, for example, utilizing fewer pesticides or composts. These sustenance's, similar to other people, can be presented to destructive microbes amid the developing and collecting process. It is vital for agriculturists and merchants to utilize great clean practices to limit nourishment defilement. Purchasers ought to dependably plan and cook sustenance appropriately, regardless of where it is from.

What Is the Hazard Analysis of Critical Control Point Framework (HACCP) and How Does HACCP Work in Sustenance Generation

HACCP, or the Hazard Analysis Critical Control Point framework, is a procedure control framework that distinguishes where risks may happen in the nourishment generation process and institute stringent activities to keep the dangers from happening. By entirely observing and controlling each progression of the procedure, there is less shot for perils to happen. HACCP is an essential piece of the current sustenance industry used to distinguish and control real nourishment dangers, for example, microbiological, compound and physical contaminants. Shoppers can actualize HACCP-like practices in the home by following appropriate capacity, taking care of, cooking and cleaning systems. The presentation of preventive methodologies, for example, HACCP, have brought about industry assuming more noteworthy liability for and control of sustenance dangers. Such an incorporated methodology encourages enhanced shopper assurance, successfully invigorates horticulture and the nourishment handling industry, and advances residential and global sustenance exchange.

What Are Sustenance Security Issues Identified With Fish and Fish?

Fish and fish can wind up tainted with pathogens, for example, vibrio cholera, salmonella, e. coli, shigella, listeria because of human action or poor cleanliness and sanitation amid nourishment creation and preparing. There have been flareups of foodborne diseases and diseases connected to the utilization of polluted fish and fish. Likewise, methyl mercury is framed by bacterial activity in an amphibian domain from the dumping of mechanical mercury just as regular wellsprings of basic mercury. Testing of fish against methyl mercury is requested by most bringing in nations. Certain parasite hatchlings can be available in fish, which is the reason most fish ought to be cooked all together.

What Is Nourishment Sullying and What Might Be Potential Reasons for Tainting?

Nourishment contaminants are any substances not purposefully added to sustenance, which are available in such nourishment because of the creation (counting tasks completed in harvest cultivating, creature farming and aquaculture), make, handling, arrangement, treatment, pressing, bundling, transport or holding of such sustenance or because of ecological sullying. Nourishment sullying alludes to the nearness of destructive synthetic substances or miniaturized scale creatures in sustenance, which can cause a few weakening diseases whenever devoured. The unexpected pollution may happen amid creation, handling, stockpiling and showcasing. Palatable oil might be debased amid handling because of spillage of mineral oil underway line.

Sustenance sullying is a significantly greater danger in nations of the South-East Asia area because of the absence of delivering collecting standards, nourishment dealing with models, and natural directions.

What Is Being Done to Lessen the Introduction to Pesticides?

It is generally realized that pesticides/bug sprays and herbicides/fungicides are utilized for nuisance and weed/deterioration control. These agrochemicals are accessible over the counter; ranchers may utilize them without legitimate comprehension or supervision. These synthetic concoctions can be perilous, and there is dependably an opportunity of tainting of farming produce with deposits of these synthetic compounds. Considering the conceivable wellbeing peril of dietary admission of buildups of these synthetic substances, the Joint FAO/WHO Meetings on Pesticide Residues gives free logical master guidance on pesticide deposits, remaining cutoff points and the adequate most extreme dietary admission (ADI) and greatest lingering limit (MRL) based on proof-based data and hazard appraisal.

What Is Satisfactory Day by Day Allow (ADI) and the Greatest Lingering Limit (MRL)?

Adequate every day consumption (ADI) of a substance is the day by day allow which, amid a whole lifetime, gives off an impression of being without apparent hazard to the wellbeing of the buyer based on all the well-established actualities at the season of the assessment of the synthetic by the Joint FAO/WHO Meeting on Pesticide Residues (JMPR). It is communicated in milligrams of the substance per kilogram of body weight. Greatest lingering limit (MRL) is the most extreme convergence of a pesticide buildup (communicated as mg/kg), prescribed by the Codex Alimentarius Commission to be legitimately allowed in nourishment items and creature bolsters. Particular MRLs are proposed to be toxicologically worthy. MRLs which are principally expected to apply in universal exchange are gotten from estimations made by the JMPR following both:

1. Toxicological evaluation of the pesticide and its buildup
2. Review of buildup information from administered preliminaries and managed utilizes including those reflecting national sustenance farming practices. Information from directed preliminaries led at the most noteworthy broadly prescribed, approved, or enlisted utilizes are incorporated into the audit. To suit varieties in national bug control necessities, ADI and MRLs are likewise decided for veterinary medication deposits and antimicrobial substances as these synthetic concoctions are utilized for development advancement and creature illness avoidance and control.

Instances of Data

Practically all product programs expect information to do anything valuable. For instance, if you are altering an archive in a word processor, for example, Microsoft Word, the report you are dealing with is the information. The word-preparing programming can control the information: make another report, copy an archive, or alter a record. Some different instances of information are an MP3 music document, a video record, a spreadsheet, a site page, and a digital book. Now and again, for example, with a digital book, you may just be able to peruse the information.

Data Types

When characterizing the fields in a database table, we should give each handle an information type. For instance, the field Birth Year is a year, so it will be a number, while the First Name will be content. Most current databases take into account a few unique information types to be put away. A portion of the more typical information types are recorded here:

1. **Text:** For putting away non-numeric information that is brief, by and large under 256 characters. The database fashioner can distinguish the greatest length of the content.

2. **Number:** For putting away numbers. There are generally a couple of various number sorts that can be chosen, contingent upon how extensive the biggest number will be.

3. **Yes/No:** A unique type of the number information type that is (typically) one byte long, with a 0 for "No" or "False" and a 1 for "Yes" or "Genuine."

4. **Date/Time:** An extraordinary type of the number information type that can be deciphered as a number or a period.

5. **Currency:** An extraordinary type of number information type that arranges all qualities with a money maker and two decimal spots.

6. **Paragraph Text:** This information type considers message longer than 256 characters.

7. **Object:** This information type takes into consideration the capacity of information that can't be entered employing console, for example, a picture or a music record.

There are two imperative reasons that we should legitimately characterize the information kind of a field. Initial, an information type tells the database what capacities can be performed with the information. For instance, on the off chance that we wish to perform scientific capacities with one of the fields, we should make certain to tell the database that the field is a number information type. So, on the off chance that we have, say, a field putting away a birth year, we can subtract the number put away in that field from the present year to get age. The second essential motivation to characterize information type is with the goal that the correct measure of the storage room is designated for our information. For instance, if the First Name field is characterized as a text (50) information type, this implies fifty characters are selected for every first name we need to store. In any case, regardless of whether the primary name is just five characters in length, fifty characters (bytes) will be designated. While this may not appear to be a major ordeal, if our table winds up holding 50,000 names, we are dispensing 50 * 50,000 = 2,500,000 bytes for the capacity of these qualities. It might be reasonable to lessen the span of the field, so we don't squander the storage room.

CASES ANALYSIS

Notwithstanding being such a popular expression as of late, huge information is as yet an entirely shapeless term. While datasets have dependably existed, with late advances in innovation, we have more routes than any time in recent memory to catch immense measures of information, (for example, through implanted frameworks like sensors) and better approaches to store them. Enormous information likewise incorporates the procedures and devices used to dissect, envision, and use this tremendous volume of information to tackle it and help individuals settle on better choices.

The prescient investigation is another word that is frequently observed with enormous information. Fundamentally, prescient investigation alludes to the utilization of verifiable information and measurable procedures, for example, machine figuring out how to make forecasts about what's to come. A precedent may be how Netflix recognizes what you need to watch (forecasts) before you do, in light of your past survey propensities (authentic information). It is likewise imperative to take note of that information doesn't such allude to lines and segments in a spreadsheet, yet additionally increasingly complex information records, for example, recordings, pictures, sensor information, etc.

The best way to see how big data applies to our food is through an example from my own life. It's no secret that I love Stacy's Pita Chips. Despite so, it was a surprise when I opened up my Kroger app the other day and found a digital coupon for these pita chips staring straight back at me. How did they know what I was thinking? Was it just a happy coincidence? Kroger was one of the first food retailers in the US to jump onto big data analytics bandwagon, by using previously collected consumer data to generate personalized offers as well as tailored pricing for its consumers. They were also the first to use infrared body-heat sensors combined with a computer algorithm to track how customers were moving through the store, and accordingly, predict how many cashiers to deploy, thus shortening check-out time for shoppers.

From the first look, it gives the idea that information examination utilized in the sustenance business is frequently based on store network the board, operational effectiveness and marketing1, for example, mining buyer information to comprehend their conduct, or making sense of how to stock items at the perfect time to give organizations a focused edge. Be that as it may, enormous information is likewise a noteworthy player in nourishment quality and wellbeing, however, isn't frequently discussed. This specific article centers around four more contextual investigations in which huge information examination are utilized for propelling nourishment wellbeing.

Chicago's Sanitation Inspections

In the city of Chicago, there are just 32 auditors in charge of the sterile examinations of more than 15,000 sustenance foundations in the city of Chicago, which comes down to approximately 470 foundations for every reviewer. Basic infringement of the sanitation code can prompt the spread of foodborne diseases, in this way getting eateries with infringement at an early stage is principal.

The program examines 10 years of verifiable information utilizing 13 primary indicators, (for example, close-by refuse objections) to recognize the high-chance foundations, with the objective of occupying valuable assets (overseers for this situation) to the more hazardous sustenance foundations so any basic infringement can be immediately distinguished and corrected before they make anybody debilitated.

Given results from the examination, a 2-month test case program in which controllers were all the more effectively apportioned was launched10. By and large, foundations with infringement were discovered 7.5 days sooner than when the monitors worked as usual11. Need to know the best part? The logical code utilized for gauging nourishment investigations is composed on an open-source programming dialect and accessible for nothing on Github, enabling clients to constantly enhance the calculation.

Whole Genome Sequencing

The approach of reasonable and quick entire genome sequencing is creating an abundance of high-goals genomic information. At the essential dimension, entire genome sequencing can separate practically any strain of pathogens, something that past systems, for example, beat field gel electrophoresis (PFGE) was not able to do. At the more elevated amount, genomic information is being created in enough high-goals to track and follow foodborne diseases crosswise over various sustenance sources, nourishment fabricating offices and clinical cases.

The FDA is likewise fronting a global exertion called the GenomeTrakr to organize, where research facilities around the globe are sequencing pathogens segregated from debased sustenance, natural sources and foodborne outbreaks12. This exertion comes full circle in a worldwide database where general wellbeing authorities can rapidly survey for data when required. Theoretically, if a nourishment episode happens, the pathogen can be secluded from the culpable sustenance, its genome sequenced and after that immediately contrasted with the database. Since the genomic information of a specific animal category or strain of foodborne pathogen is not quite the same as one geographic region to another, knowing the geographic zone of the obscure pathogen can be instrumental in deciding the root wellspring of sullying.

Given our inexorably worldwide sustenance supply and the way that nourishment items are regularly multi-fixing, this will be a vigorous instrument for following sustenance pollution rapidly and expelling any debased nourishment items from the sustenance supply.

What's Next?

Foodborne ailments slaughter practically a large portion of a million people for each year13, with a lot more hospitalized, and even a lot more who are influenced however did not report their side effects. Given late advancements in our capacity to catch, store and process information, the nourishment business is exceptionally situated to take measures to lessen foodborne sicknesses. The contextual investigations here are disengaged to give a case of what prescient examination and enormous information can mean for nourishment wellbeing. It isn't just about what specific innovation, sensor, or calculation that can do something amazing, however it is likewise about the collection of extensive, apparently random datasets, can uncover examples and help us inventively enhance nourishment wellbeing.

Encouraging the selection of information driven culture in sustenance science and security requires the help of the scholarly world as well as contributing to the administration and industry. There are numerous energetic scholastic establishments and network software engineers who are eager to help. Work that should be possible today incorporates building up the enormous information framework, preparing and mindfulness for future nourishment experts.

What Is R?

R is a coordinated suite of programming offices for information control, estimation and graphical show. In addition to other things it has

1. A compelling information taking care of and storeroom,
2. A suite of administrators for estimations on exhibits, specifically networks,
3. A substantial, reasonable, coordinated gathering of moderate devices for information investigation,
4. Graphical offices for information investigation and show either straightforwardly at the PC or on the printed version, and
5. A very much created, straightforward and viable programming dialect (called 'S') which incorporates conditionals, circles, client characterized recursive capacities and info and yield offices. (Surely the vast majority of the framework provided capacities are themselves written in the S dialect.)

The expression "condition" is expected to describe it as a completely arranged and rational framework, as opposed to a steady, gradual addition of unmistakable and firm devices, as is every now and again the case with other information investigation programming.

R is particularly a vehicle for recently creating techniques for intuitive information investigation. It has grown quickly and has been reached out by a substantial accumulation of bundles. Notwithstanding, most programs written in R are transient, composed for a solitary bit of information examination.

Basic Features of R

In the good old days, a key element of R was that its language structure is fundamentally the same as S, making it simple for S-PLUS clients to switch over. While the R's sentence structure is about indistinguishable to that of S's, R's semantics, while externally like S, is very extraordinary. Indeed, R is a lot nearer to the Scheme dialect than it is to the first S dialect with regards to how R functions in the engine.

Today R keeps running on practically any standard registering stage and working framework. Its open source nature implies that anybody is allowed to adjust the product to whatever stage they pick. For sure, R has been accounted for to keep running on current tablets, telephones, PDAs, and diversion supports.

One decent component that R imparts to numerous mainstream open source ventures is visited discharges. These days there is a noteworthy yearly discharge, normally in October, where major new highlights are consolidated what's more, discharged to people in general. Consistently, littler scale bugfix discharges will be made as required. The successive discharges and normal discharge cycle demonstrates dynamic improvement of the product and guarantees that bugs will be tended to in an auspicious way. While the center designers control the essential source tree for R, numerous individuals around the globe make commitments as new include, bug fixes, or both. Another key preferred standpoint that R has over numerous other factual bundles (even today) is its advanced designs abilities. R's capacity to make "distribution quality" illustrations has existed since the earliest reference point and has for the most part been exceptional than contending bundles. Today, with some more perception bundles accessible than previously, that slant proceeds. R's base designs framework permits for fine power over basically every part of a plot or chart. Other more up to date illustrations frameworks, like cross section and ggplot2 consider perplexing and advanced representations of high-dimensional information.

R has kept up the first S theory, which is that it gives a dialect that is both helpful for intelligent work yet contains an amazing programming dialect for growing new instruments. This permits the client, who takes existing instruments and applies them to information, to gradually yet without a doubt turn into a designer who is making new instruments.

At last, one of the delights of utilizing R has nothing to do with the dialect itself, yet rather with the dynamic and energetic client network. From numerous points of view, a dialect is fruitful see that it makes a stage with which numerous individuals can make new things. R is that stage, and a large number of individuals around the globe have met up to make commitments to R, to create bundles, and help each other use R for a wide range of utilizations. The R-help and R-devel mailing records have been very dynamic for over ten years now, and there is significant movement on sites like Stack Overflow.

Limitations of R

No programming dialect or factual investigation framework is flawless. R has various disadvantages. First of all, R is founded on very nearly multi-year-old innovation, returning to the unique S framework created at Bell Labs. There was initially minimal worked in help for dynamic or 3-D illustrations (yet things have enhanced enormously since the "days of yore"). Another ordinarily referred to the impediment of R is that objects should, for the most part, be put away in physical memory. This is to a limited extent because of the perusing standards of the dialect, yet R by and large is, even more, a memory hoard than other measurable bundles. Be that as it may, there have been various headways to manage this, both in the R center and furthermore in various bundles created by benefactors. Additionally, figuring power and limit has kept on developing after some time and measure of physical memory that can be introduced on even a buyer level workstation is generous. While we will probably never have enough physical memory on a PC to deal with the undeniably substantial datasets that are being produced, the circumstance has gotten significantly less demanding after some time. At a larger amount one "impediment" of R is that its usefulness depends on customer request and (willful) client commitments. On the off chance that nobody has a craving for actualizing your most loved technique, it's your employment to execute it (or you have to pay somebody to do it) — the abilities of the R framework for the most part mirror the interests of the R client network. As the network has expanded in size over the past ten years, the abilities have correspondingly expanded. When I previously began utilizing R, there was practically nothing in the method for usefulness for the physical sciences (material science, stargazing, and so on.). Be that as it may, presently a few of those networks have embraced R, and we are seeing more code being composed for those sorts of applications.

SUMMARY

The imminent value of Big Data Analytics has been proved profoundly as global wide business opportunities have opened up ensuring new future and also thereby assuring a great deal of security too. The knowledge that has been revealed through big data has proven to easily convert into valuable busi- ness. Decisions that are highly effectual could be made with the available data analysis techniques and tactical data administration by the corporate organizations. The recent emergence of Big Data Analytics is seen to be replacing these old methods and puts on a fresh face to the situation with more productive and effective results. The commercial market dataset used for our proposed research is passed under several contingencies tests using R-studio and R-programming language. The predictive accuracies will be combined and used for future predictions of healthy and unhealthy food for unknown food records. The decision tree suggested for this experiment will be J48 and Random Forest. Ctree and RPART are old fashion and does not give sufficient results for predictions with a dull classification model. The future scope for our research can be widely expanded to huge market company's dataset and prevention of illness by classifying the food products even before they are revealed to the buyers or customers in the stores.

REFERENCES

Ahmed, M. (2019). Intelligent Big Data Summarization for Rare Anomaly Detection. *IEEE Access: Practical Innovations, Open Solutions, 7*, 68669–68677. doi:10.1109/ACCESS.2019.2918364

Anandakumar, H., & Umamaheswari, K. (2017). Supervised machine learning techniques in cognitive radio networks during cooperative spectrum handovers. *Cluster Computing, 20*(2), 1505–1515. doi:10.100710586-017-0798-3

Anandakumar, H., & Umamaheswari, K. (2018). A bio-inspired swarm intelligence technique for social aware cognitive radio handovers. *Computers & Electrical Engineering, 71*, 925–937. doi:10.1016/j.compeleceng.2017.09.016

Haldorai, A., & Kandaswamy, U. (2019). Energy Efficient Network Selection for Cognitive Spectrum Handovers. In *Intelligent Spectrum Handovers in Cognitive Radio Networks* (pp. 41–64). Springer; doi:10.1007/978-3-030-15416-5_3

Haldorai, A., & Kandaswamy, U. (2019). Software Radio Architecture: A Mathematical Perspective. In Intelligent Spectrum Handovers in Cognitive Radio Networks (pp. 65-86). Springer.

Haldorai, A., & Ramu, A. (Eds.). (2019). Cognitive Social Mining Applications in Data Analytics and Forensics. Hershey, PA: IGI Global. doi:10.4018/978-1-5225-7522-1

Haldorai, A., & Kandaswamy, U. (2019). Intelligent Spectrum Handovers in Cognitive Radio Networks. Springer International Publishing. doi:10.1007/978-3-030-15416-5

Harerimana, G., Jang, B., Kim, J. W., & Park, H. K. (2018). Health Big Data Analytics: A Technology Survey. *IEEE Access, 6*, 65661–65678. doi:10.1109/ACCESS.2018.2878254

Jang, B., Park, S., Lee, J., & Hahn, S.-G. (2018). Three Hierarchical Levels of Big-Data Market Model Over Multiple Data Sources for Internet of Things. *IEEE Access, 6*, 31269–31280. doi:10.1109/ACCESS.2018.2845105

Lee, D. (2019). Big Data Quality Assurance Through Data Traceability: A Case Study of the National Standard Reference Data Program of Korea. *IEEE Access, 7*, 36294–36299. doi:10.1109/ACCESS.2019.2904286

Li, X., Wang, L., Lian, Z., & Qin, X. (2018). Migration-Based Online CPSCN Big Data Analysis in Data Centers. *IEEE Access: Practical Innovations, Open Solutions, 6*, 19270–19277. doi:10.1109/ACCESS.2018.2810255

Lv, D., Zhu, S., & Liu, R. (2019). Research on Big Data Security Storage Based on Compressed Sensing. *IEEE Access*, 7, 3810–3825. doi:10.1109/ACCESS.2018.2889716

Mokhtari, G., Anvari-Moghaddam, A., & Zhang, Q. (2019). A New Layered Architecture for Future Big Data-Driven Smart Homes. *IEEE Access*, 7, 19002–19012. doi:10.1109/ACCESS.2019.2896403

Salloum, S., Huang, J. Z., He, Y., & Chen, X. (2019). An Asymptotic Ensemble Learning Framework for Big Data Analysis. *IEEE Access*, 7, 3675–3693. doi:10.1109/ACCESS.2018.2889355

She, R., Liu, S., Wan, S., Xiong, K., & Fan, P. (2019). Importance of Small Probability Events in Big Data: Information Measures, Applications, and Challenges. *IEEE Access*. doi:10.1109/access.2019.2926518

Xiao, C., Li, P., Zhang, L., Liu, W., & Bergmann, N. (2018). ACA-SDS: Adaptive Crypto Acceleration for Secure Data Storage in Big Data. *IEEE Access*, 6, 44494–44505. doi:10.1109/ACCESS.2018.2862425

Chapter 12
"Saksham Model" Performance Improvisation Using Node Capability Evaluation in Apache Hadoop

Ankit Shah
Shankersinh Vaghela Bapu Institute of Technology, India

Mamta C. Padole
(iD) https://orcid.org/0000-0002-0695-5970
The Maharaja Sayajirao University of Baroda, India

ABSTRACT

Big Data processing and analysis requires tremendous processing capability. Distributed computing brings many commodity systems under the common platform to answer the need for Big Data processing and analysis. Apache Hadoop is the most suitable set of tools for Big Data storage, processing, and analysis. But Hadoop found to be inefficient when it comes to heterogeneous set computers which have different processing capabilities. In this research, we propose the Saksham model which optimizes the processing time by efficient use of node processing capability and file management. The proposed model shows the performance improvement for Big Data processing. To achieve better performance, Saksham model uses two vital aspects of heterogeneous distributed computing: Effective block rearrangement policy and use of node processing capability. The results demonstrate that the proposed model successfully achieves better job execution time and improves data locality.

DOI: 10.4018/978-1-5225-9750-6.ch012

INTRODUCTION

In the current digital era, several terabytes of data is generated on daily basis, due to the advances in High Performance Computing, IoT devices, Sensors, Entertainment and Communicating devices and variety of applications. Big Data is a term coined for such a huge magnitude of data. Due to high speed data generation, it is difficult to handle storage and processing of big data, using individual computing systems. But, the data, its processing and analysis have become vital from all perspectives of human life. For big data processing, distributed computing is the widely adopted approach, by researchers and scientists.

Distributed computing allows us to break big data processing tasks or jobs among multiple computing devices. Big data processing jobs can be executed on homogeneous or heterogeneous distributed systems. On distributed systems, we may need to dispense these jobs on thousands of machines for computing and finally are required to collect the results. In order to attain rapid outcomes, various tools and techniques need to be adopted for storage, processing and analysis of big data in distributed environment. These tools are required to handle various issues like fault tolerance, reliability, scalability, performance issues and many more. In the prevailing times, Apache Hadoop seems to be promising choice that is capable of handling the enormous amount of data, using HDFS combined with MapReduce.

The paper discusses features of Apache Hadoop and how it manages storage and scheduling of jobs. The existing approach in Hadoop comprises of some limitations, which are resolved using Block Rearrangement and Node Labeling for storage and scheduling, thus, improving performance.

The paper is structured as follows. Section 2 describes briefly about Apache Hadoop and the HDFS block placement policy. Section 3 describes the literature review on related work done for Hadoop performance improvement using different approaches. Section 4 gives an insight into the motivation of our work. Section 5 and 6 explains our proposed approach and Saksham: Block Rearrangement algorithm. Section 7 shows the experimental setup of Grid'5000. Sections 8 explain the results of the proposed approach compared with Hadoop default specifications. Finally, in section 9, the paper is concluded and future enhancements are mentioned.

APACHE HADOOP

Apache Hadoop (Hadoop.apache.org, 2018) is an open-source framework especially developed for the purpose of distributed computing for big data. Hadoop has become widely popular due to its adaptability of commodity hardware. Hadoop

Figure 1. Hadoop 2.0 architecture

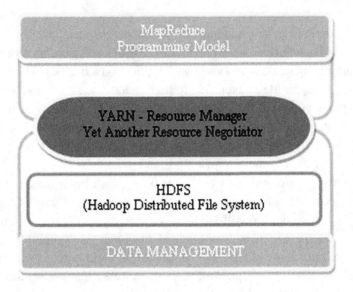

has a better edge in terms of performance in homogeneous environment rather than the heterogeneous one (Dean and Ghemawat, 2008). Hadoop comprises of three important components: Hadoop Distributed File System (HDFS), Yet Another Resource Negotiator (YARN) and MapReduce.

1. HDFS (Shvachko et al., 2010): It allows to split the dataset holding big data into multiple blocks and stores them to various datanodes in the distributed file system. Namenode maintains the metadata for the distributed blocks.
2. YARN (Vavilapalli et al., 2013): It separates the resource management layer and processing components layer. YARN is responsible for managing resources of Hadoop cluster.
3. MapReduce (Dean and Ghemawat, 2008): It is a programming framework on top of YARN, responsible for the processing of big data that enables enormous scalability across thousands of computing devices run on a Hadoop cluster.

Hadoop uses HDFS block placement policy (Shvachko et al., 2010) for placing the data blocks on datanodes. Whenever the client requests to store data blocks in HDFS, it first splits the dataset into blocks according to block size specified (default: 64/128 MB) and also generates the replicas of the blocks as per the specified replication factor (default: 3). This policy tries to place blocks evenly amongst the list of available nodes. In Hadoop, Data locality plays a prominent role in HDFS reliability and performance of MapReduce. Data locality (Team, 2018) relies on moving the computation close to data rather than moving large data blocks to computation. Data locality minimizes network congestion, achieves high performance and reliability.

HDFS Block Placement Policy

"Rack Awareness" is the key concept which HDFS block placement policy relies on. When the client sends a request to place the blocks into Hadoop cluster, HDFS checks whether the client node is in the cluster list of datanodes or not. If it is part of the cluster, then it places the first replica of a data block on that client node itself. If client node is not the part of the cluster, then it randomly chooses the node based on availability status. If each block is having three replicas, it places the second replica of the same block on random datanode of another rack of the cluster, if available. If more than one rack is not available in the cluster, then, it places the data block on any random node, other than the node which already contains a copy of that block. For the third replica of a block, it chooses random node of the same rack, on which the second replica of data block is placed. Figure 2 demonstrates the block placement policy.

Figure 2. HDFS Block Placement Policy [A]: Two Racks [B] Single Rack

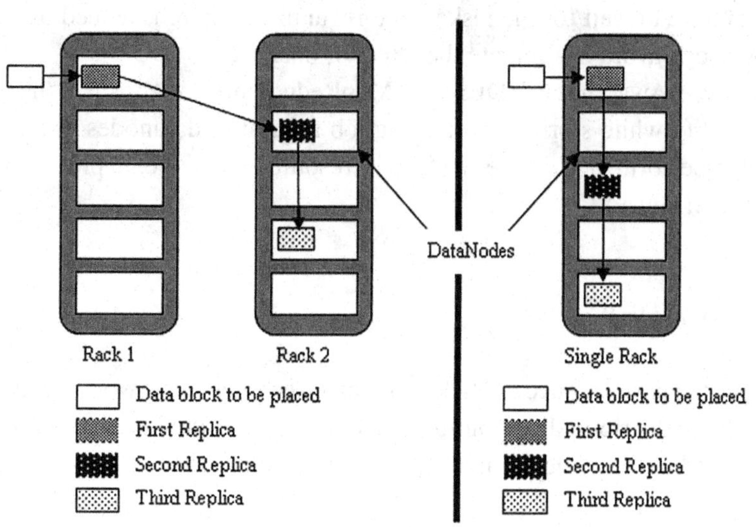

Hadoop Performance Challenges

Hadoop cluster configuration is challenging since the Hadoop framework is a complex distributed environment that involves a combination of hardware and software which affects the performance of Big Data application. On the hardware side, HDFS performance relies on data storage, access and data transfer between datanodes. Datanode hardware specification like processors, memory, and storage space also plays a major role in it. On the software side, Hadoop can be customized and tuned to achieve better performance. There are various challenges must take into account to achieve better Hadoop performance is discussed below:

- Heterogeneous Environment: Hadoop is specifically designed for homogeneous nodes only. In today's era of computing, we cannot imagine having cluster made up of homogeneous nodes only. Data locality variation on the heterogeneous cluster is the biggest challenge to answer. To achieve better Hadoop performance on the heterogeneous cluster is one of the major challenges to exhibit.
- HDFS Block Placement Policy: Hadoop default HDFS block placement strategy can be improvised, as it does not distribute blocks uniformly based on nodes processing capability. Default policy requires major changes specifically under heterogeneous Big Data application processing.
- Load Balancing: Though Hadoop handles load balancing automatically, it is also one of the major concern for the researchers and scientists. Sometimes, the load balancing issue occurs as data is not distributed evenly, so finished tasks have to wait for the task which is running. There is a need of technique which can avoid or mitigate the effect of data skew.
- Resource Awareness: HDFS and MapReduce do not consider the resource capability while storing and putting job request to datanodes. It can achieve better performance if the system is resource-aware (e.g. processor, no of cores, memory).

RELATED WORK

To improve the performance of Hadoop many researchers have worked with diverse approaches. In distributed computing, load balancing is the key area which affects significantly the overall performance, since the system may consist of thousands of computers in the cluster. Many researchers have worked on performance improvement through effective load balancing using various custom-designed algorithms and programming models. In paper (Shah and Padole, 2018), have summarized notable research contribution for load balancing by scheduling (Zaharia et al., 2008; 2010), load balancing during job processing (Liu et al., 2016; 2017) and load balancing using custom block placement (Dharanipragada et al., 2017; Hadaps, 2018; Xie et al., 2010; Hsiao, 2013). In this section, we summarize some of the noteworthy work done to achieve better performance in Hadoop using load balancing and custom block placement strategy.

In the paper (Muthukkaruppan et al., 2016) authors propose the approach which places the blocks based on region placement policy. Data is stored into the plurality of regions rather than the plurality of nodes. Therefore, the complete replica of the region can be stored in a contiguous portion of data. This policy achieves fault-tolerance and data locality for region-based cluster storage. Authors of paper (Qureshi et al., 2016) propose heterogeneous storage media aware strategy which collects storage media, processing capacity and stores them on different storage media types (i.e. HDD, SSD, RAM) according to workload balance. The experiment proves that it reduces imbalancing of the cluster. In the paper (Qu et al., 2016) authors propose dynamic replica placement which works on Markov probability model and places replica homogeneously across the racks. Results show better job completion time compare to HDFS and CDRM and also distribute the replica uniformly across all the nodes. In the paper (Meng et al., 2015) authors propose a strategy which considers network load and disk utilization for placing data blocks. Proposed strategy outperforms default and real-time block placement policy and achieves better performance in terms of throughput and storage space utilization. In the paper (Dai et al., 2017) authors propose improved slot replica placement policy which considers the heterogeneity of nodes and partitions all nodes in 4 sections to store data blocks. Section wise partition scheme achieves greater load balancing and eliminates the use of HDFS balancer. In the paper (Fahmy et al., 2016) authors propose a strategy which tracks spatial characteristics of data to co-locate them. If data blocks are geographically distributed across multiple data centers without concern where a job is running then it degrades the performance tremendously. Here authors have achieved better query execution time by adding spatial data awareness which effectively reduces the job execution time. In paper (Park et al., 2016) authors propose probability based DLMT (Data Local Map Task Slot) approach which adjusts the data placement rate in along with replica eviction policy to improve Hadoop performance and cluster space utilization respectively. In paper (Herodotou et al., 2011) authors propose a model called "Starfish" which dynamically adjusts the Hadoop parameter according to the workload of the job. Starfish work with each phase of Hadoop, starting with job level tuning, real-time parameter adjustment and finally process scheduling. It achieves great performance compare to default Hadoop setup, placement policy, and scheduling scheme. Below table 1 summarizes the work done by the researchers.

MOTIVATION

HDFS block placement policy does not perform optimally for heterogeneous cluster. In today's era of computing, it is impractical to envisage the cluster comprising of homogeneous nodes only. Hence, there is a need for better block placement approach in Hadoop which leverages over the heterogeneous cluster.

In Hadoop, we do not have control over block placement which may result in poor load balancing and may affect MapReduce performance. In MapReduce load unbalancing may create two major problems: First, if MapReduce containers are running on the datanodes which have low processing capability then it job may get skewed. Second, If MapReduce containers are not able to find data blocks where a job is running, then block automatically gets transferred from the nodes of same rack or other racks. In both the cases, overall execution time will increase and which results in high latency and less data locality respectively. Default block placement policy doesn't consider processing capability of nodes while placing the data as discussed in section 2. Hadoop default HDFS block placement strategy needs to be improvised, as it does not consider node processing capability or heterogeneity of system.

PROPOSED MODEL

To achieve to better performance for big data processing, we target upon two important aspects of heterogeneous distributed computing: file system management and process management.

First, file system management basically controls the block placement and allows us to rearrange the blocks on specified nodes based upon two important approaches of load balancing:

1. Balance the load among heterogeneous and homogeneous nodes of the cluster.
2. Balance the load within the cluster based on the processing capability of each node by giving priority to each node.

Table 1. Related Research Contribution

	Performance Improvisation Factors	Research Contribution	Remarks
A region-based placement policy	Fault-tolerance and data locality	Designed region-based cluster storage system which stored once complete replica of the region on single node	This scheme is helpful when plurality of region servers is required.
Robust Data Placement Scheme (RDP)	Load balancing and optimal network congestion	Proposed RDP scheme considers the storage type (i.e. SSD, HDD and RAM) and processing speed of node for balancing.	Authors have successfully demonstrates how storage type and computing capacity prediction can achieve better load balancing and reduce network overhead. Pre-processing for RDP scheme takes significant amount of time when multiple clusters with variety of nodes are there.
Dynamic Replication Strategy (DRS)	Job scheduling time and disk utilization rate	Proposed dynamic replica placement based on Markov model.	Authors have successfully tested model on homogeneous cluster. Authors have not considered the time for replication adjustment which is important justification.
Network sensitive strategy	Strong fault-tolerance block placement and high throughput	Designed scheme which considers network load for data placement. Try to place replica on low network loaded group of nodes.	Proposed strategy reduces the inter-rack transfers which eventually increase the performance also works with heterogeneous cluster. Authors have not considered the load imbalancing issue in Hadoop.
Improved replica placement policy	Load balancing	Designed policy which evenly distributes the replicas into section.	Proposed policy achieves even load balancing across nodes which eliminates the use of HDFS balancer. Policy only proposed for homogeneous cluster.
CoS*-HDFS	Reduce total execution time and network bandwidth.	Proposed algorithm which is aware of geo-spatial data blocks.	Proposed algorithm improves performance of MapReduce query execution and reduces network traffic.
Data Replication Method	Data locality and replication method	Proposed LRFA* policy effectively uses storage space of cluster to achieve better data locality.	Effectiveness and performance is not evaluated which they've claimed.
Starfish	Self-tuning approach	Proposed self-tuning Hadoop model to achieve better performance.	Improved block placement policy significantly improves job running time. Dynamic tuning also tested successfully.

*CoS- Co-Locating Geo-Distributed Spatial Data, LRFA- Least Recently Frequently Access

Our proposed algorithm allows the user to select the nodes based on its individual data processing capability and rearrange the blocks which are placed using the default policy. Default block placement policy of HDFS fails to achieve optimized performance as it does not check the processing capability of the node while placing blocks on the node. Our proposed algorithm achieves that by considering processing capability of nodes and places blocks on nodes which has higher processing capability. If there are two or more nodes having same processing capability then it checks the utilization of the node, and considers the less utilized node first, for block placement. By doing this, we have control over data to be put on selected nodes, considering processing capacity and utilization of nodes.

Second, we use the concept of node labeling to achieve better process management. YARN Node label (Hadoop.apache.org, 2018) allows partitioning the single cluster among multiple sub-clusters. Using this concept, we can mark nodes with meaningful labels i.e. nodes with higher processing capability may be labeled as "high_cpu" and with high memory may be labeled as "high_mem". By combining the proposed algorithm with node label, it can be actually decided where to put jobs. To achieve better data locality the job can be submitted to the nodes where data is actually rearranged using proposed algorithm. Later, Hadoop scheduling can be used to put jobs in queues for processing. It limits the overhead of internode and inter-rack data transfer since process (containers) and data blocks are on to the same nodes. Figure 3 represents the proposed model.

SAKSHAM: BLOCK REARRANGEMENT ALGORITHM

Hadoop uses "Rack Awareness" while placing data blocks for fault tolerance and to achieve better performance. "Rack Awareness" is a concept Hadoop uses to place read/write request to the same rack or nearby rack (Team, 2018). This concept helps to achieve better data locality as discussed in section 2. MapReduce *de facto* standard tries to move the job where data is stored. That node may not have sufficient processing capability or job may get skewed due to less processing/memory capability. Hence, we propose "Saksham: Resource Aware" algorithm which rearranges the data blocks according to user defined processing capability or heterogeneity of environment.

We can apply custom block rearrangement policy by considering two distinct ways. First, we have heterogeneous nodes with different computational capability. Second, we can assign two separate groups for processing depending upon needs of application, homogeneous and heterogeneous nodes. Initially default HDFS block placement policy places data blocks as shown in fig. 4. Figure 4 shows how data placement would place 8 blocks, if client requests from node1 considering replication factor 3.

Figure 3. Proposed "Saksham" Model for Load Balancing

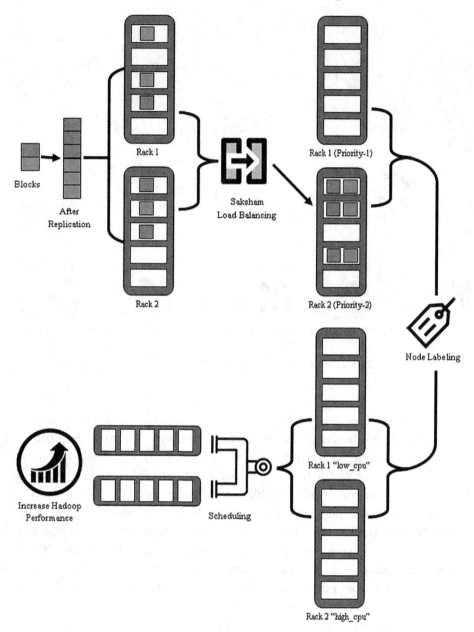

For the first way, we will consider processing capability of nodes for forming a group. For this case, we have considered heterogeneous nodes so nodes are having different processing capability. Few nodes are comparatively slower which may

Figure 4. HDFS Default Block Placement Example

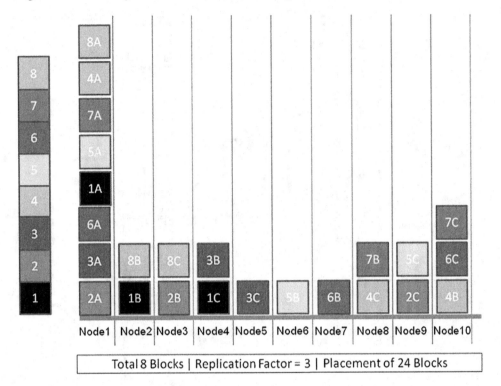

degrade the overall performance of processing. We've divided nodes into two groups priority=1 and priority=2. Assigned priority=2 for nodes which have more processing capability and priority=1 which has lower processing capability. These settings will take place in config.xml file. Once priority is set our "Saksham" algorithm will rearrange the blocks of specified HDFS file path and store all blocks onto the nodes which has priority=2 and remove all the blocks from nodes which have priority=1.

For the second way, we will formulate the group of homogeneous and heterogeneous nodes. We can assign priority 1 or 2 to either of the group. Depends upon big data processing application need we can rearrange all blocks to heterogeneous nodes or homogeneous nodes only. Only nodes with priority=2 will store the blocks and with priority=1 will not store any of them.

While placing all blocks our proposed algorithm also take care that blocks of a file will distribute equally over all the nodes by considering disk usage of each node. Each time before placing the block of file it checks that node should not contain a replica of the same block. The fact that Hadoop works better for the homogeneous environment, fulfilled by our strategy even though cluster is heterogeneous. Figure 5

Figure 5. "Saksham" Approach: Group-1: Priority=2; Group-2: Priority=1

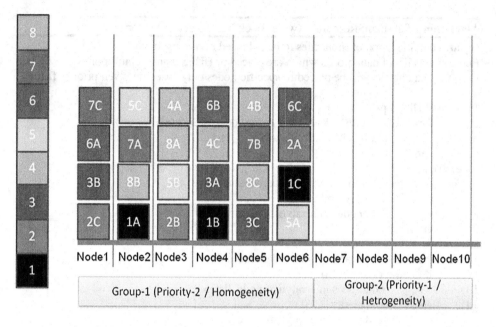

demonstrates how our proposed "Saksham: Resource Aware Block Rearrangement" policy can rearrange blocks according to a priority assigned.

Below fig. 6 is the proposed "Sakasham: Resource Aware Block Rearrangement" algorithm.

- Firstly, algorithm checks the HDFS path contains blocks and also collects the list of datanodes from the DatanodeInfo, Hadoop API and stored them in arraylist.
- Secondly, based upon config.xml file it checks the priority assigned to each node and segregates the nodes in two lists i.e. node_list1 (priority-1) and node_list2 (priority-2).
- In last step blocks along with each replica will be rearranged in nodes which are having priority-2. For rearrangement, it checks the disk utilization and processing capability of each node.

217

Figure 6. Proposed "Saksham" algorithm

Algorithm 1 Saksham: Resource Aware Block Rearrangement algorithm

---

Input: HDFS location of input files to be balanced / rearranged
File contains list of data blocks which are placed in HDFS using default policy.
Output: Data blocks will be placed to specific nodes only based on given priority factor.

1) **if** input HDFS path != null
2)   **foreach** locatedBlocks block : nameNode.getLocatedBlocks() **do**
3)   Put blocks in arraylist<block_list>
4)   **endfor**
5) **endif**
6) **foreach** DatanodeInfo node : getDatanodeStats(Live) **do**
7)   **if** nodes in config.xml != null
8)   Add nodes in arralylist<datanodes>
9)   **endif**
10) **endfor**
11) **foreach** BalancerDataNode node : datanodes **do**
12)   **if** nodes.priority = 1.0
13)   Add nodes in arralylist<node_list1>
14)   **elseif** nodes.priority = 2.0
15)   Add nodes in arralylist<node_list2>
16)   **endif**
17) **endfor**
18) Sort *node_list2* by disk utilization in ascending order
19) **for** each block replica **do**
20)   Initialize <block_list> queue with all blocks
21)   Initialize <node_list2> nodes with priority=2
22)   **for** each block replica in <block_list> **do**
23)   **if** (find first node form <node_list2>) doesn't contains(block)
24)   Put block onto selected node
25)   Remove node from <node_list2>
26)   **if** node_list2 is empty
27)   Initialize with all nodes with priority=2
28)   **endif**
29)   **endif**
30)   **endfor**
31) **endfor**

EXPERIMENT SETUP

We have tested our experiment on Grid'5000 (Grid5000, 2018) heterogeneous cluster. Grid'5000 is large-scale distributed testbed for the researchers to experiment their research on high configurable cluster. We have used 10 nodes for our experiment.

The cluster is configured for Hadoop 2.7.2 version. The configuration of nodes is shown in below table 2. Table 2 shows the heterogeneity of nodes in terms of CPU, memory, storage, number of cores and networks. Table 3 shows priority and node label settings for block rearrangement and the job processing respectively. In Table 3 parasilo and parapide are the name of the nodes in cluster.

EXPERIMENT RESULTS

Initially, we have placed blocks using the default HDFS block placement policy. Afterward, we have applied "Saksham" block rearrangement policy according to settings described in table 3. We have tested our "Saksham" algorithm using 2 datasets of different sizes. First, "Bag of words" text data set of 5 GB and 10 GB. Second 5 GB and 10 GB data generated using TeraGen utility. TeraGen generates random data containing a set of A-Z characters for a subsequent TeraSort run. Text data set is placed using the default HDFS placement policy while TeraGen generates data using MapReduce and places accordingly. In both, the case replication factor is

Table 2. Hadoop 2.7.2 heterogeneous cluster configuration

CPU	Detail Specifications	No of Nodes
Intel Xeon E5-2630 v3 **CPU:** 2 CPUs/node	**Cores:** 8 cores/CPU **Memory:** 128 GB memory **Storage:** 558 GB/node, **Network:** 10 Gbps	Parasilo-[1-6] Total - 6
Intel Xeon X5570 **CPU:** 2 CPUs/node	**Cores:** 4 cores/CPU **Memory:** 24 GB memory **Storage:** 465 GB/node, **Network:** 20 Gbps	Parapide-[1-4] Total - 4

Table 3. Data placement priority and node label settings

Priority-2	Priority-1
Node Label – "high_cpu"	Node Label – "low_cpu"
parasilo-1.rennes.grid5000.fr	parapide-1.rennes.grid5000.fr
parasilo-2.rennes.grid5000.fr	parapide-2.rennes.grid5000.fr
parasilo-3.rennes.grid5000.fr	parapide-3.rennes.grid5000.fr
parasilo-4.rennes.grid5000.fr	parapide-4.rennes.grid5000.fr
parasilo-5.rennes.grid5000.fr	
parasilo-6.rennes.grid5000.fr	

three (3), so total block size for rearrangement is 15 GB and 30 GB. Figure 7 [A-B] and fig. 8 [A-B] shows how blocks are rearranged from default placement to our selected nodes only (i.e. parasilo-[1-6]) with priority is set to 2.

Results of table 4 also show that our "Saksham" algorithm is successfully configured and all the blocks are rearranged to the nodes which have prirority-2 and disk utilization of nodes is also merely same. Figure 9 shows rearrangement time taken by "Saksham" algorithm.

We successfully achieved control over block rearrangement based upon the priority assigned to the nodes. Next, we have assigned Node Labels to the nodes according to table 3 and using YARN resource manager we schedule the jobs according to given labels. This approach will prove the effectiveness of the proposed algorithm.

We have used two standard job applications for testing to prove the effectiveness of our proposed approach.

Figure 7. Saksham Balancing: Text dataset (A) Size-15 GB (B) Size- 30 GB

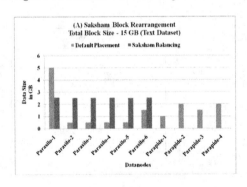
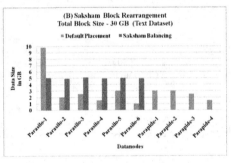

Figure 8. Saksham Balancing: TeraGen dataset (A) Size- 15 GB (B) Size-30 GB

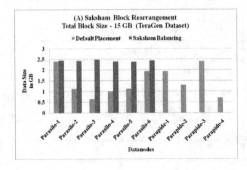
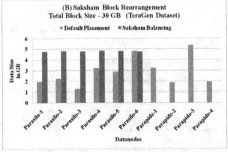

Table 4. Disk utilization of all nodes for different datasize

Datanodes	Text Data 15 GB		Text Data 30 GB		TeraGen 15 GB		TeraGen 30 GB	
	Default Placement	Saksham Balancing	Default Placement	Saksham Balancing	Default Placement	Saksham Balancing	Default Placement	Saksham Balancing
Parasilo-1	5.04	2.55	9.85	5.08	2.41	2.45	1.94	4.77
Parasilo-2	0.50	2.53	2.02	4.93	1.12	2.43	2.23	4.80
Parasilo-3	0.50	2.51	2.52	5.09	0.65	2.49	1.29	4.79
Parasilo-4	0.50	2.51	1.51	4.95	1.01	2.39	3.23	4.85
Parasilo-5	0.50	2.51	3.02	5.01	1.12	2.38	2.87	4.80
Parasilo-6	1.51	2.52	1.01	4.96	1.94	2.44	4.81	4.76
Parapide-1	1.01	28 kb	3.03	28 kb	1.94	28 kb	3.23	28 kb
Parapide-2	2.02	28 kb	3.02	28 kb	1.29	28 kb	1.87	28 kb
Parapide-3	1.51	28 kb	2.52	28 kb	2.41	28 kb	5.35	28 kb
Parapide-4	2.02	28 kb	1.51	28 kb	0.70	28 kb	1.94	28 kb

Figure 9. Saksham block rearrangement time

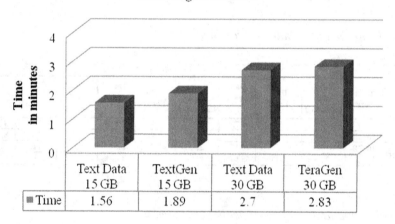

Rearrangement Time

	Text Data 15 GB	TextGen 15 GB	Text Data 30 GB	TeraGen 30 GB
Time	1.56	1.89	2.7	2.83

1. **WordCount:** Standard "bag of words" static test dataset is used for the counting job. Wordcount application counts the total no. of words from the file using MapReduce programming to achieve parallelism.
2. **TeraSort:** The TeraSort benchmark is the most well-known Hadoop benchmark for stress testing. To perform the sorting on data generated by TeraGen using MapReduce programming.

221

We use two datasets of size 10 GB and 20 GB for our experiment. We focus on two important parameters of performance improvement in Hadoop, data locality and job execution time. If data locality gets improve proportionally, it improves MapReduce job processing time. We compare our strategy with default placement execution and after applying only node labeling without "Saksham" balancing. Table 5 shows the result of total tasks launched, data local found and data locality in percentage. Figure 10 shows the comparative result of data locality achieved by various strategies. Results prove that our "Saksham" algorithm with node labeling approach achieves almost 90% data locality which is far better than other strategies.

Last, we use default Hadoop schedulers for our test. We combine our "Saksham" algorithm plus node labeling and schedule the jobs for testing. We test using following schedulers to see the effectiveness: capacity and fair scheduler. Fair scheduler has three policies: Fair-FIFO, Fair-Fair and Fair-DRF. Figure 11 shows our test cycle that we have implemented for comparison. We compare the job execution time of our propose approach with default MapReduce execution, executing using node

Table 5. Data locality results for various strategies

Jobs	Data Size	Default			Node Label			Saksham		
		Total Task Launched	Data Local	Data Locality %	Total Task Launched	Data Local	Data Locality %	Total Task Launched	Data Local	Data Locality %
Word Count	10 GB	128	88	68.75%	122	74	60.66%	120	112	93.33%
	20 GB	240	178	74.17%	227	140	61.67%	233	208	89.27%
TeraSort	10 GB	134	102	76.12%	126	89	70.63%	127	111	87.40%
	20 GB	267	183	68.54%	250	186	74.40%	236	213	90.25%

Figure 10. Comparison of data locality achieved

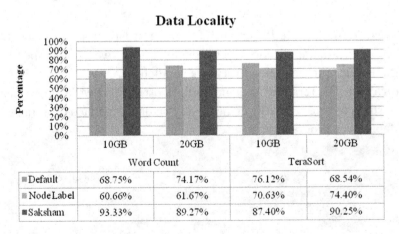

Data Locality

	10GB	20GB	10GB	20GB
	Word Count		TeraSort	
Default	68.75%	74.17%	76.12%	68.54%
NodeLabel	60.66%	61.67%	70.63%	74.40%
Saksham	93.33%	89.27%	87.40%	90.25%

Figure 11. Test cycle of all results

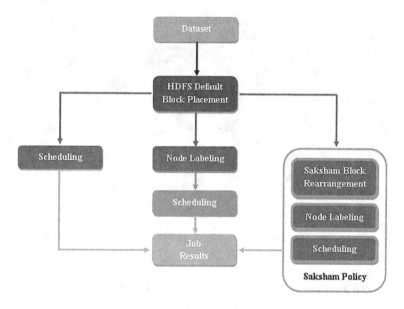

labeling w/o "Saksham" balancing. Figure [12-15] shows results of job execution time of two jobs (i.e. wordcount and terasort) using different schedulers.

Results show that mere implementation of node labeling creates overhead of the internode and interrack block transfer and increase the job execution time. But our "Saksahm" algorithm in combination with node labeling achieves optimized

Figure 12. Job Execution Time using Capacity Scheduler

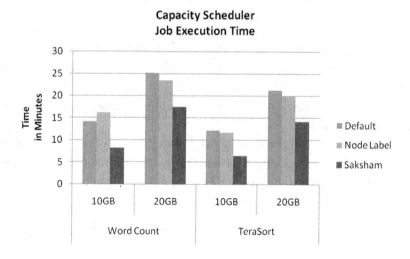

Figure 13. Job Execution Time using Fair-FIFO Scheduler

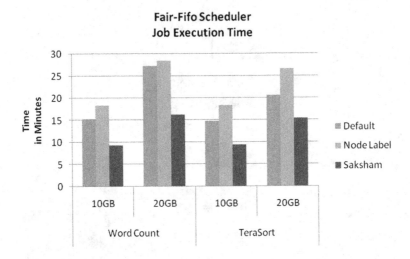

Figure 14. Job Execution Time using Fair-Fair Scheduler

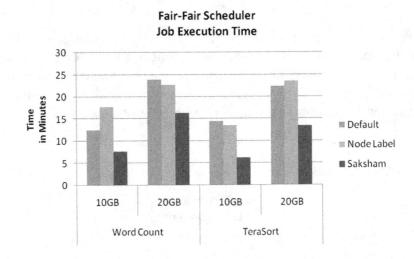

result. Below fig. 16 proves that Fair-Fair scheduling strategy outsmart capacity, fair-fair, fair-drf policies.

Results prove that "Saksham" policy successfully achieves better job execution time and improves the Hadoop performance. But at the same time, it is important to consider the amount of time required for the rearrangement of the blocks. Figure

Figure 15. Job Execution Time using Fair-DRF Scheduler

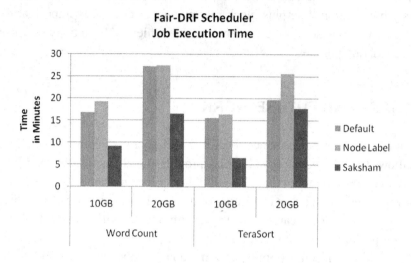

Figure 16. Job Execution time of all scheduling policy

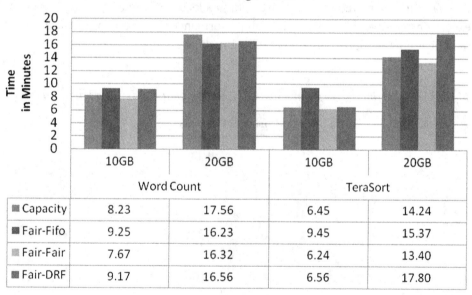

	Word Count		TeraSort	
	10GB	20GB	10GB	20GB
■ Capacity	8.23	17.56	6.45	14.24
■ Fair-Fifo	9.25	16.23	9.45	15.37
■ Fair-Fair	7.67	16.32	6.24	13.40
■ Fair-DRF	9.17	16.56	6.56	17.80

17 shows the total time comparison in fair-fair scheduling policy. Here total time means job execution time plus block rearrangement time. It is important to note that even if we consider rearrangement time we achieve substantially better results than the existing policies.

SUMMARY AND FUTURE WORK

To improve Hadoop performance, HDFS is an imperative component. HDFS not only allows to store the big data but also provides handy support to distribute and process the huge amount of data. Default HDFS block placement policy requires a major improvement in terms of placing of data replicas and processing. This work contributes to the block rearrangement algorithm along with proposed "Saksham" policy for performance optimization of big data processing.

Default block placement policy does not consider the cluster heterogeneity and processing capability of nodes while placing data blocks. MapReduce job tries to place the process, where data blocks are stored but it might be possible that the few nodes which are having data blocks, may not have processing capability. Therefore, it is required to shift the process, where processing capability is available and in that case, it may be required to move data blocks too where the process is put for execution. This would affect the overall performance in Hadoop, which is a matter of concern, particularly while processing big data.

Figure 17. Total time (Execution Time + Rearrangement Time) using Fair-Fair policy

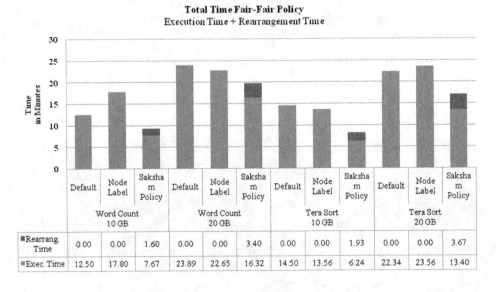

	Word Count 10 GB			Word Count 20 GB			Tera Sort 10 GB			Tera Sort 20 GB		
	Default	Node Label	Saksham Policy	Default	Node Label	Saksham Policy	Default	Node Label	Saksham Policy	Default	Node Label	Saksham Policy
■Rearrang. Time	0.00	0.00	1.60	0.00	0.00	3.40	0.00	0.00	1.93	0.00	0.00	3.67
■Exec. Time	12.50	17.80	7.67	23.89	22.65	16.32	14.50	13.56	6.24	22.34	23.56	13.40

The proposed approach, Saksham: block rearrangement policy leverages the processing capacity of CPU, during block placement. This approach helps MapReduce to minimize the internode and inter-rack transfer. The paper demonstrates that data blocks of a specific file can be placed on the specified nodes. This approach will not affect the overall load balancing of a cluster as other remaining files will not be affected. Experimental results prove that with the use of proposed scheme and Fair-Fair scheduler, Hadoop can achieve better performance for Big Data processing.

Considering all cluster nodes' processing capability along with node labeling and scheduling is a key feature in Saksham policy. It is proved that based on nodes processing capability, replica rearrangement on desired cluster nodes achieves better data locality and turns into better job execution time.

Thus, "Saksham" block rearrangement policy successfully achieves better load balancing compared to default policy and "Saksham" policy combined with node labeling yields a greater performance over Hadoop default performance.

As a future enhancement, it is proposed to use "Saksham" policy for direct process scheduling, without using Hadoop Scheduler for actually scheduling of the job. However, that would require a lot of modification in existing API. It is also possible to think of implementing assigning priorities to jobs dynamically, based on processing capability or hardware specifications.

REFERENCES

Dai, W., Ibrahim, I., & Bassiouni, M. (2017), June. An improved replica placement policy for Hadoop Distributed File System running on Cloud platforms. *Proceedings of the 2017 IEEE 4th International Conference on Cyber Security and Cloud Computing (CSCloud)* (pp. 270-275). IEEE.

Dean, J., & Ghemawat, S. (2008). MapReduce: Simplified data processing on large clusters. *Communications of the ACM, 51*(1), 107–113. doi:10.1145/1327452.1327492

Dharanipragada, J., Padala, S., Kammili, B., & Kumar, V. (2017). Tula: A disk latency aware balancing and block placement strategy for Hadoop. *Proceedings of the 2017 IEEE International Conference on Big Data (Big Data)* (pp. 2853-2858). IEEE. 10.1109/BigData.2017.8258253

Fahmy, M. M., Elghandour, I., & Nagi, M. (2016), December. CoS-HDFS: co-locating geo-distributed spatial data in hadoop distributed file system. *Proceedings of the 3rd IEEE/ACM International Conference on Big Data Computing, Applications and Technologies* (pp. 123-132). ACM.

Grid5000. (2018). *Grid5000*. Retrieved from https://www.grid5000.fr/mediawiki/index.php/Grid5000:Home

Hadaps. (2018). Retrieved from https://github.com/fluxroot/hadaps

Hadoop.apache.org. (2018). *Apache Hadoop 2.7.2 – YARN Node Labels*. Retrieved from https://hadoop.apache.org/docs/r2.7.2/hadoop-yarn/hadoop-yarn-site/NodeLabel.html

Hadoop.apache.org. (2018). *Hadoop – Apache Hadoop 2.7.2*. Retrieved from https://hadoop.apache.org/docs/r2.7.2/index.html

Herodotou, H., Lim, H., Luo, G., Borisov, N., Dong, L., Cetin, F. B., & Babu, S. (2011). Starfish: a self-tuning system for big data analytics. In CIDR (Vol. 11, pp. 261-272).

Hsiao, H. C., Chung, H. Y., Shen, H., & Chao, Y. C. (2013). Load rebalancing for distributed file systems in clouds. *IEEE Transactions on Parallel and Distributed Systems, 24*(5), 951–962. doi:10.1109/TPDS.2012.196

Liu, Q., Cai, W., Shen, J., Fu, Z., Liu, X., & Linge, N. (2016). A speculative approach to spatial-temporal efficiency with multi-objective optimization in a heterogeneous cloud environment. *Security and Communication Networks*, *9*(17), 4002–4012. doi:10.1002ec.1582

Liu, Y., Jing, W., Liu, Y., Lv, L., Qi, M., & Xiang, Y. (2017). A sliding window-based dynamic load balancing for heterogeneous Hadoop clusters. *Concurrency and Computation*, *29*(3), e3763. doi:10.1002/cpe.3763

Meng, L., Zhao, W., Zhao, H., & Ding, Y. (2015). A Network Load Sensitive Block Placement Strategy of HDFS. *Transactions on Internet and Information Systems (Seoul)*, *9*(9).

Muthukkaruppan, K., Ranganathan, K., & Tang, L. (2016). U.S. Patent No. 9,268,808. Washington, DC: U.S. Patent and Trademark Office.

Park, D., Kang, K., Hong, J., & Cho, Y. (2016), April. An efficient Hadoop data replication method design for heterogeneous clusters. *Proceedings of the 31st Annual ACM Symposium on Applied Computing* (pp. 2182-2184). ACM. 10.1145/2851613.2851945

Qu, K., Meng, L., & Yang, Y. (2016), August. A dynamic replica strategy based on Markov model for Hadoop distributed file system (HDFS). *Proceedings of the 2016 4th International Conference on Cloud Computing and Intelligence Systems (CCIS)* (pp. 337-342). IEEE.

Qureshi, F., Muhammad, N., & Shin, D. R. (2016). RDP: A storage-tier-aware robust data placement strategy for Hadoop in a cloud-based heterogeneous environment. *Transactions on Internet and Information Systems (Seoul)*, *10*(9).

Shah, A., & Padole, M. (2018). Load Balancing through Block Rearrangement Policy for Hadoop Heterogeneous Cluster. Paper presented at the *7th International Conference on Advances in Computing, Communication and Informatics*, Bangalore, India, September 19-22. Academic Press. 10.1109/ICACCI.2018.8554404

Shvachko, K., Kuang, H., Radia, S., & Chansler, R. (2010). The hadoop distributed file system. *Proceedings of the 2010 IEEE 26th symposium on mass storage systems and technologies (MSST)* (pp. 1-10). IEEE. 10.1109/MSST.2010.5496972

Team, D. (2018). *Data locality in Hadoop: The Most Comprehensive Guide – DataFlair*. Data-flair.training. Retrieved from https://data-flair.training/blogs/data-locality-in-hadoop-mapreduce/

Vavilapalli, V. K., Murthy, A. C., Douglas, C., Agarwal, S., Konar, M., Evans, R., ... Saha, B. (2013). Apache hadoop yarn: Yet another resource negotiator. *Proceedings of the 4th annual Symposium on Cloud Computing* (p. 5). ACM. 10.1145/2523616.2523633

Xie, J., Yin, S., Ruan, X., Ding, Z., Tian, Y., Majors, J., ... Qin, X. (2010). Improving mapreduce performance through data placement in heterogeneous hadoop clusters. *Proceedings of the 2010 IEEE International Symposium on Parallel & Distributed Processing, Workshops and Phd Forum (IPDPSW)* (pp. 1-9). IEEE.

Zaharia, M., Borthakur, D., Sen Sarma, J., Elmeleegy, K., Shenker, S., & Stoica, I. (2010). Delay scheduling: a simple technique for achieving locality and fairness in cluster scheduling. *Proceedings of the 5th European conference on Computer systems* (pp. 265-278). ACM. 10.1145/1755913.1755940

Zaharia, M., Konwinski, A., Joseph, A. D., Katz, R. H., & Stoica, I. (2008). Improving MapReduce performance in heterogeneous environments. In OSDI (Vol. 8, No. 4, p. 7).

Compilation of References

Abbasi, A., Sarker, S., & Chiang, R. H. (2016). Big data research in information systems: Toward an inclusive research agenda. *Journal of the Association for Information Systems*, *17*(2), I–XXXII. doi:10.17705/1jais.00423

Abdellatif, M., Capretz, F., & Ho, D. (2015). *Software Analytics to Software Practice: A Systematic Literature Review*. Academic Press.

Abdullah, A. S., & Selvakumar, S. (2018). An Improved Medical Informatic Decision Model by Hybridizing Ant colony Optimization Algorithm with Decision Trees for Type II Diabetic Prediction. *Proceedings of the International Conference on Business Analytics and Intelligence*. Academic Press.

Abdullah, A. S., Gayathri, N., & Selvakumar, S. (2017). Determination of the Risk of Heart Disease using Neural Network Classifier. *Proceedings of the National Conference on Big Data Analytics and Mobile Technologies (NCBM 2017)*, Thiagarajar College of Engineering, Madurai. Academic Press.

Abdullah, A. S., Rishi, K. V., Karthickbabu, M., Prathap, D., & Selvaumar, S. (2019). Heart Disease Prediction using Data Mining. *Proceedings of the Fifth International Conference on Biosignals, Images and Instrumentation (ICBSII 2019)*, Chennai, India. Springer India.

Abdullah, A. S., Selvakumar, S., Parkavi, R., Suganya, R., & Venkatesh, M. (2019). An Introduction to Survival Analytics, Types, and Its Applications. UK: Intech Open Publishers. doi:10.5772/intechopen.80953

Abdullah, A. S., Selvakumar, S., & Abirami, A. M. (2017). An Introduction to Data Analytics: Its Types and Its Applications. In *Handbook of Research on Advanced Data Mining Techniques and Applications for Business Intelligence*. Hershey, PA: IGI Global; doi:10.4018/978-1-5225-2031-3.ch001

Abdullah, A. S., Selvakumar, S., Abirami, A. M., Parkavi, R., & Suganya, R. (2018). Big data Analytics in Healthcare Sector. In *Machine Learning Techniques for Improved Business Analytics*. Hershey, PA: IGI Global; doi:10.4018/978-1-5225-3534-8.ch005

Abdullah, A. S., Selvakumar, S., Karthikeyan, P., & Venkatesh, M. (2017). Comparing the Efficacy of Decision Tree and its Variants using Medical Data. *Indian Journal of Science and Technology*, *10*(18), 1–8. doi:10.17485/ijst/2017/v10i18/111768

Abdullah, A. S., Selvakumar, S., & Ramya, C. (2017). Descriptive Analytics. In *Applying Predictive analytics within the service sector*. Hershey, PA: IGI Global; doi:10.4018/978-1-5225-2148-8.ch006

Abdullah, A. S., Suganya, R., Selvakumar, S., & Rajaram, S. (2017). Data Classification: Its Techniques and Big data. In *Handbook of Research on Advanced Data Mining Techniques and Applications for Business Intelligence*. Hershey, PA: IGI Global; doi:10.4018/978-1-5225-2031-3.ch003

Abdullah, A. S., Varshini, R., & Niveditha, J. P. (2017). Sentiment Analysis of Movie Reviews using Twitter data. *Proceedings of the International Conference on Big data and Data Analytics*. Academic Press.

Abirami, A. M., Abdullah, A. S., & Selvakumar, S. (2017). Sentiment Analysis. In *Handbook of Research on Advanced Data Mining Techniques and Applications for Business Intelligence*. Hershey, PA: IGI Global; doi:10.4018/978-1-5225-2031-3.ch009

Aderaldo, C. M., Mendonça, N. C., Pahl, C., & Jamshidi, P. (2017, May). Benchmark requirements for microservices architecture research. *Proceedings of the 1st International Workshop on Establishing the Community-Wide Infrastructure for Architecture-Based Software Engineering* (pp. 8-13). IEEE Press.

Adil, A., Kar, H. A., Jangir, R., & Sofi, S. A. (2015, December). Analysis of multi-diseases using big data for improvement in healthcare. *Proceedings of the 2015 IEEE UP Section Conference on Electrical Computer and Electronics (UPCON)* (pp. 1-6). IEEE.

Afendi, F. M., Ono, N., Nakamura, Y., Nakamura, K., Darusman, L. K., Kibinge, N., ... Kanaya, S. (2013). Data mining methods for omics and knowledge of crude medicinal plants toward big data biology. *Computational and Structural Biotechnology Journal*, *4*(5), 1–14. doi:10.5936/csbj.201301010 PMID:24688691

Ahangama, S., & Poo, C. C. D. (2015). Improving health analytic process through project, communication and knowledge management.

Ahmad, J., Muhammad, K., Lloret, J., & Baik, S. W. (2018). Efficient Conversion of Deep Features to Compact Binary Codes using Fourier Decomposition for Multimedia Big Data. *IEEE Transactions on Industrial Informatics*, *14*(7), 3205–3215. doi:10.1109/TII.2018.2800163

Ahmed, M. (2019). Intelligent Big Data Summarization for Rare Anomaly Detection. *IEEE Access: Practical Innovations, Open Solutions*, *7*, 68669–68677. doi:10.1109/ACCESS.2019.2918364

Akhtar, N. (2014, April). Social network analysis tools. *Proceedings of the 2014 Fourth International Conference on Communication Systems and Network Technologies* (pp. 388-392). IEEE.

Akinola, S. O., & Oyabugbe, O. J. (2015). Accuracies and training times of data mining classification algorithms: An empirical comparative study. *Journal of software Engineering and Applications*, *8*(9), 470.

Aktas, M. S., Aydin, G., Fox, G. C., Gadgil, H., Pierce, M., & Sayar, A. (2005, June). Information services for grid/web service oriented architecture (soa) based geospatial applications. *Proceedings of the 1st International Conference*, Beijing, China (pp. 27-29). Academic Press.

Aktas, M. S. (2018). Hybrid cloud computing monitoring software architecture. Concurrency and Computation. *Practice and Experience*, *30*(21), e4694.

Aktas, M. S., & Astekin, M. (2019). Provenance aware run-time verification of things for self-healing Internet of Things applications. *Concurrency and Computation, Practice and Experience*, *31*(3), e4263.

Aktas, M. S., Fox, G. C., & Pierce, M. (2005, November). Information services for dynamically assembled semantic grids. *Proceedings of the 2005 First International Conference on Semantics, Knowledge and Grid* (pp. 10-10). IEEE. 10.1109/SKG.2005.83

Aktas, M. S., Fox, G. C., & Pierce, M. (2007). Fault tolerant high performance Information Services for dynamic collections of Grid and Web services. *Future Generation Computer Systems*, *23*(3), 317–337. doi:10.1016/j.future.2006.05.009

Aktas, M. S., Fox, G. C., Pierce, M., & Oh, S. (2008). Xml metadata services. Concurrency and Computation. *Practice and Experience*, *20*(7), 801–823.

Aktas, M. S., & Pierce, M. (2010). High-performance hybrid information service architecture. Concurrency and Computation. *Practice and Experience*, *22*(15), 2095–2123.

Aktas, M., Aydin, G., Donnellan, A., Fox, G., Granat, R., Lyzenga, G., & Rundle, J. (2005, June). Implementing geographical information system grid services to support computational geophysics in a service-oriented environment. Proceedings of the *NASA Earth-Sun System Technology Conference*. Adelphi, MD: University of Maryland.

Akter, S., & Wamba, S. F. (2016). Big data analytics in E-commerce: A systematic review and agenda for future research. *Electronic Markets*, *26*(2), 173–194. doi:10.100712525-016-0219-0

Albert, R., Jeong, H., & Barabasi, A. (1999). Diameter of the World Wide Web. *Nature*, *401*(6749), 130–131. doi:10.1038/43601

Alexandrov, A., Bergmann, R., Ewen, S., Freytag, J.-C., Hueske, F., Heise, A., . . . Warneke, D. (2014). *The Stratosphere platform for big data analytics*. Academic Press.

Allouche, G. (2014). *How Big Data can Save Health Care*. Innovation Excellence. Retrieved from [REMOVED HYPERLINK FIELD]http://www.innovationexcellence.com/blog/2014/11/14/how-big-data-can-save-health-care/

Al-Radaideh, Q. A., Al-Shawakfa, E. M., & Al-Najjar, M. I. (2006, December). Mining student data using decision trees. *Proceedings of the International Arab Conference on Information Technology (ACIT'2006)*, Yarmouk University, Jordan. Academic Press.

Alsghaier, H., Akour, M., Shehabat, I., & Aldiabat, S. (2017). The Importance of Big Data Analytics in Business: A Case Study. *American Journal of Software Engineering and Applications*, *6*(4), 111. doi:10.11648/j.ajsea.20170604.12

Anandakumar, H., & Umamaheswari, K. (2017). Supervised machine learning techniques in cognitive radio networks during cooperative spectrum handovers. *Cluster Computing*, *20*(2), 1505–1515. doi:10.100710586-017-0798-3

Anandakumar, H., & Umamaheswari, K. (2018). A bio-inspired swarm intelligence technique for social aware cognitive radio handovers. *Computers & Electrical Engineering*, *71*, 925–937. doi:10.1016/j.compeleceng.2017.09.016

Ang, J., & Teo, T. S. (2000). Management issues in data warehousing: Insights from the Housing and Development Board. *Decision Support Systems*, *29*(1), 11–20. doi:10.1016/S0167-9236(99)00085-8

Anguita, D., Ghelardoni, L., Ghio, A., Oneto, L., & Ridella, S. (2012). The 'K' in k-fold cross validation. *Proceedings of the European Symposium on Artificial Neural Networks, Computational Intelligence and Machine Learning ESANN 2012* (pp. 441-445). i6doc.com publ.

Armstrong, J. (2017, December 4). The Journey to 150,000 Containers at PayPal. Docker. Retrieved from https://blog.docker.com/2017/12/containers-at-paypal

Arulkumar, C. V., & Vivekanandan, P. (2015). Multi-feature based automatic face identification on kernel eigen spaces (KES) under unstable lighting conditions. *Proceedings of the 2015 International Conference on Advanced Computing and Communication Systems*. IEEE.

Arulkumar, C. V., Selvayinayagam, G., & Vasuki, J. (2012). Enhancement in face recognition using PFS using Matlab. *International Journal of Computer Science & Management Research*, *1*(1), 282–288.

Arulkumar, V., & Vivekanandan, P. (2018). An Intelligent Technique for Uniquely Recognizing Face and Finger Image Using Learning Vector Quantisation (LVQ)-based Template Key Generation. *International Journal of Biomedical Engineering and Technology*, *26*(3/4), 237–249. doi:10.1504/IJBET.2018.089951

Atsa'am, D. D., & Bodur, E. K. (2019). Knowledge mining on the association between psychological capital and educational qualifications among hospitality employees. *Current Issues in Tourism*, 1–5. doi:10.1080/13683500.2019.1597026

Austin, P. C., Tu, J. V., Ho, J. E., Levy, D., & Lee, D. S. (2013). Using methods from the data-mining and machine-learning literature for disease classification and prediction: A case study examining classification of heart failure subtypes. *Journal of Clinical Epidemiology.*

Aydin, G., Aktas, M. S., Fox, G. C., Gadgil, H., Pierce, M., & Saya, A. (2005, November). SERVO Grid complexity computational environments (CCE) integrated performance analysis. *Proceedings of the 6th IEEE/ACM International Workshop on Grid Computing.* IEEE.

Aydin, G., Pierce, M., Fox, G., Aktas, M., & Sayar, A. (2004). Implementing GIS Grid Services for the International Solid Earth Research Virtual Observatory. *Pure and Applied Geophysics.*

Bagherzade-Khiabani, F., Ramezhankani, A., Aiziz, F., Hadaegh, F., Steyerberg, E. W., & Khalili, D. (2016). A tutorial on variable selection for clinical prediction models: Feature selection methods in data mining could improve the results. *Journal of Clinical Epidemiology, 71*, 76–85. doi:10.1016/j.jclinepi.2015.10.002 PMID:26475568

Bansal, S., & Gupta, D. (2009). Remote Sensing Image Classification by Improved Swarm Inspired Techniques. *International Conference on Artificial Intelligence and Pattern Recognition (AIPR-09).*

Baruffa, G., Femminella, M., Pergolesi, M., & Reali, G. (2018). A Big Data architecture for spectrum monitoring in cognitive radio applications. *Annales des Télécommunications, 73*(7-8), 451–461. doi:10.100712243-018-0642-7

Bermejo, P., Ossa, L., Gamez, J. A., & Puerta, J. M. (2012). Fast wrapper feauture subset selection in high-dimensional datasets by means of filter re-ranking. *Knowledge-Based Systems, 25*(1), 35–44. doi:10.1016/j.knosys.2011.01.015

Bernstein, D. (2014). Containers and cloud: From lxc to docker to kubernetes. *IEEE Cloud Computing, 1*(3), 81–84. doi:10.1109/MCC.2014.51

Bifet, A., & Frank, E. (2010, October). Sentiment knowledge discovery in twitter streaming data. *Proceedings of the International conference on discovery science* (pp. 1-15). Berlin: Springer.

Bodur, E. K., & Atsa'am, D. D. (2019). Filter variable selection algorithm using risk ratios for dimensionality reduction of healthcare data for classification. *Processes, 7*(4), 222. doi:10.3390/pr7040222

Bonabeau, E., Dorigo, M., & Theraulaz, G. (1999). *Swarm Intelligence from Natural to Artificial System* (1st ed.). Oxford University Press.

Boone, C. A., Skipper, J. B., & Hazen, B. T. (2017). A framework for investigating the role of big data in service parts management. *Journal of Cleaner Production, 153*, 687–691. doi:10.1016/j.jclepro.2016.09.201

Boyd, J., Ferrante, A., Brown, A., Randall, S., & Semmens, J. (2017). Implementing privacy-preserving record linkage: Welcome to the real world. *International Journal of Population Data Science, 1*(1). doi:10.23889/ijpds.v1i1.153

Breiman, L. (2001). Random Forests. *Machine Learning, 45*(1), 5–32. doi:10.1023/A:1010933404324

Brijain, M., Patel, R., Kushik, M., & Rana, K. (2014). A survey on decision tree algorithm for classification.

Brindha, S., Prabha, K., & Sukumaran, S. (2016, January). A survey on classification techniques for text mining. *Proceedings of the 2016 3rd International Conference on Advanced Computing and Communication Systems (ICACCS)* (Vol. 1, pp. 1-5). IEEE. https://www.analyticsvidhya.com/blog/2015

Burg, N. (2014). How Big Data Will Help Save Healthcare. *Forbes Magazine, 10.*

Canty, A., & Ripley, B. (2017). *boot: Bootstrap R (S-Plus) functions. R package version 1.3-20.* Retrieved from https://cran.r-project.org/web/packages/boot/boot.pdf

Cao, M., Chychyla, R., & Stewart, T. (2015). Big Data analytics in financial statement Audits. *Accounting Horizons, 29*(2), 423–429. doi:10.2308/acch-51068

Catena, S., Colla, V., & Vannucci, M. (2014). A hybrid feature selection method for classification purposes. *Proceedings of the UKSim-AMSS 8th European Modeling Symposium on Mathematical Modeling and Computer Simulation* (EMS2014), Pisa, Italy (pp. 39-44). IEEE Computer Society. 10.1109/EMS.2014.44

Catena, S., Colla, V., & Vannucci, M. (2016). A fuzzy system for combining filter features selection methods. *International Journal of Fuzzy Systems, 19*(4), 1168–1180. doi:10.100740815-016-0208-7

Cebr. (2012). *The Value of Big Data and the Internet of Things to the UK Economy.* Retrieved from https://www.sas.com/content/dam/SAS/en_gb/doc/analystreport/cebr-value-of-big-data.pdf

Chakrabarty, T. (2017). *Towards an ideal eGovernance scenario in India.* Retrieved from Tata Consultancy Services: https://www.tcs.com/towards-an-ideal-governance-scenario-in-india

Chambers, C., Raniwala, A., Perry, F., Adams, S., Henry, R., Bradshaw, R., & Weizenbaum, N. (2010). *FlumeJava: Easy.* Efficient Data-Parallel Pipelines. doi:10.1145/1806596.1806638

Chandrashekar, G., & Sahin, F. (2014). A survey on feature selection methods. *Computers & Electrical Engineering, 40*(1), 16–28. doi:10.1016/j.compeleceng.2013.11.024

Chang-Sik, S., Kim, Y. N., Kim, H. S., Park, H. S., & Kim, M. S. (2012). Decision-making model for early diagnosis of congestive heart failure using rough set and decision tree approaches. *Journal of Biomedical Informatics, 45*(5), 999–1008.

Chen, H., Chiang, R., Storey, V., & Robinson, J. (2014). *Business intelligence research business intelligence and analytics: From big data to big impact.* Academic Press.

Chen, N. J. Y., Sha, J., & Zhang, M. (2015). Hadoop-based Distributed Computing Algorithms for Healthcare and Clinic Data Processing. *Proceedings of the Eighth International Conference on Internet Computing for Science and Engineering.* Academic Press.

Chen, H., Chiang, R. H., & Storey, V. C. (2012). Business intelligence and analytics: From big data to big impact. *Management Information Systems Quarterly, 36*(4), 1165–1188. doi:10.2307/41703503

Chen, H., Cohen, P., & Chen, S. (2007). Biased odds ratios from dichotomization of age. *Statistics in Medicine, 26*(18), 3487–3497. doi:10.1002im.2737 PMID:17066378

Chen, J., Chen, Y., Du, X., Li, C., Lu, J., Zhao, S., & Zhou, X. (2013). Big data challenge: A data management perspective. *Frontiers of Computer Science, 7*(2), 157–164. doi:10.100711704-013-3903-7

Chen, P., Plale, B., & Aktas, M. S. (2014). Temporal representation for mining scientific data provenance. *Future Generation Computer Systems, 36,* 363–378. doi:10.1016/j.future.2013.09.032

Christianini, N., & Taylor, J. S. (2000). *An Introduction to support vector machines and other kernel based learning methods.* Cambridge University Press. doi:10.1017/CBO9780511801389

Çığşar, B., & Ünal, D. (2019). Comparison of Data Mining Classification Algorithms Determining the Default Risk. *Scientific Programming.*

Clauset, A., Newman, M., & Moore, C. (2004). Finding community structure in very large networks. *Physical Review. E, 70*(6), 066111. doi:10.1103/PhysRevE.70.066111 PMID:15697438

Crone, S. F., & Kourentzes, N. (2010). Feature selection for time series prediction – A combined filter and wrapper approach for neural networks. *Neurocomputing, 73*(10-12), 1923–1936. doi:10.1016/j.neucom.2010.01.017

Cukier, K. (2010). *Data, data everywhere.* Retrieved from The Economist: https://www.economist.com/special-report/2010/02/27/data-data-everywhere

Dai, W., & Ji, W. (2014). A mapreduce implementation of C4. 5 decision tree algorithm. International journal of database theory and application, 7(1), 49-60.

Dai, W., Ibrahim, I., & Bassiouni, M. (2017), June. An improved replica placement policy for Hadoop Distributed File System running on Cloud platforms. *Proceedings of the 2017 IEEE 4th International Conference on Cyber Security and Cloud Computing (CSCloud)* (pp. 270-275). IEEE.

Das, M., Cui, R., Campbell, D. R., Agrawal, G., & Ramnath, R. (2015). Towards methods for systematic research on big data. *Proceedings of the 2015 IEEE International Conference on Big Data* (pp. 2072-2081). IEEE. 10.1109/BigData.2015.7363989

Davison, A. C., & Hinkley, D. V. (1997). *Bootstrap Methods and their Applications*. Cambridge: Cambridge University Press. doi:10.1017/CBO9780511802843

Dean, J., & Ghemawat, S. (2008). *MapReduce: Simplified Data Processing on Large Clusters*. Academic Press.

Dean, J., & Ghemawat, S. (2008). MapReduce: Simplified data processing on large clusters. *Communications of the ACM, 51*(1), 107–113. doi:10.1145/1327452.1327492

Desjardins, B., Crawford, T., Good, E., Oral, H., Chugh, A., Pelosi, F., ... Bogun, F. (2009). Infarct architecture and characteristics on delayed enhanced magnetic resonance imaging and electro anatomic mapping in patients with post infarction ventricular arrhythmia. *Heart Rhythm, 6*(5), 644–651. doi:10.1016/j.hrthm.2009.02.018 PMID:19389653

Dharanipragada, J., Padala, S., Kammili, B., & Kumar, V. (2017). Tula: A disk latency aware balancing and block placement strategy for Hadoop. *Proceedings of the 2017 IEEE International Conference on Big Data (Big Data)* (pp. 2853-2858). IEEE. 10.1109/BigData.2017.8258253

Dimopoulos, S., Krintz, C., & Wolski, R. (2016). Big data framework interference in restricted private cloud settings. *Proceedings of the 2016 IEEE International Conference on Big Data* (pp. 335-340). IEEE. 10.1109/BigData.2016.7840620

Dong, W., & Xiang-bin, W. (2008). Particle Swarm Intelligence Classification Algorithm for Remote Sensing Images. *IEEE Pacific-Asia Workshop on Computational Intelligence and Industrial Application*. 10.1109/PACIIA.2008.26

Dpkp. (2019). Dpkp/kafka-python. Retrieved from https://github.com/dpkp/kafka-python

Dragoni, N., Lanese, I., Larsen, S. T., Mazzara, M., Mustafin, R., & Safina, L. (2017, June). Microservices: How to make your application scale. *Proceedings of the International Andrei Ershov Memorial Conference on Perspectives of System Informatics* (pp. 95-104). Springer, Cham.

Dragoni, N., Giallorenzo, S., Lafuente, A. L., Mazzara, M., Montesi, F., Mustafin, R., & Safina, L. (2017). Microservices: yesterday, today, and tomorrow. In *Present and ulterior software engineering* (pp. 195–216). Cham: Springer.

Drowning in numbers – Digital data will flood the planet—and help us understand it better. (2011). Retrieved from The Economist: https://www.economist.com/graphic-detail/2011/11/18/drowning-in-numbers

Du, M., Wang, K., Xia, Z., & Zhang, Y. (2018). Differential privacy preserving of training model in wireless Big Data with edge computing. *IEEE Transactions on Big Data*. doi:10.1109/tbdata.2018.2829886

Dunbar, R. (1998). *Grooming, gossip, and the evolution of language*. Harvard University Press.

Du, Z. (2013). Inconsistencies in big data: Cognitive Informatics & Cognitive Computing (ICCI* CC), 2013. *Proceedings of the 12th IEEE International Conference. IEEE.*

Ebner, K., Buhnen, T., & Urbach, N. (2014, January). Think big with Big Data: Identifying suitable Big Data strategies in corporate environments. *Proceedings of the 2014 47th Hawaii International Conference on System Sciences (HICSS)* (pp. 3748-3757). IEEE.

Ehrenstein, V., Nielsen, H., Pedersen, A. B., Johnsen, S. P., & Pedersen, L. (2017). Clinical epidemiology in the era of big data: New opportunities, familiar challenges. *Clinical Epidemiology, 9,* 245–250. doi:10.2147/CLEP.S129779 PMID:28490904

Enticott, J. C., Kandane-Rathnayake, R. K., & Phillips, L. E. (2012). Odds ratios simplified. *Transfusion, 52*(3), 467–469. doi:10.1111/j.1537-2995.2011.03429.x PMID:22070765

Erikson, E. H. E. (1950). *Childhood and society.* New York: Norton.

Erwin, R. (2015). Data literacy: Real-world learning through problem-solving with data sets. *American Secondary Education, 43*(2), 18–26.

Esposito, C., Ficco, M., Palmieri, F., & Castiglione, A. (2015). A knowledge-based platform for Big Data analytics based on publish/subscribe services and stream processing. *Knowledge-Based Systems, 79,* 3–17. doi:10.1016/j.knosys.2014.05.003

Fahmy, M. M., Elghandour, I., & Nagi, M. (2016), December. CoS-HDFS: co-locating geo-distributed spatial data in hadoop distributed file system. *Proceedings of the 3rd IEEE/ACM International Conference on Big Data Computing, Applications and Technologies* (pp. 123-132). ACM.

Fernandes, L. M., O'Connor, M., & Weaver, V. (2012). Big data, bigger outcomes. *Journal of American Health Information Management Association, 83*(10), 38–43. PMID:23061351

Fesenmaier, D. R., Kuflik, T., & Neidhardt, J. (2016). Rectour 2016: workshop on recommenders in tourism. *Proceedings of the 10th ACM Conference on Recommender systems* (pp. 417-418). ACM.

Fleuret, F. (2004). Fast binary feature selection with conditional mutual information. *Journal of Machine Learning Research, 5,* 1531–1555.

Fortunato, S. (2010). Community detection in graphs. *Physics Reports, 486*(3-5), 75–174. doi:10.1016/j.physrep.2009.11.002

Fox, G. C., Aktas, M. S., Aydin, G., Gadgil, H., Pallickara, S., Pierce, M. E., & Sayar, A. (2009). Algorithms and the Grid. *Computing and visualization in science, 12*(3), 115-124.

Fox, J., Weisberg, S., & Price, B. (2018). *carData: Companion to applied regression data sets. R package version 3.0-2.* Retrieved from https://CRAN.R-project.org/package=carData

Fox, G. C., Aktas, M. S., Aydin, G., Bulut, H., Pallickara, S., Pierce, M., & Zhai, G. (2006). Real time streamingdatagridapplications. In *Distributed Cooperative Laboratories: Networking, Instrumentation, and Measurements* (pp. 253–267). Boston, MA: Springer. doi:10.1007/0-387-30394-4_17

Frenay, B., Doquire, G., & Verleysen, M. (2013). Is mutual information adequate for feature selection in regression? *Neural Networks*, *48*, 1–7. doi:10.1016/j.neunet.2013.07.003 PMID:23892907

Frenkiel, R., Badrinath, B., Borres, J., & Yates, R. (2000). 4). The Infostations challenge: Balancing cost and ubiquity in delivering wireless data. *IEEE Personal Communications*, *7*(2), 66–71. doi:10.1109/98.839333

Gamage, P. (2016). New development: Leveraging 'big data' analytics in the public sector. *Public Money & Management*, *36*(5), 385–390. doi:10.1080/09540962.2016.1194087

Gandhi, B. S., & Deshpande, L. A. (2016, August). The survey on approaches to efficient clustering and classification analysis of big data. *Proceedings of the 2016 International Conference on Computing Communication Control and automation (ICCUBEA)* (pp. 1-4). IEEE. 10.1109/ICCUBEA.2016.7859993

Gandomi, A., & Haider, M. (2015). Beyond the hype: Big data concepts, methods, and analytics. *International Journal of Information Management*, *35*(2), 137–144. doi:10.1016/j.ijinfomgt.2014.10.007

Gao, S., & Li, H. (2012, August). Breast cancer diagnosis based on support vector machine. *Proceedings of the 2012 2nd International Conference on Uncertainty Reasoning and Knowledge Engineering* (pp. 240-243). IEEE.

Garg, N. (2013). *Learning Apache Kafka: start from scratch and learn how to administer Apache Kafka effectively for messaging.* Academic Press.

George, G., Osinga, E. C., Lavie, D., & Scott, B. A. (2016). Big data and data science methods for management research.

Gobble, M. M. (2013). Creating change. *Research Technology Management*, *56*(5), 62–66. doi:10.5437/08956308X5605005

Godfrey, D., Johns, C., Meyer, C. D., Race, S., & Sadek, C. (2014). *A case study in text mining: Interpreting twitter data from world cup tweets.*

Goel, Gupta, & Panchal. (2011). Hybrid bioinspired techniques for land cover feature extraction: A remote sensing perspective. *Applied Soft Computing, 12*(2), 832-849.

Goel, L., Gupta, D., Panchal, V. K., & Abraham, A. (2012). Taxonomy of nature inspired computational intelligence: A remote sensing perspective. *Fourth World Congress on Nature and Biologically Inspired Computing (NaBIC)*. 10.1109/NaBIC.2012.6402262

Compilation of References

Golub, T. R., Slonim, D. K., Tamayo, P., Huard, C., Gaasenbeek, M., Mesirov, J. P., ... Lander, E. S. (1999). Molecular classification of cancer: Class discovery and class prediction by gene expression monitoring. *Science*, *286*(5439), 531–537. doi:10.1126cience.286.5439.531 PMID:10521349

Goodman, D., Borras, J., Mandayam, N., & Yates, R. (2000). INFOSTATIONS: a new system model for data and messaging services. *1997 IEEE 47th Vehicular Technology Conference. Technology in Motion, 2*, 969-973.

Goodwin, K. (2011). *Designing for the digital age: How to create human-centered products and services*. John Wiley & Sons.

Gorade, S. M., Deo, A., & Purohit, P. (2017). A study of some data mining classification techniques. *International Research J. of Engineering and Technology (IRJET), 4*.

Grand View Research. (2016). *Big Data Market Size, Share Forecast, Industry Research Report, 2025*. Retrieved from https://www.grandviewresearch.com/industry-analysis/big-data-industry?utm_source=Pressrelease&utm_medium=referral&utm_campaign=abnewswire_05oct&utm_content=content

Grid5000. (2018). *Grid5000*. Retrieved from https://www.grid5000.fr/mediawiki/index.php/Grid5000:Home

Groves, P., Kayyali, B., Knott, D., & Van Kuiken, S. (2013). The 'big data'revolution in healthcare. *The McKinsey Quarterly, 2*(3).

Gu, D., Li, J., Li, X., & Liang, C. (2017). Visualizing the knowledge structure and evolution of big data research in healthcare informatics. *International Journal of Medical Informatics*, *98*, 22–32. doi:10.1016/j.ijmedinf.2016.11.006 PMID:28034409

Gudivada, V. N., Baeza-Yates, R. A., & Raghavan, V. V. (2015). Big Data: Promises and Problems. *IEEE Computer, 48*(3), 20–23. doi:10.1109/MC.2015.62

Gupta & Kamalapur. (2014). Study of Classification of Remote Sensing Images using Particle Swarm Optimization based approach. *International Journal of Application or Innovation in Engineering & Management, 3*(10).

Gupta, V., Kaur, K., & Kaur, S. (2017). Performance comparison between lightweight virtualization using docker and heavy weight virtualization. *Mar, 2*, 211-216.

Gupta, D., Das, B., & Panchal, V. K. (2011). *A Methodical Study for the Extraction of Landscape Traits Using Membrane Computing technique, GEM*. WORLDCOMP.

Hackman, J. R. (1987). The design of work teams. In J. W. Lorsch (Ed.), Handbook of organizational behavior (pp. 315-342). Englewood Cliffs, NJ: Prentice-Hall.

Hadaps. (2018). Retrieved from https://github.com/fluxroot/hadaps

Hadoop.apache.org. (2018). *Apache Hadoop 2.7.2 – YARN Node Labels*. Retrieved from https://hadoop.apache.org/docs/r2.7.2/hadoop-yarn/hadoop-yarn-site/NodeLabel.html

Hadoop.apache.org. (2018). *Hadoop – Apache Hadoop 2.7.2*. Retrieved from https://hadoop.apache.org/docs/r2.7.2/index.html

Halaweh, M., & Massry, A. E. (2015). Conceptual model for successful implementation of big data in organizations. *Journal of International Technology and Information Management, 24*(2), 2.

Haldorai, A., & Kandaswamy, U. (2019). Intelligent Spectrum Handovers in Cognitive Radio Networks. Springer International Publishing. doi:10.1007/978-3-030-15416-5

Haldorai, A., & Kandaswamy, U. (2019). Software Radio Architecture: A Mathematical Perspective. In Intelligent Spectrum Handovers in Cognitive Radio Networks (pp. 65-86). Springer.

Haldorai, A., & Ramu, A. (Eds.). (2019). Cognitive Social Mining Applications in Data Analytics and Forensics. Hershey, PA: IGI Global. doi:10.4018/978-1-5225-7522-1

Haldorai, A., & Kandaswamy, U. (2019). Energy Efficient Network Selection for Cognitive Spectrum Handovers. In *Intelligent Spectrum Handovers in Cognitive Radio Networks* (pp. 41–64). Springer; doi:10.1007/978-3-030-15416-5_3

Hancock, P., & Kent, P. (2016). Interpretation of dichotomous outcomes: Risk, odds, risk ratios, odds ratios and number needed to treat. *Journal of Physiotherapy, 62*(3), 172–174. doi:10.1016/j.jphys.2016.02.016 PMID:27320830

Han, J., Pei, J., & Kamber, M. (2010). *Data mining: concepts and techniques* (3rd ed.). Elsevier.

Harerimana, G., Jang, B., Kim, J. W., & Park, H. K. (2018). Health Big Data Analytics: A Technology Survey. *IEEE Access, 6*, 65661–65678. doi:10.1109/ACCESS.2018.2878254

Harsheni, S. K., & Souganthika, S. GokulKarthik, K., Abdullah, S.A., & Selvakumar, S. (March 2019). Analysis of the Risk factors of Heart disease using Step-wise Regression with Statistical evaluation. Proceedings of the International Conference on Emerging Current Trends in Computing and Expert Technology (COMET 2019) (pp. 22-23). Springer.

Hashem, I. A. T., Yaqoob, I., Anuar, N. B., Mokhtar, S., Gani, A., & Khan, S. U. (2015). The rise of "big data" on cloud computing: Review and open research issues. *Information Systems, 47*, 98–115. doi:10.1016/j.is.2014.07.006

Hastie, T., Tibshrani, R., & Friedman, J. (2001). *Elements of statistical learning: Data mining, Inference and prediction*. Berlin: Springer Verlag. doi:10.1007/978-0-387-21606-5

Herodotou, H., Lim, H., Luo, G., Borisov, N., Dong, L., Cetin, F. B., & Babu, S. (2011). Starfish: a self-tuning system for big data analytics. In CIDR (Vol. 11, pp. 261-272).

He, W., Shen, J., Tian, X., Li, Y., Akula, V., Yan, G., & Tao, R. (2015). Gaining competitive intelligence from social media data: Evidence from two largest retail chains in the world. *Industrial Management & Data Systems, 115*(9), 1622–1636. doi:10.1108/IMDS-03-2015-0098

Hilbert, M. (2016). Big data for development: A review of promises and challenges. *Development Policy Review, 34*(1), 135–174. doi:10.1111/dpr.12142

Hoenisch, P., Weber, I., Schulte, S., Zhu, L., & Fekete, A. (2015, November). Four-foldauto-scaling on a contemporary deployment platform using docker containers. *Proceedings of the International Conference on Service-Oriented Computing* (pp. 316-323). Springer. 10.1007/978-3-662-48616-0_20

Hou, B., Li, K. L., Shi, Y., Tao, L., & Liu, J. (2016). MongoDB NoSQL Injection Analysis and Detection. *Proceedings of the International Conference on Cyber Security and Cloud Computing.* Academic Press.

Hsiao, H. C., Chung, H. Y., Shen, H., & Chao, Y. C. (2013). Load rebalancing for distributed file systems in clouds. *IEEE Transactions on Parallel and Distributed Systems, 24*(5), 951–962. doi:10.1109/TPDS.2012.196

Huang, J., Wang, C.-X., Bai, L., Sun, J., Yang, Y., Li, J., Zhou, M. (2018). A Big Data Enabled Channel Model for 5G Wireless Communication Systems. *IEEE Transactions on Big Data.* doi:10.1109/tbdata.2018.2884489

Huang, S. H., Wulsin, L. R., Li, H., & Guo, J. (2009). Dimensionality reduction for knowledge discovery in medical claims database: Application to antidepressant medication utilization study. *Computer Methods and Programs in Biomedicine, 93*(2), 115–123. doi:10.1016/j.cmpb.2008.08.002 PMID:18835058

Hussain, S., & Lee, S. (2015). Semantic transformation model for clinical documents in big data to support healthcare analytics. *Proceedings of the Tenth International Conference on Digital Information Management.* Academic Press.

Hu, Z., Bao, Y., Xiong, T., & Chiong, R. (2015). Hybrid filter–wrapper feature selection for short-term load forecasting. *Engineering Applications of Artificial Intelligence, 40,* 17–27. doi:10.1016/j.engappai.2014.12.014

IDC. (2015). *Double-Digit Growth Forecast for the Worldwide Big Data and Business Analytics Market Through 2020 Led by Banking and Manufacturing Investments, According to IDC.* Retrieved from https://www.idc.com/url.do?url=/includes/pdf_download.jsp?containerId=prUS41826116&position=51

Ives, Z. G., Florescu, D., Friedman, M., Levy, A., & Weld, D. S. (1999, June). An adaptive query execution system for data integration. *SIGMOD Record, 28*(2), 299–310. doi:10.1145/304181.304209

Jamil, N., Ishak, I., Sidi, F., Affendey, L., & Mamat, A. (2015). A Systematic Review on the Profiling of Digital News Portal for Big Data Veracity. *Procedia Computer Science*, *72*, 390–397. doi:10.1016/j.procs.2015.12.154

Jangade, R., & Chauhan, R. (2016). Big Data with Integrated Cloud Computing For Healthcare Analytics. *Proceedings of the International Conference on Computing for Sustainable Global Development*. Academic Press.

Jang, B., Park, S., Lee, J., & Hahn, S.-G. (2018). Three Hierarchical Levels of Big-Data Market Model Over Multiple Data Sources for Internet of Things. *IEEE Access*, *6*, 31269–31280. doi:10.1109/ACCESS.2018.2845105

Javed, K., Babri, H. A., & Saeed, M. (2014). Impact of a metric of association between two variables on performance of filters for binary data. *Neurocomputing*, *143*, 248–260. doi:10.1016/j.neucom.2014.05.066

Jee, K., & Kim, G. H. (2013). Potentiality of big data in the medical sector: Focus on how to reshape the healthcare system. *Healthcare Informatics Research*, *19*(2), 79–85. doi:10.4258/hir.2013.19.2.79 PMID:23882412

Jin, Y., Deyu, T., & Yi, Z. (2011). A Distributed Storage Model for HER Based on HBase. *Proceedings of the International Conference on Information Management, Innovation Management and Industrial Engineering*. Academic Press.

Jing Zhao, J., & Guohong Cao, G. (2008). VADD: Vehicle-Assisted Data Delivery in Vehicular *Ad Hoc* Networks. *IEEE Transactions on Vehicular Technology*, *57*(3), 1910–1922. doi:10.1109/TVT.2007.901869

Jin, K., Cheng, H., & Wang, W. (2018). Using odds ratios to detect differential item functioning. *Applied Psychological Measurement*, *42*(8), 613–629. doi:10.1177/0146621618762738 PMID:30559570

Jobs, C. G., Aukers, S. M., & Gilfoil, D. M. (2015). The impact of big data on your firms marketing communications: A framework for understanding the emerging marketing analytics industry. *Academy of Marketing Studies Journal*, *19*(2).

Jung, Y., & Hu, J. (2015). A k-fold averaging cross-validation procedure. *Journal of Nonparametric Statistics*, *27*(2), 1–13. doi:10.1080/10485252.2015.1010532 PMID:27630515

Junqué de Fortuny, E., Martens, D., & Provost, F. (2013). Predictive modeling with big data: Is bigger really better? *Big Data*, *1*(4), 215–226. doi:10.1089/big.2013.0037 PMID:27447254

K., R., & K., M. (2017). e-Governance using Data Warehousing and Data Mining. *International Journal of Computer Applications, 169*(8), 28-31.

Kaisler, S., Armour, F., Espinosa, J. A., & Money, W. (2013). Big data: Issues and challenges moving forward. *Proceedings of the 2013 46th Hawaii international conference on System sciences (HICSS)* (pp. 995-1004). IEEE.

Kankanhalli, A., Hahn, J., Tan, S., & Gao, G. (2016). Big data and analytics in healthcare: Introduction to the special section. *Information Systems Frontiers, 18*(2), 233–235.

Karaolis, A., Moutiris, A., Hadjipanayi, D., & Pattichis, S. (2010, May). Assessment of the Risk Factors of Coronary Heart Events Based on Data Mining With Decision Trees. *IEEE Transactions on Information Technology in Biomedicine, 14*(3).

Kaushik, S. (2016). *Introduction to feature selection methods with an example.* Analytics Vidhya. Retrieved from https://www.analyticsvidhya.com/blog/2016/12/introduction-to-feature-selection-methods-with-an-example-or-how-to-select-the-right-variables/

Keller, S. A., Koonin, S. E., & Shipp, S. (2012). Big data and city living–what can it do for us? *Significance, 9*(4), 4–7. doi:10.1111/j.1740-9713.2012.00583.x

Kelly, J., & Kaskade, J. (2013). CIOS & Big Data what your IT team wants you to know. Retrieved from http://blog.infochimps.com/2013/01/24/cios-big-data

Kimble, C., & Milolidakis, G. (2015). Big data and business intelligence: Debunking the myths. *Global Business and Organizational Excellence, 35*(1), 23–34. doi:10.1002/joe.21642

Kim, M., Zimmermann, T., DeLine, R., & Begel, A. (2016). The emerging role of data scientists on software development teams. *Proceedings of the 38th International Conference on Software Engineering* (pp. 96-107). ACM. 10.1145/2884781.2884783

Kitchin, R., & McArdle, G. (2016). What makes Big Data, Big Data? Exploring the ontological characteristics of 26 datasets. *Big Data & Society, 3*(1).

Kitchin, R., Lauriault, T. P., & McArdle, G. (2015). Knowing and governing cities through urban indicators, city benchmarking and real-time dashboards. *Regional Studies. Regional Science, 2*(1), 6–28.

Krawatzeck, R., Dinter, B., & Thi, D. A. P. (2015, January). How to make business intelligence agile: The Agile BI actions catalog. *Proceedings of the 2015 48th Hawaii International Conference on System Sciences (HICSS)* (pp. 4762-4771). IEEE.

Kreps, J., Narkhede, N., & Rao, J. (2011, June). Kafka: A distributed messaging system for log processing. *Proceedings of the NetDB* (pp. 1-7). Academic Press.

Kuhn, M., Wing, J., Weston, S., Williams, A., Keefer, C., Engelhardt, A., . . . Kenkel, B. (2019). *caret: Classification and regression training. R package version 6.0-82.* Retrieved from https://CRAN.R-project.org/package=caret

Kullback, S., & Leibler, R. A. (1951). On information and sufficiency. *Annals of Mathematical Statistics, 22*(1), 79–86. doi:10.1214/aoms/1177729694

Kumar, M., & Nagar, M. (2017). Big data analytics in agriculture and distribution channel. In *2017 International Conference on Computing Methodologies and Communication (ICCMC)* (pp. 384-387). IEEE. 10.1109/ICCMC.2017.8282714

Kwon, O., Lee, N., & Shin, B. (2014). Data quality management, data usage experience and acquisition intention of big data analytics. *International Journal of Information Management, 34*(3), 387–394. doi:10.1016/j.ijinfomgt.2014.02.002

Labor Relations dataset. (n.d.). UCI. Retrieved from https://archive.ics.uci.edu/ml/datasets/Labor+Relations

Labrinidis, A., & Jagadish, H. V. (2012). Challenges and opportunities with big data. *Proceedings of the VLDB Endowment International Conference on Very Large Data Bases, 5*(12), 2032–2033. doi:10.14778/2367502.2367572

Lary, D. J., Alavi, A. H., Gandomi, A. H., & Walker, A. L. (2016). Machine learning in geosciences and remote sensing. *Geoscience Frontiers, 7*(1), 3–10. doi:10.1016/j.gsf.2015.07.003

Laudon, K. C., & Laudon, J. P. (2016). *Management information system*. Pearson Education India.

Lazar, C., Taminau, J., Meganck, S., Steenhoff, D., Coletta, A., Molter, C., ... Nowe, A. (2012). A survey on filter techniques for feature selection in gene expression microarray analysis. *IEEE/ACM Transactions on Computational Biology and Bioinformatics, 9*(4), 1106–1119. doi:10.1109/TCBB.2012.33 PMID:22350210

Lee, D. (2019). Big Data Quality Assurance Through Data Traceability: A Case Study of the National Standard Reference Data Program of Korea. *IEEE Access, 7*, 36294–36299. doi:10.1109/ACCESS.2019.2904286

Lee, J. H., Clarke, R. I., & Perti, A. (2015). Empirical evaluation of metadata for video games and interactive media. *Journal of the Association for Information Science and Technology, 66*(12), 2609–2625. doi:10.1002/asi.23357

Lewis, J., & Fowler, M. (2014). Microservices. Retrieved from https://martinfowler.com/-articles/microservices.html

Li, J., Liu, H., Tung, A., & Wong, L. (2014). The practical bioinformatician. In L. Wong (Ed.), Data mining techniques for the practical bioinformatician (pp. 35-70). 5 Toh Tuck Link, Singapore: World Scientific Publishing.

Limit a container's resources. (2019, May 25). Docker. Retrieved from https://docs.docker.com/config/containers/resource_constraints

Liu, D., Li, T., & Liang, D. (2014). Incorporating logistic regression to decision-theoretic rough sets for classifications. *International Journal of Approximate Reasoning*, *55*(1), 197–210. doi:10.1016/j.ijar.2013.02.013

Liu, Q., Cai, W., Shen, J., Fu, Z., Liu, X., & Linge, N. (2016). A speculative approach to spatial-temporal efficiency with multi-objective optimization in a heterogeneous cloud environment. *Security and Communication Networks*, *9*(17), 4002–4012. doi:10.1002ec.1582

Liu, Y., Jing, W., Liu, Y., Lv, L., Qi, M., & Xiang, Y. (2017). A sliding window-based dynamic load balancing for heterogeneous Hadoop clusters. *Concurrency and Computation*, *29*(3), e3763. doi:10.1002/cpe.3763

Liu, Y., Wang, Q., & Chen, H. Q. (2015). Research on IT Architecture of Heterogeneous Big Data. *J. Appl. Sci. Eng.*, *18*, 135–142.

Li, X., Wang, L., Lian, Z., & Qin, X. (2018). Migration-Based Online CPSCN Big Data Analysis in Data Centers. *IEEE Access: Practical Innovations, Open Solutions*, *6*, 19270–19277. doi:10.1109/ACCESS.2018.2810255

Lohr, S. (2012). *Big Data's Impact in the World - The New York Times*. Retrieved from The New York Times: https://www.nytimes.com/2012/02/12/sunday-review/big-datas-impact-in-the-world.html

Lu, J., Li, L., Chen, G., Shen, D., Pham, K., & Blasch, E. (2017). Machine learning based Intelligent cognitive network using fog computing. *Sensors and Systems for Space Applications*, *X*. doi:10.1117/12.2266563

Lv, D., Zhu, S., & Liu, R. (2019). Research on Big Data Security Storage Based on Compressed Sensing. *IEEE Access*, *7*, 3810–3825. doi:10.1109/ACCESS.2018.2889716

Maindonald, J. H., & Braun, J. W. (2019). *DAAG: Data analysis and graphics data and functions. R package version 1.22.1*. Retrieved from https://CRAN.R-project.org/package=DAAG

Maldonado, S., & Weber, R. (2009). A wrapper method for feature selection using support vector machines. *Information Sciences*, *179*(13), 2208–2217. doi:10.1016/j.ins.2009.02.014

Manyika, J., Chui, M., Brown, B., Bughin, J., Dobbs, R., Roxburgh, C., & Hung Byers, A. (2011). *Big data: The next frontier for innovation, competition, and productivity*. Academic Press.

Manyika, J., Chui, M., Brown, B., Bughin, J., Dobbs, R., Roxburgh, C., & Byers, A. H. (2011). *Big data: The next frontier for innovation, competition, and productivity*. McKinsey Global Institute.

Marvin, H. J., Janssen, E. M., Bouzembrak, Y., Hendriksen, P. J., & Staats, M. (2017). Big data in food safety: An overview. *Critical Reviews in Food Science and Nutrition*, *57*(11), 2286–2295. doi:10.1080/10408398.2016.1257481 PMID:27819478

Mastrogiannis, N., Boutsinas, B., & Giannikos, I. (2009). A method for improving the accuracy of data mining classification algorithms. *Computers & Operations Research*, *36*(10), 2829–2839. doi:10.1016/j.cor.2008.12.011

Mcafee, A., & Brynjolfsson, E. (2012). *HBR.ORG Spotlight on Big Data Big Data: The Management Revolution.* Academic Press.

McAfee, A., & Brynjolfsson, E. (2012). Big Data: The Management Revolution. *Harvard Business Review*, *90*(10), 60-66. PMID:23074865

Meng, L., Zhao, W., Zhao, H., & Ding, Y. (2015). A Network Load Sensitive Block Placement Strategy of HDFS. *Transactions on Internet and Information Systems (Seoul)*, *9*(9).

Menon, S. P., & Hegde, N. P. (2015, January). A survey of tools and applications in big data. *Proceedings of the 2015 IEEE 9th International Conference on Intelligent Systems and Control (ISCO)* (pp. 1-7). IEEE. 10.1109/ISCO.2015.7282364

Merkel, D. (2014). Docker: lightweight linux containers for consistent development and deployment. *Linux Journal*, (239), 2.

MGI. (2012). *Big Data: The next frontier for innovation, competition, and productivity.* Retrieved from https://www.mckinsey.com/~/media/McKinsey/Business%20Functions/McKinsey%20Digital/Our%20Insights/Big%20data%20The%20next%20frontier%20for%20innovation/MGI_big_data_exec_summary.ashx

Mokhtari, G., Anvari-Moghaddam, A., & Zhang, Q. (2019). A New Layered Architecture for Future Big Data-Driven Smart Homes. *IEEE Access*, *7*, 19002–19012. doi:10.1109/ACCESS.2019.2896403

Murugan, S., & Sumithra M. G. (2019). Efficient Space Communication and Management (SCOaM) Using Cognitive Radio Networks Based on Deep Learning Techniques. *Cognitive Social Mining Applications in Data Analytics and Forensics*, 65–76. doi:10.4018/978-1-5225-7522-1.ch004

Muthukkaruppan, K., Ranganathan, K., & Tang, L. (2016). U.S. Patent No. 9,268,808. Washington, DC: U.S. Patent and Trademark Office.

Nacar, M. A., Aktas, M. S., Pierce, M., Lu, Z., Erlebacher, G., Kigelman, D., ... Yuen, D. A. (2007). VLab: collaborative Grid services and portals to support computational material science. Concurrency and Computation. *Practice and Experience*, *19*(12), 1717–1728.

Nambiar, R., Bhardwaj, R., Sethi, A., & Vargheese, R. (2013). A look at challenges and opportunities of Big Data analytics in healthcare. *Proc. of the 2013 IEEE Int. Conf. Big Data* (pp. 17–22). IEEE. 10.1109/BigData.2013.6691753

Nardelli, M. (2017). Elastic Allocation of Docker Containers in Cloud Environments. In ZEUS (pp. 59-66). Academic Press.

Newman, S. (2015). *Building micro services: designing fine-grained systems*. O'Reilly Media, Inc.

Nichols, W. (2013). Advertising Analytics 2.0. *Harvard Business Review*, *91*(3), 60–68. PMID:23593768

Nimmagadda, S. L., & Dreher, H. V. (2013). Big-data integration methodologies for effective management and data mining of petroleum digital ecosystems. *Proceedings of the 2013 7th IEEE International Conference on Digital Ecosystems and Technologies (DEST)* (pp. 148-153). IEEE. 10.1109/DEST.2013.6611345

Noguchi, Y. (2011a). *Following Digital Breadcrumbs To 'Big Data' Gold: NPR*. Retrieved from www.npr.org: https://www.npr.org/2011/11/29/142521910/the-digital-breadcrumbs-that-lead-to-big-data

Noguchi, Y. (2011b). *The Search For Analysts To Make Sense Of 'Big Data': NPR*. Retrieved from The National Public Radio: https://www.npr.org/2011/11/30/142893065/the-search-for-analysts-to-make-sense-of-big-data

Oh, Y. K., & Min, J. (2015). The mediating role of popularity rank on the relationship between advertising and in-app purchase sales in mobile application market. *Journal of Applied Business Research*, *31*(4), 1311. doi:10.19030/jabr.v31i4.9318

Oliverio, V., & Poli-Neto, O. B. (2017, April). Case Study: Classification Algorithms Comparison for the Multi-Label Problem of Chronic Pelvic Pain Diagnosing. *Proceedings of the 2017 IEEE 33rd International Conference on Data Engineering (ICDE)* (pp. 1507-1509). IEEE.

Omar, A. (2015). Improving Data Extraction Efficiency of Cache Nodes in Cognitive Radio Networks Using Big Data Analysis. *Proceedings of the 9th International Conference on Next Generation Mobile Applications, Services and Technologies*. Academic Press. 10.1109/NGMAST.2015.15

Opresnik, D., & Taisch, M. (2015). The value of big data in servitization. *International Journal of Production Economics*, *165*, 174–184. doi:10.1016/j.ijpe.2014.12.036

Owais, S. S., & Hussein, N. S. (2016). Extract five categories CPIVW from the 9V's characteristics of the big data. *International Journal of Advanced Computer Science and Applications*, *7*(3), 254–258.

Pal, K. (2016). *Why the World Is Moving Toward NoSQL Databases*. Retrieved from Techopedia: https://www.techopedia.com/2/32000/trends/big-data/why-the-world-is-moving-toward-nosql-databases

Pandey, A., & Jain, A. (2017). Comparative analysis of knn algorithm using various normalization techniques. *International Journal of Computer Network and Information Security*, *11*(11), 36–42. doi:10.5815/ijcnis.2017.11.04

Park, D., Kang, K., Hong, J., & Cho, Y. (2016), April. An efficient Hadoop data replication method design for heterogeneous clusters. *Proceedings of the 31st Annual ACM Symposium on Applied Computing* (pp. 2182-2184). ACM. 10.1145/2851613.2851945

Piao, Y., Park, H. W., Jin, C. H., & Ryu, K. H. (2014, January). Ensemble method for classification of high-dimensional data. *Proceedings of the 2014 International Conference on Big Data and Smart Computing (BIGCOMP)* (pp. 245-249). IEEE. 10.1109/BIGCOMP.2014.6741445

Pierce, M. E., Fox, G. C., Aktas, M. S., Aydin, G., Gadgil, H., Qi, Z., & Sayar, A. (2008). The Quake Sim project: Web services for managing geophysical data and applications. In Earthquakes: Simulations, Sources and Tsunamis (pp. 635-651). Birkhäuser Basel.

Pitre, R., & Kolekar, V. (2014). A Survey Paper on Data Mining With Big Data. *International Journal of Innovative Research in Advanced Engineering, 1*(1), 178–180.

Plödereder, E., (2014). Gesellschaft für Informatik, T., Tagung der Gesellschaft für Informatik. *Informatik 2014 Big Data - Komplexität meistern ; Tagung der Gesellschaft für Informatik.*

Polato, I., Ré, R., Goldman, A., & Kon, F. (2014). A comprehensive view of Hadoop research-A systematic literature review. *Journal of Network and Computer Applications, 46,* 1–25. doi:10.1016/j.jnca.2014.07.022

Poria, S., Cambria, E., Winterstein, G., & Huang, G.-B. (2014). Sentic patterns: Dependency-based rules for concept-level sentiment analysis. *Knowledge-Based Systems, 69,* 45–63. doi:10.1016/j.knosys.2014.05.005

Provost, F., & Fawcett, T. (2013). Data science and its relationship to big data and data-driven decision making. *Big Data, 1*(1), 51–59. doi:10.1089/big.2013.1508 PMID:27447038

Purdam, K. (2016). Task-based learning approaches for supporting the development of social science researchers' critical data skills. *International Journal of Social Research Methodology, 19*(2), 257–267. doi:10.1080/13645579.2015.1102453

Qu, K., Meng, L., & Yang, Y. (2016), August. A dynamic replica strategy based on Markov model for Hadoop distributed file system (HDFS). *Proceedings of the 2016 4th International Conference on Cloud Computing and Intelligence Systems (CCIS)* (pp. 337-342). IEEE.

Qureshi, F., Muhammad, N., & Shin, D. R. (2016). RDP: A storage-tier-aware robust data placement strategy for Hadoop in a cloud-based heterogeneous environment. *Transactions on Internet and Information Systems (Seoul), 10*(9).

Raghupathi, W., & Raghupathi, V. (2014). Big data analytics in healthcare: Promise and potential. *Health Inform. Sci. Syst., 2*(1), 3. doi:10.1186/2047-2501-2-3 PMID:25825667

Rajan, K. (2015). Materials informatics: The materials "gene" and big data. *Annual Review of Materials Research, 45*(1), 153–169. doi:10.1146/annurev-matsci-070214-021132

Rallapalli, S., Gondkar, R. R., & Kumar, U. P. (2016). Impact of processing and analyzing healthcare big data on cloud computing environment by implementing Hadoop Cluster. *Procedia Computer Science*, *85*, 16–22. doi:10.1016/j.procs.2016.05.171

Rani, P. R. S., Rao, M. R. N., & Lakshmi, D. T. V. (2014). A study on data mining classification algorithms for medical data. *International Journal of Advanced Research in Computer Science*, *5*(2), 13–16.

Reimsbach-Kounatze, C. (2015). *"The Proliferation of "Big Data" and Implications for Official Statistics and Statistical Agencies: A Preliminary Analysis", OECD Digital Economy Papers, No. 245.* Paris: OECD Publishing. doi:10.1787/5js7t9wqzvg8-

Revathy, R., & Lawrance, R. (2017). Comparative Analysis of C4. 5 and C5. 0 Algorithms on Crop Pest Data. *Int. J. Innov. Res. Comput. Commun. Eng*, *5*(1), 50–58.

Rice, J. A. (2007). *Mathematical Statistics and Data Analysis* (3rd ed.). Belmont, CA: Thomson Books/Cole.

Riggins, F. J., & Wamba, S. F. (2015). Research directions on the adoption, usage, and impact of the internet of things through the use of big data analytics. *Proceedings of the 2015 48th Hawaii International Conference on System Sciences (HICSS)* (pp. 1531-1540). IEEE. 10.1109/HICSS.2015.186

Rijmenam, M. (2014). *Think bigger: Developing a successful big data strategy for your business.* Amacom.

Rubin, V., & Lukoianova, T. (2013). Veracity roadmap: Is big data objective, truthful and credible? *Advances in Classification Research Online*, *24*(1), 4. doi:10.7152/acro.v24i1.14671

Salloum, S., Huang, J. Z., He, Y., & Chen, X. (2019). An Asymptotic Ensemble Learning Framework for Big Data Analysis. *IEEE Access*, *7*, 3675–3693. doi:10.1109/ACCESS.2018.2889355

Saltz, J. S. (2015). The need for new processes, methodologies and tools to support big data teams and improve big data project effectiveness. *Proceedings of the 2015 IEEE International Conference on Big Data (Big Data)* (pp. 2066-2071). IEEE. 10.1109/BigData.2015.7363988

Saltz, J. S., & Shamshurin, I. (2016). Big data team process methodologies: A literature review and the identification of key factors for a project's success. *Proceedings of the 2016 IEEE International Conference on Big Data (Big Data)* (pp. 2872-2879). IEEE. 10.1109/BigData.2016.7840936

Sarkhel, A., & Alawadhi, N. (2017). *Data Brokerage: How data brokers are selling all your personal info for less than a rupee to whoever wants it.* Retrieved from The Economic Times: https://economictimes.indiatimes.com/tech/internet/how-data-brokers-are-selling-all-your-personal-info-for-less-than-a-rupee-to-whoever-wants-it/articleshow/57382192.cms

Savitz, E. (2013). *Gartner: Top 10 Strategic Technology Trends For 2013*. Retrieved from https://www.forbes.com/sites/ericsavitz/2012/10/23/gartner-top-10-strategic-technology-trends-for-2013/#343d0d64b761

Schroeder, R. (2016). Big data business models: Challenges and opportunities. Cogent Social Sciences, 2(1), 1166924.

Seay, C., Agrawal, R., Kadadi, A., & Barel, Y. (2015, April). Using hadoop on the mainframe: A big solution for the challenges of big data. *Proceedings of the 2015 12th International Conference on Information Technology-New Generations (ITNG)* (pp. 765-769). IEEE. 10.1109/ITNG.2015.135

Seddon, J. J., & Currie, W. L. (2017). A model for unpacking big data analytics in high-frequency trading. *Journal of Business Research, 70*, 300–307. doi:10.1016/j.jbusres.2016.08.003

Shah, A., & Padole, M. (2018). Load Balancing through Block Rearrangement Policy for Hadoop Heterogeneous Cluster. Paper presented at the *7th International Conference on Advances in Computing, Communication and Informatics*, Bangalore, India, September 19-22. Academic Press. 10.1109/ICACCI.2018.8554404

She, R., Liu, S., Wan, S., Xiong, K., & Fan, P. (2019). Importance of Small Probability Events in Big Data: Information Measures, Applications, and Challenges. *IEEE Access*. doi:10.1109/access.2019.2926518

Shin, D. H., & Choi, M. J. (2015). Ecological views of big data: Perspectives and issues. *Telematics and Informatics, 32*(2), 311–320. doi:10.1016/j.tele.2014.09.006

Shvachko, K., Kuang, H., Radia, S., & Chansler, R. (2010). The hadoop distributed file system. *Proceedings of the 2010 IEEE 26th symposium on mass storage systems and technologies (MSST)* (pp. 1-10). IEEE. 10.1109/MSST.2010.5496972

Sookhak, M., Gani, A., Khan, M. K., & Buyya, R. (2017). Dynamic remote data auditing for securing big data storage in cloud computing. *Information Sciences, 380*, 101–116. doi:10.1016/j.ins.2015.09.004

Sperandei, S. (2014). Lessons in biostatistics: Understanding logistic regression analysis. *Biochemical Medicine, 24*, 12–18. doi:10.11613/BM.2014.003

Sroka, C. J., & Nagaraja, H. N. (2018). Odds ratios from logistic, geometric, Poisson, and negative binomial regression models. *BMC Medical Research Methodology, 18*(112), 1–11. PMID:30342488

Stathakis & Vasilakos. (2006). *Comparison of computational Intelligence based Classification Techniques for Remotely Sensed optical Image Classification* (Vol. 44). IEEE Transactions on and Remote Sensing.

Suganya, R., Rajaram, S., Abdullah, A. S., & Rajendran, V. (2016). A Novel Feature Selection method for Predicting Heart Diseases with Data mining Techniques. *Asian Journal of Information Technology, 15*(8), 1314–1321.

Sun, H., Chen, C., Ling, Y., Huang, J., & Lin, X. (2018). The Study of Cognitive Radio Prediction Based on Big Data. *Proceedings of the 2018 International Conference on Mechanical, Electronic, Control and Automation Engineering (MECAE 2018).* Academic Press. 10.2991/mecae-18.2018.70

Sun, F., Huang, G. B., Wu, Q. J., Song, S., & Wunsch, D. C. II. (2017). Efficient and rapid machine learning algorithms for big data and dynamic varying systems. *IEEE Transactions on Systems, Man, and Cybernetics. Systems, 47*(10), 2625–2626. doi:10.1109/TSMC.2017.2741558

Suriya, M., & Sumithra, M. G. (2018). Efficient Evolutionary Techniques for Wireless Body Area Using Cognitive Radio Networks. *EAI/Springer Innovations in Communication and Computing,* 61–70. doi:10.1007/978-3-030-02674-5_4

Suriya, M., & Sumithra, M. G. (2019). Efficient Evolutionary Techniques for Wireless Body Area Using Cognitive Radio Networks. In *Computational Intelligence and Sustainable Systems* (pp. 61–70). Springer.

Tamhane, A. R., Westfall, A. O., Burkholder, G. A., & Cutter, G. R. (2016). Prevalence odds ratio versus prevalence ratio: Choice comes with consequences. *Statistics in Medicine, 35*(30), 5730–5735. doi:10.1002im.7059 PMID:27460748

Team, D. (2018). *Data locality in Hadoop: The Most Comprehensive Guide – DataFlair.* Dataflair.training. Retrieved from https://data-flair.training/blogs/data-locality-in-hadoop-mapreduce/

TechAmerica Foundation. (2012). *Demystifying Big Data: A practical guide to transforming the business of government.* Retrieved from http://www.techamerica.org/Docs/fileManager.cfm?f=techamerica-bigdatareport-final.pdf

Thakor, H. R. (2017). A Survey Paper on Classification Algorithms in Big Data. International Journal Of Research Culture Society, 1(3).

Thein, K. M. M. (2014). Apache kafka: Next generation distributed messaging system. *International Journal of Scientific Engineering and Technology Research, 3*(47), 9478–9483.

Tormay, P. (2015). Big data in pharmaceutical R&D: Creating a sustainable R&D engine. *Pharmaceutical Medicine, 29*(2), 87–92. doi:10.100740290-015-0090-x PMID:25878506

Toshniwal, A., Taneja, S., Shukla, A., Ramasamy, K., Patel, J., Kulkarni, S., . . . Ryaboy, D. (2014). *Storm @Twitter.* Academic Press.

Tran, T. N., Afanador, N. L., Buydens, L. M. C., & Blanchet, L. (2014). Interpretation of variable importance in partial least squares with significance multivariate correlation (sMC). *Chemometrics and Intelligent Laboratory Systems, 138,* 153–160. doi:10.1016/j.chemolab.2014.08.005

Travers, J., & Milgram, S. (1969). An experimental study small world problem, (1969). *Sociometry, 32*(4), 425–443. doi:10.2307/2786545

Vanderweele, T. J., & Vansteelandt, S. (2010). Odds ratios for mediation analysis for a dichotomous outcome. *American Journal of Epidemiology*, *172*(12), 1339–1348. doi:10.1093/aje/kwq332 PMID:21036955

Vatsalan, D., Sehili, Z., Christen, P., & Rahm, E. (2017). Privacy-preserving record linkage for big data: Current approaches and research challenges. In *Handbook of Big Data Technologies* (pp. 851–895). Cham: Springer. doi:10.1007/978-3-319-49340-4_25

Vavilapalli, V. K., Murthy, A. C., Douglas, C., Agarwal, S., Konar, M., Evans, R., ... Saha, B. (2013). Apache hadoop yarn: Yet another resource negotiator. *Proceedings of the 4th annual Symposium on Cloud Computing* (p. 5). ACM. 10.1145/2523616.2523633

Venables, W. N., & Ripley, B. D. (2002). *Modern Applied Statistics with S* (4th ed.). New York: Springer. doi:10.1007/978-0-387-21706-2

Wadhwa, P., & Bhatia, M. P. S. (2012). Social networks analysis: trends, techniques and future prospects. *Springer open journal, 455*, 19-32.

Wang, C. H. (2016). A novel approach to conduct the importance-satisfaction analysis for acquiring typical user groups in business-intelligence systems. *Computers in Human Behavior*, *54*, 673–681. doi:10.1016/j.chb.2015.08.014

Wang, Y., Kung, L. A., Wang, W. Y., & Cegielski, C. G. (2017). An integrated big data analytics-enabled transformation model: Application to health care. Information & Management, 55(1), 64–79.

Wasan, P. S., Uttamchandani, M., Moochhala, S., Yap, V. B., & Yap, P. H. (2013). Application of statistics and machine learning for risk stratification of heritable cardiac arrhythmias. *Expert Systems with Applications*, *40*(7), 2476–2486.

Watts, D. J. (2004). *Six degrees: The science of a connected age.* WW Norton & Company.

White, T. (2012). *Hadoop: The definitive guide.* O'Reilly Media, Inc.

Wicks, P., Massagli, M., Frost, J., Brownstein, C., Okun, S., Vaughan, T., ... Heywood, J. (2010). Sharing health data for better outcomes on PatientsLikeMe. *Journal of Medical Internet Research*, *12*(2), e19. doi:10.2196/jmir.1549 PMID:20542858

Wikipedia. (n.d.). Weka (machine learning). Retrieved from https://en.wikipedia.org/wiki/Weka_(machine_learning)

Wixom, B., Ariyachandra, T., Douglas, D. E., Goul, M., Gupta, B., Iyer, L. S., . . . Turetken, O. (2014). The current state of business intelligence in academia: The arrival of big data. CAIS, 34, 1.

Wu, X., Zhu, X., Wu, G. Q., & Ding, W. (2013). Data mining with big data. *IEEE Transactions on Knowledge and Data Engineering*, *26*(1), 97–107.

Xiao, C., Li, P., Zhang, L., Liu, W., & Bergmann, N. (2018). ACA-SDS: Adaptive Crypto Acceleration for Secure Data Storage in Big Data. *IEEE Access, 6*, 44494–44505. doi:10.1109/ACCESS.2018.2862425

Xie, J., Yin, S., Ruan, X., Ding, Z., Tian, Y., Majors, J., . . . Qin, X. (2010). Improving mapreduce performance through data placement in heterogeneous hadoop clusters. *Proceedings of the 2010 IEEE International Symposium on Parallel & Distributed Processing, Workshops and Phd Forum (IPDPSW)* (pp. 1-9). IEEE.

Xu, W., Huang, R., Zhang, H., El-Khamra, Y., & Walling, D. (2016). Empowering R with high performance computing resources for big data analytics. In *Conquering Big Data with High Performance Computing* (pp. 191–217). Cham: Springer. doi:10.1007/978-3-319-33742-5_9

Xu, Z., Liu, Y., Mei, L., Hu, C., & Chen, L. (2015). Semantic based representing and organizing surveillance big data using video structural description technology. *Journal of Systems and Software, 102*, 217–225. doi:10.1016/j.jss.2014.07.024

Yang, C., Li, C., Wang, Q., Chung, D., & Zhao, H. (2015). Implications of pleiotropy: Challenges and opportunities for mining big data in biomedicine. *Frontiers in Genetics, 6*, 229. doi:10.3389/fgene.2015.00229 PMID:26175753

Yin, S., & Kaynak, O. (2015). Big data for modern industry: Challenges and trends [point of view]. *Proceedings of the IEEE, 103*(2), 143–146. doi:10.1109/JPROC.2015.2388958

Yu, H., Yang, J., & Han, J. (2003, August). Classifying large data sets using SVMs with hierarchical clusters. *Proceedings of the ninth ACM SIGKDD international conference on Knowledge discovery and data mining* (pp. 306-315). ACM. 10.1145/956750.956786

Zaharia, M., Konwinski, A., Joseph, A. D., Katz, R. H., & Stoica, I. (2008). Improving MapReduce performance in heterogeneous environments. In OSDI (Vol. 8, No. 4, p. 7).

Zaharia, M., Borthakur, D., Sen Sarma, J., Elmeleegy, K., Shenker, S., & Stoica, I. (2010). Delay scheduling: a simple technique for achieving locality and fairness in cluster scheduling. *Proceedings of the 5th European conference on Computer systems* (pp. 265-278). ACM. 10.1145/1755913.1755940

Zaharia, M., Chowdhury, M., Franklin, M., & Shenker, S. (n.d.). Spark. *Cluster Computing with Working Sets.*

Zhang, Q., Yang, L. T., Chen, Z., & Li, P. (2019). Incremental Deep Computation Model for Wireless Big Data Feature Learning. *IEEE Transactions on Big Data*. doi:10.1109/tbdata.2019.2903092

Zhao, R., Liu, Y., Zhang, N., & Huang, T. (2017). An optimization model for green supply chain management by using a big data analytic approach. *Journal of Cleaner Production, 142*, 1085–1097. doi:10.1016/j.jclepro.2016.03.006

Zhou, L., Pan, S., Wang, J., & Vasilakos, A. V. (2017). Machine learning on big data: Opportunities and challenges. *Neurocomputing, 237*, 350–361. doi:10.1016/j.neucom.2017.01.026

About the Contributors

Anandakumar Haldorai, Professor (Associate) and Research Head in Department of Computer Science and Engineering, Sri Eshwar College of Engineering, Coimbatore, Tamilnadu, India. He has received his Master's in Software Engineering from PSG College of Technology, Coimbatore and PhD in Information and Communication Engineering from PSG College of Technology under, Anna University, Chennai. His research areas include Big Data, Cognitive Radio Networks, Mobile Communications and Networking Protocols. He has authored more than 82 research papers in reputed International Journals and IEEE conferences. He has authored 7 books and many book chapters with reputed publishers such as Springer and IGI. He is editor of Inderscience IJISC and served as a reviewer for IEEE, IET, Springer, Inderscience and Elsevier journals. He is also the guest editor of many journals with Elsevier, Springer, Inderscience, etc. He has been the General Chair, Session Chair, and Panelist in several conferences. He is senior member of IEEE, IET, ACM and Fellow member of EAI research group.

Arulmurugan Ramu Received his PhD. degrees in Information and Communication Engineering from Anna University, Chennai, Tamil Nadu, India. He is currently working as Assistant Professor in the Department of Computer Science and Engineering, Presidency University, India. He received Young Faculty Award for 2018. He published many paper in Scopus indexed and SCI journals with Google scholar 61 citations.His research interests include Digital Image Processing, Biomedical Image Processing Computer vision, pattern recognition, and machine learning.

***

Sheik Abdullah A. is working as an Assistant Professor, Department of Information Technology, Thiagarajar College of Engineering, Madurai, Tamil Nadu, India. He completed his Post Graduate in M.E (Computer Science and Engineering) at

Kongu Engineering College under Anna University, Chennai. He is pursuing his Ph.D in the domain of Medical Data Analytics at Anna University Chennai. He has been awarded as gold medalist for his excellence in the degree of Post Graduate, in the discipline of Computer Science and Engineering by Kongu Engineering College. He is an active member of the ACM (Association for Computing and Machinery) and being rewarded as ACM Coach Award for the ACM World level International Collegiate Programming contest for the year 2013 and 2014. He has handled various e-governance government projects such as automation system for tracking community certificate, birth and death certificate, DRDA and income tax automation systems. He has published research articles in various reputed journals and International Conferences. He has received the Honorable chief minister award for excellence in e-governance for the best project in e-governance for the academic year 2015-16. He has been assigned as a reviewer for various reputed journals such as European Heart Journal, International Journal of Fuzzy Systems, and NASA Springer. He has delivered various guest lecturers in the area of predictive analytics, data prediction using R tools and so on. He is working interactively with various industries like CTS, IBM, Xerox Research labs. He has authored various books under IGI Global Publishers, USA.

Donald Atsa'am is a lecturer of Computer Science with the University of Agriculture, Makurdi, Nigeria. He holds a PhD in Applied Mathematics and Computer Science from the Eastern Mediterranean University, North Cyprus. His research interests are in data mining and knowledge discovery. He is also an experienced Information Systems Auditor.

Tolga Büyüktanır received his BSc degree in Computer Engineering from Erciyes University in 2014. In 2017, he got MS degree from the Electrical and Computer Engineering Department of Ankara Yildirim Beyazit University. He is now a PhD student at Yildiz Technical University in the Computer Engineering Department. Distributed real-time stream processing and complex event processing are in his major interest areas.

Selvan C. received the B.E. degree in Computer Science and Engineering in Manonmaniam Sundaranar University, India, in 2002, the M.E. degree in Computer Science and Engineering from Anna University, Chennai, India, in 2007 and the Ph.D. degree in Information and Communication Engineering from Anna University, Chennai, India in 2013. During his Ph.D. degree he was a JRF, SRF under University Grant Commission (UGC, New Delhi) in Government College of Technology, Coimbatore. He had been working as a software developer from 2002 to 2005 and has been engaging in various responsibilities in the Engineering colleges, in Tamil Nadu since 2007. He is currently a Post-Doctoral Fellow in National Institute of Technology, Tiruchirappalli, under UGC, New Delhi, India since 2017. His current research interests include Mobile Computing, Data Analytics, and Graph Analytics. Dr. Selvan C is an IEEE member and a member of the Indian Society for Technical Education.

Pradeep Reddy Ch is currently working as Associate Professor in VIT-AP University, Amaravati, India. He has a total of thirteen years' experience in both teaching and research. He received his B.Tech in Computer Science and Engineering from PBR VITS, JNTU Andhra Pradesh, India and M.Tech in Computer Science and Engineering from VIT University, Vellore, India. He did his PhD in Computer Science and Engineering from VIT University, Vellore. He has published various journals and served as reviewer and editor for reputed journals. His research interests include wireless networks, IoT, security systems and Cloud computing.

Sumit Hirve is a full-time professor at M.E.S College of Engineering, Pune. A computer science professional and Big data researcher. I would like to thank Mr. Ajinkya Kunjir, who is a student at Lakehead University and currently pursuing master's in computer science for his constant help and support at providing resources and contents for achieving the precise quality of this article.

Sumithra M. G. received her B.E. degree in Electronics and Communication Engineering from Government College of Engineering, Salem, India in 1994, she obtained her M.E. Degree in Medical Electronics from College of Engineering, Gundy, Anna University Chennai, India in 2001 and received PhD (information and communication engineering) Anna University Chennai, India in 2011. She has 24 years and 8 months of teaching experience. Her areas of interest include signal/image processing, biomedical engineering, wireless communications, and artificial intelligence. She has published 66 technical papers in refereed journals, 3 book chapters and 129 research papers in national and International conferences in India and 5 in abroad. In addition, she has published 3 book chapters and she is NVIDIA Deep learning Institute certified Instructor for "Computer vision". She is a recognized supervisor of Anna University, Chennai, and 5 research scholars pursuing PhDs under her supervision and one has been awarded a Ph.D. degree.

Suriya Murugan has received her B.E in Information Technology from Avinashilingam University, Coimbatore in 2008 and Master's in Computer Science and Engineering from Anna University of Technology, Coimbatore in 2010. She is pursuing PhD in Information and Communication under Anna University, Chennai. She has about 9 years of teaching experience and her areas of interest include artificial intelligence, Big Data, and wireless communication. She has authored more than 25 research papers in refereed International Journals and IEEE conferences and has published 6 book chapters with reputed publishers. She has obtained one patent and is serving as a reviewer for more than 6 peer journals like Inderscience, Taylor and Francis, MONET, IGI etc. She is certified NVIDIA DLI Ambassador for "Fundamentals of Computer Vision." She has delivered special lectures at FDPs and workshops on machine learning and deep learning.

Saranya N. is an Assistant Professor in the Department of Computer Science & Engineering at Sri Eshwar College of Engineering in Coimbatore, India. She has completed her master's degree under Anna University, Chennai and bachelor's degree at Avinashilingam University, Coimbatore. She is currently pursuing her PhD affiliated to Anna University. Her research interests include database systems, data analytics, and machine learning.

Priyadharshini P. is studying ME: computer science and information technology in Thiagarajar collage of engineering. Her area of interest is Internet of Things (IOT), now she is starting her project literature survey for IOT in big data analytic security. She learned about big data analytics and how to perform the IOT platform. Her UG project domain is network security.

Mamta Padole is currently working as an Associate Professor, Department of Computer Science and Engineering, The Maharaja Sayajirao University of Baroda. Research area includes distributed computing, fog computing, and IoT. She also has been a bioinformatics invited speaker/resource person to national/international conferences/workshops, a paper reviewer in international conferences, PhD thesis reviewer in some national universities, and an EC Member of Local Chapters of Professional Organizations.

Ankit Shah received his bachelor's in information & technology engineering in 2009. He received his master's in computer science & engineering in 2013. Currently, he is pursuing his Ph.D. in the Computer Science & Engineering from The Maharaja Sayajirao University of Baroda, India. His research interests include big data processing, distributed computing, and IoT.

Vinay Shankarnarayan is a professor of Industrial Production at Dayananda Sagar College of Engineering. His work focus mainly on Big Data analytics and energy management for Business and Agriculture. He is researching on use and applications of Big Data analytics in the Indian Agriculture system.

Abiramie Shree T. G. R. pursued her bachelor's degree in information technology at National Engineering College, Kovilpatti. She did her UG project on BigData with the help of Hadoop. She is now pursuing master's degree in computer science and Information Security which is a specialization course in security on Thiagarajar College of Engineering, Madurai. She is very much interested in the security related domain. She is currently doing her PG project on Blockchain technology. She already made a book chapter proposal in review on machine learning and deep learning for cyber security.

Aykut Hamit Turan is a professor in the School of Management, Department of Management Information Systems at Sakarya University, Sakarya, Turkey. His research interests include Management Information Systems education, technology acceptance and usage, technology adoption in small and medium size enterprises, and internet shopping.

Hakan Tüzün received BS degree in Computer Science Engineering from Yildiz Technical University 1999. Started his professional career in SFS as Software Specialist in 1995. He has been working for Link Bilgisayar starting from 1999. ERP applications, distribution/supply chain management systems, B2B processes, retail marketing, mobile applications, business process management, software infrastructure are main subjects he has been dealing with. Currently, he is working as Chief Technology Officer in Link Bilgisayar. Cloud computing, multi-tenancy, Big Data, SaaS methodology are the latest topics he is working on. Besides his professional career in Link, he continues his MS education on Computer Engineering in Gebze Technical University.

Naciye Güliz Uğur is a faculty member of the Department of Management Information Systems at Sakarya University. Uğur received her Ph.D. in the field of MIS. She has more than five years of industry experience in management and teaches courses on information systems and system analysis and design. Her research interests include technology acceptance and behavioral aspects of emerging technologies.

Index

Ensure Quality Research is Introduced to the Academic Community

Become an IGI Global Reviewer for Authored Book Projects

The overall success of an authored book project is dependent on quality and timely reviews.

In this competitive age of scholarly publishing, constructive and timely feedback significantly expedites the turnaround time of manuscripts from submission to acceptance, allowing the publication and discovery of forward-thinking research at a much more expeditious rate. Several IGI Global authored book projects are currently seeking highly-qualified experts in the field to fill vacancies on their respective editorial review boards:

Applications and Inquiries may be sent to:
development@igi-global.com

Applicants must have a doctorate (or an equivalent degree) as well as publishing and reviewing experience. Reviewers are asked to complete the open-ended evaluation questions with as much detail as possible in a timely, collegial, and constructive manner. All reviewers' tenures run for one-year terms on the editorial review boards and are expected to complete at least three reviews per term. Upon successful completion of this term, reviewers can be considered for an additional term.

If you have a colleague that may be interested in this opportunity, we encourage you to share this information with them.

IGI Global's Transformative Open Access (OA) Model:
How to Turn Your University Library's Database Acquisitions Into a Source of OA Funding

In response to the OA movement and well in advance of Plan S, IGI Global, early last year, unveiled their OA Fee Waiver (Offset Model) Initiative.

Under this initiative, librarians who invest in IGI Global's InfoSci-Books (5,300+ reference books) and/or InfoSci-Journals (185+ scholarly journals) databases will be able to subsidize their patron's OA article processing charges (APC) when their work is submitted and accepted (after the peer review process) into an IGI Global journal.*

How Does it Work?

1. When a library subscribes or perpetually purchases IGI Global's InfoSci-Databases including InfoSci-Books (5,300+ e-books), InfoSci-Journals (185+ e-journals), and/or their discipline/subject-focused subsets, IGI Global will match the library's investment with a fund of equal value to go toward subsidizing the OA article processing charges (APCs) for their patrons.

   Researchers: Be sure to recommend the InfoSci-Books and InfoSci-Journals to take advantage of this initiative.

2. When a student, faculty, or staff member submits a paper and it is accepted (following the peer review) into one of IGI Global's 185+ scholarly journals, the author will have the option to have their paper published under a traditional publishing model or as OA.

3. When the author chooses to have their paper published under OA, IGI Global will notify them of the OA Fee Waiver (Offset Model) Initiative. If the author decides they would like to take advantage of this initiative, IGI Global will deduct the US$ 1,500 APC from the created fund.

4. This fund will be offered on an annual basis and will renew as the subscription is renewed for each year thereafter. IGI Global will manage the fund and award the APC waivers unless the librarian has a preference as to how the funds should be managed.

Hear From the Experts on This Initiative:

"I'm very happy to have been able to make one of my recent research contributions, 'Visualizing the Social Media Conversations of a National Information Technology Professional Association' featured in the *International Journal of Human Capital and Information Technology Professionals*, freely available along with having access to the valuable resources found within IGI Global's InfoSci-Journals database."

– **Prof. Stuart Palmer**,
Deakin University, Australia

For More Information, Visit: www.igi-global.com/publish/contributor-resources/open-access or contact IGI Global's Database Team at eresources@igi-global.com